AF710495

PROPERTY IN A HUMANE ECONOMY

WITHDRAWN

PROPERTY
IN A HUMANE ECONOMY

A Selection of Essays Compiled by the
INSTITUTE FOR HUMANE STUDIES

Edited by
Samuel L. Blumenfeld

Open Court LaSalle, Illinois

Copyright © 1974 by the Institute for Humane Studies, Inc. All rights reserved. No part of this book may be reproduced in any form or by any means without permission from the publisher, except for brief excerpts to be included in a review or scholarly paper.

Library of Congress Cataloging in Publication Data
Main entry under title:

Property in a humane economy.

Includes bibliographical references.
CONTENTS: Cunningham, R. L. Introduction.—Harper, F. A. Property and its primary form.—Henry, C. F. H. Christian perspective on private property. [etc.]
1. Property—Addresses, essays, lectures.
I. Blumenfeld, Samuel L., ed. II. Institute for Humane Studies.
HB711.P73 1975 333.3 74-22455
ISBN 0-87548-321-6

Published in 1974 by Open Court Publishing Company, LaSalle, Illinois 61301.

Printed in the United States of America.

Grateful acknowledgment is made to *The Personalist* for permission to reprint "Property" by George I. Mavrodes, which was published in the Summer 1972 issue of that review.

DEDICATION

When "Baldy" Harper was among us he used his time exceedingly well—Dr. F. A. Harper was a teacher. The dedication of this volume to him is a recognition of the gratitude felt by those whose lives he touched. He was awed and humble as he contemplated the ripple effect of phenomena, correctly described and understood.

More successfully than almost anyone in his time, he showed that a love of human freedom, inherent in man's nature, could be nurtured; it could be taught. He further showed that the means to human liberty could be learned.

Gentle and persuasive in his ways, his adherence to principle made him essentially a disciplinarian, but only a self-disciplinarian. Although he saw liberty in man's nature, he recognized that it was to be enjoyed only as a luxury of self-discipline. He recognized that the institution of private property was one of man's most disciplined responses.

So the essays on property in this volume acknowledge the influence of the ripple of "Baldy" Harper's passion and dedication to the proposition of human liberty. "Baldy" might have said with Montaigne, "I gather the flowers by the wayside, by the brooks and in the meadows, and only the string with which I bind them together is my own."

A. Neil McLeod

The INSTITUTE FOR HUMANE STUDIES, INC., Menlo Park, California, was founded in 1961 as an independent center to encourage basic research and advanced study for the strengthening of a free society. Through seminars, fellowships, publications, and other activities, the Institute seeks to serve a worldwide community of scholars in education, business, and the professions who are interested in broadening the knowledge and practice of the principles of liberty.

CONTENTS

INTRODUCTION
by
Robert L. Cunningham

This volume, dedicated as a memorial to Dr. F. A. "Baldy" Harper, consists of a number of papers delivered at several symposia sponsored by the Institute for Humane Studies. The papers were selected principally on the basis of the directness with which they focus on basic issues relating to property rights.

What follows is an attempt to offer the reader a preview of the intellectual attractions in store for him in the papers themselves.

Dr. Harper's paper is devoted primarily to answering the question: Why is there so disappointing a neglect and disparagement of private property and ownership? In the course of answering this question, Dr. Harper touches on nearly all of the deep concerns of the other authors. A convenient way of providing the reader with the promised preview of the papers is to group their views, whether they amplify or contrast with Dr. Harper's, around the themes which Dr. Harper himself develops. These might be put as follows:

Property and Freedom—has the connection between the two been sufficiently analyzed?

The Alleged Injustice of Ownership—is property *theft* as socialists maintain?

The Economic Function of Private Property—can we solve the problem of scarcity by redistributing property?

Definitions of "Ownership" and "Property"—how are we to understand these terms?

The Origin of Property: The Legal View—is property the creation of the law?

The Origin of Property: The Theocratic View—what implications for our understanding of ownership and property follow from the view that God is creator, and so "owner" of everything?

The Origin of Property: The Self-Ownership View—is it conceptually and analytically helpful to see self-ownership as the prior and superior form of property?

Property and Freedom

Dr. Harper writes that "property underlies every aspect of human liberty." And why? Because trespassing upon the liberty of another is possible only by depriving him of the scarce goods he owns.

A good number of the papers contribute to our understanding of the problems and relations between property and freedom. Carl Henry looks at private property as conferring upon each person a province of liberty that promotes human discipline and maturity.

Sylvester Petro looks at the connection between property and freedom mainly from a historical point of view. He finds considerable evidence in medieval English law to support his hypothesis that the hallmarks of Western civilization will be imperfectly realized where private property rights are weak or anomalous.

In the early part of his paper, James Smith tries to account for a decline in the view that property rights are central or fundamental among human rights. The eighteenth century belief that property rights served to protect central human interests rested on an individualist view of human nature and the good life, a view crucially different from that held by many today, notably collectivists.

Leopold Kohr sees property not so much as an extension of freedom or an area within which one is able freely to act, but as the source of freedom. Like James Smith, Kohr notes that the Marxists agree that property is fundamental to freedom, for the thrust of their moral stance is that the bourgeoisie have expropriated what belongs to the worker, have taken from the worker what he needs to be free.

In his paper on environmental policy and property rights, Edwin Dolan devotes a good deal of his attention to comparing the economic efficiency of private property solutions with regulatory solutions, and on this ground, finds no clear-cut victory for either side. But more importantly, he argues that the regulatory solution, whereby government allocates to individuals rights to use common property, is incompatible with the maintenance of a free society.

James Wiggins's view that private property is best seen as an extension, and so a part of the person, has the implication that an attack on private property is also an attack on the human person. He offers evidence of such person-property identification both from ordinary experience and language, and from anthropological literature.

Alleged Injustice of Ownership

Dr. Harper points to a number of causes for the questioning that we witness of the justice of private property. One is historical: Originally ownership rested with the tribe, then later with the family, and only relatively recently with the individual; some, therefore, seem to feel "in their bones" that for an individual to own property is somehow to deprive a larger group, perhaps especially "the tribe," of what is due it. Dr. Harper goes on to point out that "unless we can establish in logic a clear title to the first owner, we are plagued with the charge of chronic theft in every subsequent claim."

James Smith notes that the paradoxical "property is theft!" cry of the socialist is meant to be a way of calling for the moral re-evaluation of the practice.

James Sadowsky argues that one should not attribute to private property and the free market the moral defects endemic to other systems. The characteristically enormous feudal land holdings were the result of conquest or state grants and so produced an unjust state of affairs—such lands should have been divided among the workers—but a defender of the free market need not defend such enormous holdings, for they were not produced by the market.

Murray Rothbard, like Sadowsky, makes the case that goods which are illegitimately acquired do not become legitimized with the passing of time. He complains that the inadequate property rights theory of the free-market utilitarians makes them rightly subject to the charge that they must of necessity endorse the status quo, and so must endorse coercive and unjust allocations or reallocations of property.

Economic Function of Private Property

Some have believed, Dr. Harper notes, that even if it could be established that John Q. Doe was the original owner of a piece of property, there would be serious questions about any increased value the property might acquire over time. However, Harper argues that one cannot solve the problem of increased scarcity by depriving the owner of his property—a chair which holds a single person will hold no more if taken away from its owner and turned into property owned by "all the people."

Israel Kirzner notes that according to both capitalist and the Marxist ethics, "a man deserves what he produces." They disagree about what "produces" means, though—the capitalist argues that a man is producing when the resources he owns are used by others, and the Marxist argues that only he who actually uses resources, the worker, can be said to be producing. Kirzner develops an alternative view. The entrepreneur is responsible for producing the whole product and deserves the whole return, subject of course to paying for the capital and labor he has bargained for and hired.

Sylvester Petro echoes Harper in observing that economic calculation is possible only within the market, and that since in the market private property is indispensable, economic calculation or efficiency demands private property.

James Sadowsky extends Kirzner's view in noting that the owner of property makes an entrepreneurial judgment when he decides, as he must, how and whether to use it or hold on to it; he is rewarded not for his "work" but for his judgment in predicting the future evaluations that he and others will make and for acting on his judgment.

Arthur Kemp writes that there are two essential institutional factors of relevance for economic behavior: the property right system, and the monetary framework; and, to be sure, the interrelations between these two differ under different systems.

Louis Spadaro's paper might be seen as an application to financial crises of the general position he shares with Kemp. Some economists, we are told, see financial crises as caused by the private property system, and the remedy is further weakening of private property rights. Spadaro argues that, on the contrary, sounder analysis would see financial crises to be the inevitable result of attempts to interfere with the proper exercise of property rights.

Defining "Property" and "Ownership"

Dr. Harper's definition of "ownership" is the usual one having to do with rights of possession, use, and disposal, but his preferred definition of "property" is worth noting. In substance, he defines "property" as anything of lasting value which is identifiable and also transferable as to features of value.

George Mavrodes believes it important to recognize that "ownership" involves a number of distinct rights and that these rights need not always be clustered together in the usual way. Ownership can be fragmented for good social purposes.

The intent of James Sadowsky's paper as a whole is to show that the notion of "collective ownership" is without meaning. Like Jeremy Bentham, Sadowsky objects to hypostatizing entities like "society," and engages in reductionist analysis of the various sorts of wholes into their parts or members.

James Wiggins, too, focuses on an aspect of the same sort of spurious identification when he distinguishes what he calls genuine private property from "counterfeit ownership." The latter is property held by an agent of the real owner, but property the agent finds it easy to think of as his own.

Leopold Kohr develops an interesting distinction between what he calls "passive property" and "active property." Now all property confers some freedom of action. But passive property is property owned as consumer goods; and freedom of action in its regard is restricted to one single exercise: consumption. It is active property, property in the means of making a living, in the means of production, that is crucial to our overall balance of freedom.

Origin of Property: The Legal View

One widespread view of the origin of property finds property the creature of the state, the creation of the law. Dr. Harper's own view is closer to that of Charles Comte: "It would, perhaps, be more correct to say that it is property which gave birth to civil laws; for it is hard to see what need a tribe of savages, among whom no property of any kind existed, could have of laws or of a government."

Kemp, like Dolan, is an adherent of "the legal view." He writes that there is no natural, simple development either of property rights or monetary arrangements.

James Smith, too, would support the legal view, though he believes that the concept of rights beyond those guaranteed by a particular legal system is coherent, morally defensible, and perhaps even essential.

For Rothbard, by contrast, the legal view could not be more dangerous. By leaving to government the power to define and allocate titles to property, we have removed the possibility of a firm roadblock to arbitrary government reallocations of property.

Origin of Property: The Theocratic View

If all creation is owned by God the Creator, it would seem to follow that no human being may acquire clear and exclusive title to any part of creation as private property. He may acquire the right to use, but not an unrestricted right to possess. Without attempting to evaluate this argument, Dr. Harper points out that both the atheist and the theist "must face the same identical problem of how we shall deal with one another here and now, while the show of earthly life is in process; how shall we resolve these problems as they arise? Neither view, *per se* and as distinct from one another, would seem to necessitate giving any privilege to one person that is denied to another in connection with property rights."

Carl Henry sees the Christian framework, which proclaims God's rights to be above human rights, as offering a firmer foundation for the inalienability of human rights, including property rights: given by God, human rights can be taken away only by God Himself.

Origin of Property: The Self-Ownership View

Dr. Harper tells us he has come to believe that to identify property with something physically separated from the human person is not sound. He prefers, rather, to say that "the primary object of property and ownership which antedates all others and is superior to all others in its importance, is the self." What attracts him, and also Spadaro and Petro, to this Lockean view is that it seems to offer a natural foundation for other property rights: I own myself, so I own my labor, so I own what I make with my labor out of the unowned materials available in creation. Kirzner contributes a very useful analysis of this Lockean argument, discussing at length what ground there is for the view that a man has a moral right to that which his labor produces. He throws light on what Locke may well have meant by his notion that title to natural resources is acquired by the "mixing of labor" with them.

For Sadowsky, the right of self-ownership is the basis of the right not to be interfered with by others; one has the right to interfere with, use violence on, only what one owns—and only I own myself.

For Rothbard, there is an absolute right of self-ownership. Otherwise either another would own me (slavery) or others would own a share in me (communism). With self-ownership as a foundation, one can see the products of one's hands and mind as an extension of oneself, of one's own personality.

Both Smith and Mavrodes find difficulty with this derivation of property rights from Lockean self-ownership and homesteading. Smith objects to self-ownership on the ground that it would entail the possibility of slavery: one can sell what one owns, and if one owns oneself, one can sell oneself. But selling oneself into slavery, he argues, is fundamentally incoherent.

Mavrodes would agree that one who brings new wealth into the world—as the sculptor does—has first claim on it. But he finds it impossible to see how one may give a simple and absolute answer to the question: Who owns the tree out of which the sculptor carved the statue? Mavrodes's own preference is for a relativistic system which makes a property private only on condition that for this privilege some benefit be conferred on others, where the judgment as to the nature and scope of the benefit is politically arrived at.

In all, the papers in this volume reveal the complexity of the subject of private property: What is involved are fundamental issues touching virtually every aspect of human existence. Perhaps this is indicative of why the subject has been neglected for so long by economists and philosophers. It is hoped that this volume represents a starting point in revitalizing a necessary discussion and provides the reader and scholar with an initial understanding of the problems inherent in creating and sustaining—in the face of unremitting attack—a humane economy based on private property.

1

F. A. Harper

PROPERTY AND ITS PRIMARY FORM

ONE DAY in the late 1940s, a former student of mine at Cornell University honored me with a visit as he was returning to complete his doctorate after a sojourn at Harvard. During our conversation he said: "I have come to believe that too little attention has been given to private property and ownership in our study of the problems of liberty."

I probably recoiled a bit from the accusation, feeling that I had always recognized its importance. But I was perfectly willing for him to give it more attention if he wanted to; that would help keep him out of mischief.

Prior experience with this quiet, thoughtful student who had an effective way of teaching his teachers must have left its impact. From whatever cause, as the days and weeks passed I found myself unable to shake off the impact of his comment. The concept of ownership began to come into focus in ways it never had before.

It is irrelevant to our purpose here to recount, step by step, the added insights into the importance of the problem. I would only point out how perplexing problems began almost to solve themselves when I finally began to analyze every question with this preparatory question: Whose it it? For when I did that, it became clear time after time that the perplexity had arisen from trying to decide for others what they should do with *their* property. To attempt that is to try to solve the unsolvable. I would usually discover that it was none of my business what the other person did with it, in addition to its being unsolvable.

What I propose to do, then, is to raise certain questions I shall not presume to answer here. And further, I should like to propose for critical analysis one aspect of property and ownership that seems to have been neglected out of all proportion to its importance by those who have studied the problems of mankind in society.

History of Property Concept

Property as a concept has a long history.

If Rousseau had spent more time in the fields, forests, and jungles rather than in the sidewalk cafés, he might not have written his famous *Discourse on the Origin of Inequality.* In his book, the "noble savage" was portrayed as ignorant of any property sense, supposedly being happy and peaceful in that animal-like existence of ignorance.

Even before the emergence of man in recorded history, evidence suggests that the property concept prevailed among animals. This is seen in the manner by which animals still treat possession of space and abode, presumably as they did in the dim and distant past. Ardrey tells us that the innate urge for "territory," which in the context is another name for property, exists widely in the animal world and is even stronger in many instances than is the sex urge. There is no government as we know it and no formal organization, yet we see the disposition to preserve domain over what is necessary for their continued existence in this animal world of property rights. Ardrey concludes: "The roles of territory, of dominance, and of society in the play of our ancestral instincts exist without question, and by their existence cast extraordinary doubt on the most precious premises of a post-Freudian, post-Marxian world."[1]

Rousseau's evident and profound error, however, was accepted by all who breathed the air saturated by his influence in those crucial early years of the nineteenth century. Hearnshaw aptly described him this way: "Rousseau, in short, was an amazing anomaly; a thinker who, because of defective training and inadequate powers of concentration, was able to hold at one and the same time radically incompatible beliefs. . . ."[2]

Faucher tells us that the distinction between mine and thine is as old as the human race, as early man sought to extend identity to things as well as to himself and other persons. I see no reason to disbelieve this early origin of the property concept, because its necessity is evidenced in even the lower forms of life. Sheer survival depends to some degree on this trait and we may assume that any species lacking it or losing it was retired to the archives of archeology. Whether the property sense was an inborn sense or came from some other means of knowing is not important to us here. We shall merely observe its existence as a functioning concept.

We, as humans, must have acted wisely for purposes of survival and advancement, and yet without any formal comprehension of property during most of our history. We did so in a manner like failing to walk off cliffs; like breathing and eating enough of the right things; like all sorts of actions necessary for survival, though without any formal knowledge of the intricacies of physics, chemistry, or nutrition.

From the standpoint of formal thought about property, Cicero was a pioneer; he developed the thought that the earth became the patrimony of labor. And shortly thereafter, Seneca in his wisdom recognized that property is an *individual* right at about the same time as the Christian religion was emphasizing the religious counterpart of the moral responsibilities of the individual. Seneca offered this view of property in an era when the rights of the state were considered to be sovereign. Yet after this helpful beginning, one can search largely in vain the writings of philosophers and embryonic economists during the intervening years for extensions and development of the concept of property and ownership; most of these authorities hardly even recognized this problem in their writings.

The physiocratic school probably pioneered in their understanding of the great importance of property in a formal sense. Of course, they failed to foresee certain important criticisms which later would be leveled at private property; but Charles Gide says of such works as Abbé Baudeau's *Philosophie économique*: "The reasons which they advanced are more worthy of quotation than almost any argument that has since been employed by conservative economists."[3] And yet even Quesnay, dean of the physiocrats, did not bother to define property except in one of his treatises on natural law.

Adam Smith apparently considered property as unworthy of much discussion and hardly mentions it, much less defines it. Nor did he analyze it in either its moral or economic aspects where he was so distinguished.

J. B. Say, in his famous work on political economy, considered matters of the origins and underlying aspects of property as unworthy of his attention. He saw little or nothing to say about it except that it exists.

The contemporary books that have devoted major attention to property and ownership are few indeed, aside from those dealing with the details of governmental processes and court cases. Even distinguished economists we revere have explored this subject very little. Why this neglect? And why has so much of what has been written either disparaged private property and ownership or progressively chiseled away the corners of its claim to merit? The work of Saint-Simon and his followers on this matter has ruled long and with little formal, intelligent challenge.

One wonders what happened to the fine beginning made by David Hume, who believed that the right of private property was the basis for the modern concept of justice in morals.[4]

As to the neglect of this important subject, I would venture to offer several reasons:

1. Failure to see why property underlies all human liberty in society, insofar as it merits our concern.

2. The historic belief that ownership is one form of sinfulness, to be avoided and prevented as much as possible; the belief that if one person owns anything, he thereby is taking it from others who have an equally valid claim to it in equity; that aside from the Creator's claim of ownership,

property should all be owned by everybody and available to everybody equally, as a collective of humanity and not as individual persons.

3. Even those who have upheld the propriety of private ownership of property have treated it as self-evident and needing no further explanation or justification.

4. As some specific extensions of the preceding point, there has been failure to identify certain underlying aspects of the right of individuals to own property, such as:

a. How could a valid claim to property by any person arise in the first instance? For without this, how could any of the subsequent claims be valid?

b. How can increases in value be allowed to become the property of a single person, since these arise solely from increasing scarcity which the single owner did nothing to create by laboring to produce it in the first place?

c. How can it be said that a private owner should hold any basic claim to the possession and use of an item of property, when it should be clear that if he fails to use it or uses it for his own purposes, he is thereby denying to all others what should equally be theirs; that, therefore, the basic control—which is the essence of ownership—should be in the hands of the collective of persons, to be administered through their agency of government?

d. If there is no economic function that ownership performs per se, how can personal gain from property be permissible in justice?

If these should be among the important reasons why the subject of property has been neglected so pathetically, and thus allowing private ownership to lose by default, they deserve some concentrated thinking by highly qualified minds. Some brief comment about them may bring the questions into clearer focus.

Scope of Property

First, on the matter of neglect in realizing the fundamental importance of property and ownership, the scope of our concern becomes impressive under the definition of property which will be presented later.

It should be clear that concerns about property underlie absolutely every aspect of economic affairs. Since economics, by definition, deals with all things that are both desired and scarce, it deals, therefore, with all things of worth—property and all its associated phenomena in society. Every item of property must be owned by somebody, or by somebodies in some form of collective arrangement. Value cannot exist without an owner. It is only *who*, not whether, that becomes the question about ownership. The popular myth of unspecified ownership in common conceals the fact that even there certain specific persons in power have control—and therefore ownership—of that property.

When it is realized that property underlies each and every aspect of economics, it is difficult to understand why it has been so much ignored throughout the history of economic and philosophic thought.

It should also be clear that property underlies every aspect of human liberty which justifies our concern.[5] Why? Because it is only by depriving us of ownership of things that are desired and scarce—economic concerns in property—that makes it possible for one person to trespass upon the liberty of another. In all other aspects of one's life his liberty is not subject to serious restriction by his fellow men, because by definition all else he desires is in ample abundance so that when some person commandeers a part of the supply there remains all anyone else wants.

I can think of no exception to this all-pervading nature of property in relation to aspects of human liberty that justify our concern. Failure to realize this and the overwhelming implications must be one important reason for historical neglect of the property question. To illustrate, no less an intellect than Max Eastman once confessed: "It seems obvious to me now—though I have been slow, I must say, in coming to the conclusion—that the institution of private property is one of the main things that have given man that limited amount of freedom and equalness that

Marx hoped to render infinite by abolishing this institution."[6] And even then, in this expression of his discovery one wonders if he saw the full significance of property, for note that he said only "one of the main things."

Alleged Sin of Ownership

The concept of private property had no function for Adam, though we may assume he wanted things he did not have, at times.

As Eve and others joined the fray, things increasingly became economic, and the issue of "mine vs. thine" came to have meaning and purpose. Property, then, has been a problem to be resolved somehow since the dimmest recesses of man's history. The earliest people in society doubtless shared in large measure our modern lack of any complete solution for the problem. The occupation of theft and marauding does not reduce the scope of property; it only evidences confusion about a code of property rights by which all should live.

It seems likely that the sense of property first arose among things of economic worth related to hunger—things nearest the stomach, so to speak. This includes the game that had been caught, the fruit and nuts that had been gathered from tree and bush, as the first items to be treated as property. Then, presumably, as tools of crude fashioning used to gather the game and other food came into being, these probably found their place among the list of property items.

Later—much later—things such as land became recognized as objects of property and lengthened the list still further. But this step must have awaited, in the main, the domestication of plants and animals and their attachment to some specific piece of land—plants and trees with their roots in the earth at one place and animals that someone restrained on a certain piece of land. When this step was taken in agriculture, specific pieces of land became objects of identification as property.

As mankind advanced more and more in an economic sense, property items increased apace to take care of the widening scope of value. Tangible tools and intangible ingredients of economic production, in all its highly complex forms, acquired value and became property. So the list lengthened still further.

In all this historical development of property about which we have speculated, another influence has been the social arrangements in which people lived. Aside from the institution of the family, mankind apparently aggregated for purposes of mutual assistance in protection and perhaps sociability at an early date when property was only in its embryonic stages. And this influenced the development of ownership units correspondingly. In any event, Faucher tells us that land was owned historically by the tribe before it was owned by the family; that it was owned by the family before it was owned by the individual.[7] In other words, ownership has tended historically to move from the larger aggregates of society down to smaller units, finally reaching the single person in relatively recent times. Even though there were distinct evidences in ancient Rome of individual ownership, no member of the family other than the patriarch himself was allowed to own and bequeath property.[8] Thus, from viewing the property concept historically, it seems fair to conclude that common and aggregative ownership is the one truly archaic; that the concept of individual ownership as a universal right is still in its infancy and "the wave of the future."

Out of those dim and distant practices of ownership by aggregates of persons we seem to have carried over the idea that it is somehow sinful or wrong for an individual to own property. In our time it is still widely asserted that for one person to own an item of property is akin to theft of it from others in society. This is clearly a remnant of the idea of collective ownership as the only just form; and that if any single person claims it, he is being unjust to his fellow men in general.

Buttressing this same view of justice embodied in collective ownership has been the continuing proclamations and interpretations of clergymen and religious leaders in numerous instances. By this type of thinking, one is being sinful to use or possess anything at all, or at least anything beyond the necessity of bare existence. Each person among the multitude is thus supposed to give his all to the multitude—and somehow increase the total as measured in justice if not in bushels. This admonition is said to arise from the concept that the Creator created everything and that we are robbing Him if we consume or possess or use economic things beyond sheer necessity for survival. And so, since all belongs to the Creator, it is argued that we are supposed to give items of value to someone else. If this seems to be stretching a point of view, it may be recalled that no less a reputed authority than Professor Richard T. Ely held that Karl Marx is a crusted Tory as compared with Jesus, and that "anyone who accepts private property in any form whatsoever, even in matters of consumption, must reject Christ."[9]

By the same terms used in this argument against the first person owning a thing, by what right could a second person have it instead? Is it not an argument, if valid, for universal suicide by starvation and exposure? The calculus of it is difficult for the mind to grasp, and yet its influence over history and still in our time cannot be denied. The ethical overtone of the archaic viewpoint still dictates many governmental laws and legal interpretations.

The long prevailing and continuing view that private ownership is sinful has another serious consequence, which is to have discouraged scientific and philosophical attention to the deserving subject. Were it similarly held, generally, that horseless carriages were a work of the devil, motor transportation would still be largely the dreams of "sinful" minds.

Property as a Self-Evident Fact

Proper credit should be given to the few great minds who perceived at an early date the importance of private property as a social organization. But many of these persons considered it to be self-evident that there was property, so that devoting any time or space to discussing it was wasteful and unnecessary. The fine work of Quesnay has already been mentioned, and yet he failed even to define it in all except perhaps one treatise on natural law; his contemporary, Turgot, seemed acutely conscious of the origin and importance of property, yet failed to deal with its principles or forms to any degree. And we have also mentioned the surprising neglect of the subject by authorities such as Smith and Say.

As to more recent times, many persons consider the classic eleventh edition of the *Encyclopaedia Britannica* as the most complete and reliable encyclopedia of information on developments up to the time of its publication. But note the extent of its treatment of "Property"—only one paragraph of 172 words! The reason for this neglect is not clear, but at best we can hope that it was not considered as sinful even to discuss it.

Coming now to the contemporary works on economics, the absence of any formal treatment of property and ownership is striking in book after book where one might expect to find extensive discussion of it. Rather than to give details here about these many fine books in other respects, I shall leave to anyone interested the task of reviewing for himself the literature from that standpoint. Few books have dealt with property, either, as a specific object. Those like the distinctive ones by C. Reinold Noyes and Gottfried Dietze have a high scarcity value.[10]

The view of property as a self-evident fact is reflected in the major emphasis on governmental processes and legal technicalities, rather than of the deeper philosophic and economic aspects, in all the books and bits of books that deal with the subject. And most of the others which dealt with it at all treated private property as sinful in some respect or degree. For all who feel otherwise, the literary arena is still critically uncrowded in that corner.

Alleged Origin by Theft

Another point of great importance is that of whether or not the institution of private ownership originated in theft.

This, it seems to me, has been seriously neglected. The assertions that property originated in theft have been so dominant that many persons may even believe it to be the meaning of original sin.

The original alleged thefts are said to have then continued throughout man's history, especially by the device of national conquest and governmental confiscation. A group of anarchists of the socialist variety, of which Proudhon is exemplary, have always held that private property is the essence of privilege and the parent of all other kinds of privilege, with the state acting in the role of bulwark for the process.

When a stork came along and set Joe Doe down in some field or forest, it is not to be denied that the land and trees and all their likes in the sense of the earth and the sea were already there when he arrived. He did not create them. At that point, he had done nothing to change them for better or for worse.

A common story goes like this, in effect: Some other Joe Doe, soon after birth, learned to walk and pick up sticks and stones. Being an inventive genius, Joe discovered that he could walk around a piece of land, drive sticks in the ground with stones at the corners, and proclaim that "This piece of land is mine forevermore."

At this point the labor theory of value enters this analysis of the "original theft" as a crucial question. Since the inventive Joe is said to have done absolutely nothing in creating the land or making it better in any way, it is thus alleged that he obviously stole it. He had ground no stones to bits to make the soil; he had not even leveled it, or moved a spoonful of dirt other than by driving the stakes into it.

I shall only say here that this theory deserves much attention, analytically. For unless we can establish in logic a clear title for the first owner, we are plagued with the charge of chronic theft in every subsequent claim to its ownership into the infinite future, in dealing with all matters of property.

Blackstone—who, incidentally, himself speaks of property as something "unconnected with his person," which raises a moot question with which I shall deal later—regrets that "few men seek to investigate the foundation of these rights. . . ."[11]

Theft in Continued Ownership

Closely akin to the question of whether the original claimant of an item acquired it by a process of theft is the question of whether the continuation of successive ownership is likewise by processes of theft. But there is a difference between the two questions that requires separate analysis.

If we accept the position that no valid ownership can arise from theft or follow any point of theft in its exchange, the reestablishment of validity in its ownership requires that we go back to the first theft and put it on the track again by restoring it to its proper owner. Or, perhaps, validity could be restored at some other point by establishing ownership which creates, in effect, someone as an *original* owner again. This means, of course, that there must be a basis for validating any first claim to any part of Creation, or otherwise there could be no valid claims to private ownership of anything anywhere. It is for this reason that I have preferred to separate the question of whether an original claimant is or is not practicing theft. Did he steal it from someone else who wanted it—valued it, economically—at that time, or did he merely use something in which nobody else saw any value as a specific item to be owned?

Once ownership of an item is originated—and for present purposes we shall assume no theft was involved—we are then confronted with a different sort of question: how about the validity of ownership after one or more other persons likewise come to value the item, and would claim it as owners if they could? The distinction between the two questions arises from the fact of there being multiple claims, in contrast to a sole and single claim of some original owner of anything.

The problem of continuing ownership, in turn, seems to me to break down into two parts:

1. With passing time and changing conditions, the value of a thing changes either up or down. If the change is upward in value and did not arise from changes made in the item by its owner, how could it be argued that the increased value should belong to him? He had done nothing to enhance its value, by this argument, so any and every other person worked no less to bring about the increase than did the owner-claimant; the others, therefore, have as much right to its appreciated value as he does, leaving him with an invalid claim to the increase.

2. Mere possession of an item by its owner creates a question in justice. The question may be posed thus: What is wrong with theft is that it strips the owner of the advantages of using the item; and isn't that all that is wrong with theft? If so, it may be said in like manner that private ownership of any item bars every other person from the advantages of using the item, for precisely the same reason.

The self-esteemed advocates of private property may assert that the answer to such questions are clearly self-evident; that, as was evidenced in the work of the classical economists of fame, these questions do not even warrant their attention.

It is neither the place nor my purpose here to deal at length with these particular questions, but perhaps the direction my answer would take might be suggested. The condition that gives rise to economic worth in the market place is that two (or more) persons want a thing when only one exists. It should be clear that there is no way to prevent this situation merely by settling ownership on one or the other. To give it to one person leaves the other bereft, whichever is chosen; and to give half to each leaves both of them in semidisownership. The best that giving it to a third party could accomplish is to leave both of them without property. The situation will be mitigated, therefore, if ownership is vested with the one who wants it most, and this is a decision to be arrived at through the market process. Any other solution will necessarily worsen the conflict of desires.

An important point to be kept in mind in any such questions is that neither of the duplicate desires for the item, nor the limitation of its supply—the two factors causing the condition leading to ownership—will ever pass away by worshiping at the wishing well. If someone chooses to speak of this unavoidable condition as "theft," he is only asserting that theft is a necessary and permanent condition in our society. In submitting any proposal to vest ownership elsewhere than with the person who bid highest in the free market, he is only nominating someone else of his own choosing to be the alleged thief instead.

The Legal View

Before attempting to define property and ownership, some prior issues need to be recognized. One of these is the legal vs. the nonlegal view of the matter.

Bentham serves to represent a long list of authorities who have asserted that property did not preexist government; that property is purely a creation of the laws which society enacts through government; that, therefore, property exists only by a grant of privilege under the power of collective political might.

Mirabeau once expressed the view this way: "*The law alone constitutes property,* because it is only the political will which can erect the renunciation of all, and give a common title, a guarantee to the use of one alone."[12]

One may hasten to conclude that this is true when it is noted that in the oldest known legal system—Egypt, running back to about 4,000 B.C.—an important function of the king's palace was to house the records of title, boundaries, wills, and contracts.[13] But this is evidence for the conclusion.

Among those who have differed sharply from this legalistic view of property was Charles Comte, who said with impressive logic: "It would, perhaps, be more correct to say that it is property which gave birth to civil laws; for it is hard to see what need a tribe of savages, among whom no property of any kind existed, could have of laws or of a government."[14]

In the opinion of Sir Henry Maine, from his distinguished and thorough studies, earliest law is itself "a habit" and not the "conscious exercise of the volition of a lawgiver or a legislature."[15]

These two sharply contrasted views have divided the great minds of all time on the nature of property and ownership. Most social scientists, I fear, have hardly advanced their thinking in this area far enough to see clearly the question, namely, whether property and ownership preexist the processes of government and are basically independent of them as such, or whether they are purely the creation of government. This would have to be resolved before any clear definitions of these concepts could be determined.

The Theocratic View

Before attempting to define property and ownership, one can hardly ignore another issue, the theocratic one.

According to one view of the matter, all of Creation is owned by the Creator. No human, by this view, may acquire a clear and exclusive title to any part of Creation as private property—legally or extralegally, formally or informally. At best it may be said, these persons aver, that we human inhabitants of this part of the universe are being allowed by the Creator to use some of His created materials for our use as tenants and for the duration of our stay on earth. For this we pay Him no rent as such, of course, and have no exclusive or enduring claim to its use that would allow us to transfer its use or ownership to some other person of our own choosing. Valid and full ownership, they say, is therefore impossible for any individual person. The theocratic view then may hold that the government is His agency here on earth for handling all conflicting claims and desires for the use of limited items of usefulness, operating as landlord or manager of the property.

It should also be observed, however, that it is possible to hold a religious view of Creation without going this far in an acceptance of any governmental function as managing director of the created property.

The view that the earth was originally owned in common to all men, and should therefore remain so, was held by the Stoics and by certain Fathers of the early Christian church.[16] The same view has been echoed since by many persons, such as Professor Ely.

The theocratic view is perhaps nowhere else so concisely expressed as in this biblical verse: "For all the earth is mine."[17]

For poetic beauty and completeness some would prefer: "The earth is the Lord's, and the fulness thereof; the world and they that dwell therein."[18]

Others may raise the interesting question of the meaning of: "Thou shalt not steal."[19]

Or how about the implied meaning of the question: "Is it not lawful for me to do what I will with mine own?"[20]

Important as are these underlying religious questions about creation, it seems to me they are not necessarily involved in our consideration of property and ownership among persons on earth for the duration. The problem of those other matters are of another dimension. Whether one be a devout atheist or a devout patron of a faith that considers all to belong to the Creator and that therefore nothing in that sense belongs to mortal man, he must face the same problem of how we shall deal with one another here and now while the show of earthly life is in process; how shall we resolve these problems as they arise? Neither the religious nor the secular view would seem to necessitate giving any property privilege to one person that is denied to another.

If the view is held that all belongs to the Creator, for instance, and that it cannot belong exclusively to you as an individual, such a limitation of your powers of ownership of created property would hardly give you a license to dictate to other human beings what they may or may not use during their lives; or what they may or may not do with their claim on property at the time of their death.

So for purposes of our present discussion, I would prefer to avoid completely this interesting theological question. And if someone should contend that all creation belongs to the Creator, and that we function only as His tenants, perhaps we can at least speak of property and ownership as being at a lower—but real—level of dealings of persons with one another. It still can be held in logic, I believe, that none of these contemporary mortals may properly assume a superior status in this creation. We could then go on with our discussion of the problem, using terms for a common problem that faces atheists and religious members of our earthly society alike.

Defining Property and Ownership

A review of the literature of economics and other treatments of interhuman affairs shows us that they are acutely lacking in definitions of property and ownership. To be sure, the physiocrats contributed some clear understanding of the importance of property, and the Scottish school of Locke and others gave us some noteworthy starts on defining its nature. All this should be rediscovered and extended. Once we definitely and clearly define our key terms and the question, we shall probably be far on the road to solutions of perplexing issues in our time.

As to the definition of ownership, it too has suffered the neglect of the ages. And what is worse, discussions of even the learned authorities have shuttled carelessly back and forth between property and ownership, as though they were two words for the same thing. It is, on the contrary, extremely important for any precise thinking to distinguish clearly between what is owned and those attributes of attachment that we call ownership. To fail in this would be like speaking indiscriminately of a picture and the nail by which it is hung on the wall.

We are now prepared, I think, to consider some definitions:

Property is anything to which value attaches and endures

in the time dimension, so long as it is susceptible to identification and is also possible of separation enough so that it may be exchanged from one person to another, insofar as its features of value are concerned; it may be either tangible or intangible, provided these features of identifiable and durable worth inhere.

Ownership is the placement of these features with some person (or persons, in a manner whereby their separate identities survive) so that he may enjoy rights of possession, use, and disposal of its worth thereby.

Irrelevant for purposes of definition is the question of why an item has value for the person. It matters only that one or more persons attach value to it, for any reason sufficient alone to him. All that is required is that the person desire it, and that a scarcity makes it unavailable to him free of cost or sacrifice in order to get it.

Duration of the economic worth beyond the present instant is one of the requirements of property. This is what gives property its capacity for identification, in part, for future possession, use, and exchange. It may be tangible or intangible, physical in nature or other, and wanted for either "consumption" or "production"; such distinctions do not matter for this purpose. There is needed, of course, something that will serve to identify who has it and who does not have it. The *who* becomes our crucial question, but beyond my purpose to resolve here.

The durability need not be permanent, in whole or in part. The value of an item of property may diminish and eventually disappear totally, and commonly does. So long as some value remains, it is still an item of property.

Property is by its nature something, of course, that exists in parts or pieces, and it is those with which we deal and of which we speak.

The Origin of Property

As my final point, I wish to suggest briefly a view I now hold about property which not so long ago I had neither accepted nor rejected, because I had never consciously considered it. I now feel, however, that it is an extremely important part of the whole question of property and ownership.

Traditionally, the issue of property and ownership have been said to arise only as the population increased to where they crowded each other for survival in items of food and the like. This view invites the common belief that property originated in the forest and stream, and that the primary objects of ownership were these essential items to preserving one's life. It has led to what might be called the *hyperopic* view of property which has always prevailed—the view that property refers to something separate from the person himself, usually of a physical nature.

I now believe this view to be wrong, basically wrong, in an important respect. The *primary* object of property and ownership which antedates all others and is superior to all others in its importance is *self*. It seems to me that all other items are secondary to this. And using this concept of primary property, questions seem to be answerable with relative ease and certainty, using self-ownership as the premise.

It may seem strange that self-ownership has been so tardy in considerations of property and ownership in general, since mankind has always lived closer to himself than to the forest and stream where property matters have always been focused. Though he could not escape from himself physically, he seems to have done so mentally in past developments of property concepts. One is reminded in this connection of the pattern of development of the physical sciences where astronomy gained a lead of thousands of years ahead of human biology. In fact, the latter has only recently begun to emerge fully. So perhaps we may be excused for our hyperopic tendencies in the social sciences.

The reason for including the person as an item of his own property is that he possesses all the required features giving rise to the condition of property:

1. Desired.
2. Scarce.

3. Durable, in the time dimension.

You are presumably desired by yourself, and hopefully in addition by your spouse and offspring and others.

You are scarce, extremely scarce, just short of not existing at all. No assembly line can conceivably resolve the problem of your scarcity.

You are durable—we hope.

The condition necessary to prove the property aspect of the person could be evidenced here and now, except for certain taboos and social amenities, merely by putting you on the auction block. For most of the history of the human race this practice has been accepted and commonly practiced. In a sense we still practice it everywhere in the world, though at the continuous auction (in effect) many of us keep bidding ourselves in as the highest bidder. Those who are not their own highest bidders customarily limit the sale of themselves to some minor proportion of their lives at some prescribed tasks—or at least some prescribed location—for a day, a week, a month, or a year, and at some specified sales price. By one view of the matter, in another form we are said to lengthen the span of the sale "until death do us part," which is perfectly legal if some town clerk or other licensed witness officiates. And still others, in unfortunate ways, fail both to be their own highest bidder or to accept higher bids of others in any form; they are the ones who jump off bridges, or otherwise terminate their property problem in some tragic way.

As I now see the matter of property and ownership, the first person singular is the *primary* form from which all other forms of property arise. It is the prior and superior form. All others are secondary, because they could not come into being without self-owned beings to make them their property; they cannot arise and stand conceptually by themselves, without the primary form of property as a pedestal on which to stand. To focus the question even better, we might ask ourselves whether a slave could own anything basically and completely from the standpoint of justice, if we start by denying the slave his self-ownership. To say that he could do so would be like saying that your cow owns her calf and the milk she produces.

Finally, I would suggest that this view of self-ownership as primary property, from which all other property arises as derivatives, does not rest on the labor theory of value; nor does it rest on any comparable value theory. It rests on the subjective evaluation of worth, with all market prices determined in the market as with other things of worth.

The origin of all economic property and claims to ownership, then, is to be found in self-ownership of persons and thence on to derived and valid claims to all other forms of property. He acquires these other things, in part, by using his own labor to "create" something from the tools made available to us by Creation. If we will approach the problem of property and ownership through this door, I believe the clouds of uncertainty and misunderstanding will fade rapidly away.

As one timely example of this approach, how would the issue of "civil rights" or "minority rights" be resolved by this approach to involuntary servitude of anybody, in whole or in part?[21]

NOTES

1. Robert Ardrey, *African Genesis* (New York, 1961), p. 167.
2. F. J. C. Hearnshaw, *A Survey of Socialism* (London, 1929), pp. 142-143.
3. Charles Gide and Charles Rist, *A History of Economic Doctrines* (London, 1915), p. 41.
4. Henry D. Aiken, *Hume's Moral and Political Philosophy* (New York, 1948), Book III.
5. For the author's meaning of liberty, see *Liberty Defined,* Mont Pelerin Society meeting of 1957, St. Moritz, Switzerland.
6. *Reader's Digest* (July 1941), p. 39.
7. L. Faucher, *Cyclopaedia of Political Science, Political Economy, and of the Political History of the United States* (New York, 1888) pp. 383-391.
8. Justinian's *Institutes* (Sandar's translation).
9. Gide and Rist, p. 538n.
10. *The Institution of Property* and *In Defense of Property,* 1936 and 1963 respectively.

11. *Blackstone's Commentaries on the Law* (Washington, 1892, Gavit edition), p. 218.

12. Faucher, p. 385.

13. John Henry Wigmore, *A Panorama of the World's Legal Systems* (Saint Paul, 1928), Volume I, p. 12.

14. Faucher, p. 385.

15. *Ancient Law* (London, 1917), p. v.

16. Bruno Leoni, *Freedom and the Law* (Princeton, 1961), pp. 52-53.

17. Exodus, 19:5.

18. Psalms, 24:1.

19. Exodus, 20:15.

20. St. Matthew, 20:15.

21. See an interesting interpretation by Alfred Avins, *Cornell Law Quarterly,* Vol. 49, No. 2, pp. 228-256.

2

Carl F. H. Henry

CHRISTIAN PERSPECTIVE ON PRIVATE PROPERTY

THE CONTROVERSY over private property has split our twentieth century world in two. In the name of economic justice the free world advocates private property; in the name of economic justice the communist world rejects it. Both the communist revolution and western political adjustments have blunted the free world's convictions about private property. The whole realm of property now staggers under problems, compromises and uncertainties. In numerous lands, nationalization is now largely a matter of public indifference, and common ownership of property is hardly a live political issue.

In lands of fairly advanced economic development the disappearance of vast disparities of wealth and poverty has lessened some of the explosive potential of the property debate. But private property remains a politically volatile issue where great masses of people are hungry, as in rural India. The use of property (what ownership exists *for*) has become as fundamental an issue as ownership itself.

Although private property is a major social concern of our century, free world literature treats the theme cavalierly, indeed, often neglects and even avoids it. Even U.S. Information Agency libraries around the world are so lacking in constructive volumes on this subject that to prepare any respectable defense of private property from their resources would be almost impossible. The same complaint can be made against many public libraries in the Anglo-Saxon world. Meanwhile communist spokesmen constantly affirm the illegitimacy of private property. Since alien views thrive in a climate of indifference, the free world is especially obliged to engage earnestly in this debate. This duty of studying the property issue is doubly incumbent upon any society that considers private property not only indispensable to a just social order but, contrary to the communist rejection of supernatural sanctions, presumes also to find a basis for ownership in man's God-given rights. In a time when the problem of property constitutes a pressing question of social morality, our generation must face the issue with new boldness and energy and in a manner that soundly probes its spiritual and theological implications.

The scriptural revelation of man's nature and destiny sets the theme of property and all other human concerns in the larger context of God's purpose in creation and redemption. In the Bible, God's sanction of private property stands in a framework that proclaims Divine Right above human rights, and only on this basis do human rights become inalienable. While the biblical view of rights and responsibilities may not be the only answer short of a planned society, it is nonetheless the only view long enough and wide enough to escape internal instability and external demolition.

In thus speaking of the biblical view of property I am not unmindful of several facts, notably the fluctuations of ecclesiastical opinion. The theologians and canonists of the Roman Catholic Church have indeed viewed private property as justified; several encyclicals by Leo XIII strongly insist on the necessity and justice of private ownership, and the encyclical *Rerum Novarum* expressly condemns as unjust the socialist design to abolish private property. The Roman Church condemned as heretical the Anabaptists and other sects that renounced private property and charged the Church—a holder of vast properties—with worldly-mindedness. In its support of private property the medieval Church largely perpetuated rather than transformed the pagan Roman view of absolute property rights—of which we shall speak later—although recognizing the existence of personal abuses. Yet, consistently with the notion of some early church fathers that private property springs from avarice, the Church from the fourth century onward from time to time also espoused community possessions and elimination of private property as normative; during the Inquisition, moreover, the Roman Church disregarded the right of personal property of the offender or his posterity.

In our own day church bodies of several denominations have acquired such extensive properties not directly related to their distinctive ministries that both municipal planners and churchmen, too, warn increasingly that this accumulation of tax-favored or tax-free properties may invite ultimate expropriation. The problem is compounded by large buildings presumably erected for spiritual ministries yet standing unused much of the week.

Not in practice only, but also in the realm of theory, the Christian witness is compromised. Modern ecclesiastical and ecumenical pronouncements on economic matters often reflect the influence of socialistic theory. The episcopate of the Anglican churches throughout the world, in the Lambeth Conference back in 1887, appealed to the clergy to emphasize "how much of what is good and true in Socialism is to be found in the precepts of Christ." In erstwhile Christian lands now dominated by communist forces, the morality of private ownership is no longer the common teaching of the churches. Textbooks on Christian social ethics generally give little thought to the theme of ownership, although German scholars show more awareness of the subject. Spokesmen for Anglo-Saxon church bodies frequently approve welfare legislation, yet neglect the exposition of scripturally revealed principles bearing on property rights as well as other social concerns. In America many clergymen shun the theme of private ownership in their pulpits, except when exhorting members to larger contributions. Even evangelical Protestants seldom express Christian conscience on this important issue, except by the occasional adoption of resolutions at annual conferences.

The socialist curtailment of the rights and functions of ownership and its institution of compulsory charity were aimed in part to overcome the misuse or abuse of property. The possibility of such abuse is encouraged whenever the use of property is undisciplined by ethical and spiritual considerations. Any doctrine of property devoid of biblical legitimation will inevitably license immoral practices. When man as a sinful creature fashions and justifies the right of property in isolation from divine prerogatives, he no longer properly balances rights and responsibilities, but will compromise the one in protecting the other. Unjustifiable excesses will incur the penalty of unjust restrictions as well-intentioned but misguided reformers seek to erase social wrongs by their techniques of compulsion. Recent modern history has certainly taught us that unless the present system of property is spiritually molded in the light of Christian principle, its alteration will be arbitrarily demanded by non-Christian speculation. In the case of communism, the stifling device of government correction and regulation promoted unjust demands in the name of justice: the wealthy were deprived of their goods and the poor have hardly found utopia.

To view the subject of private property from the standpoint of the biblical revelation is therefore imperative. We must do so not simply in order to anchor the Christian community firmly to the biblical view of life, but also to apprise the human race of the norm or criterion by which mankind will be divinely judged in regard to property relationships. Neglect of the scriptural view created a climate in which even some secular theorists could misrepresent as authentically biblical their speculative views of property that lacked true scriptural sensitivity. Think, for example, of the ease with which such writers conjoined the words "Christian Socialism." Or consider their description of the author of Luke's Gospel as "the socialist among the evangelists" (H. Holstzmann in *Protest. Kirchenzeit,* 1894, No. 45). A German socialist insisted that if Jesus were on earth he would affiliate with the Social Democrats. Early in this century A. Kalthoff depicted Christianity as a socioeconomic movement and Jesus as the ideal hero of a communistic proletarian revolution (*Das Christusproblem: Grundlinien zu einer Sozialtheologie,* Leipzig, 1902). Such perverse attachment of communist and socialist speculations to Christian motifs and their arbitrary misrepresentation as the proper climax of Protestant Reformation thought ought to spur the Western world to probe anew the biblical treatment of property.

Property rights must indeed be viewed in relationship to the whole social system in which they stand; they cannot long be preserved apart from other social ingredients. Nor can the social environment escape fundamental alteration when property rights are in jeopardy. But the property question must not be assessed today simply within socio-economic horizons. The subject arises within the context of the broad religious and cultural crisis facing our world; it must therefore be considered in the larger realm of both theological and anthropological realities. In fact, biblical religion deals with the property question not simply as an isolated economic concern but rather in the context of the will of God. F. C. Grant's reminder is timely that "it is less than ever possible, nowadays, to represent early Christianity as a revolutionary social (or social-economic) movement....It is clear that Christianity was from the very beginning a purely religious movement."[1] But Christianity was not, because of this central spiritual vision, therefore indifferent to human rights and duties; rather, as pure religion, it summoned every human activity under the rule of God. Judaeo-Christian revelation lifts the discussion of property above the merely horizontal perspective of an abstract antagonism between individual and society. Instead, its perspective is vertical, stressing at once the practical responsibility of all men to their Creator and under God to one another. The clash between individual and group interests, in which contemporary theory abstractly locates economic conflict, is thus challenged by an even more fundamental dimension of relationships, subjecting individual and social behavior alike to divine judgment.

In such a setting the absolute contrast between individual right and social right disappears: all human rights are for the individual, and every individual right is also a human right. The transcendent Creator stands above all as the ultimate source, sanction and support of enduring rights; and on earth, every man and all things are seen as God's own—God's creatures and his creation. In a word, God is their absolute owner, and man's possessions are a contingent and limited entrustment.

Here the contrast of the biblical with the ancient pagan view of property is immediately apparent. The Roman or Justinian view derives ownership from a natural right; it defines ownership as the individual's unconditional and exclusive power over property. It implies an owner's right to use property as he pleases (even to spoil or destroy it) irrespective of the will of others, and to do so continually. This view, preserved well into the Middle Ages, still remains the silent presupposition of much of the free world's common practice today.

The biblical view, as we shall see, differs in important respects from this pagan view. But it is a contrary view rather than a contradictory one. Sometimes the contrast between the Judaeo-Christian and Roman views has been stated so sharply as to create sympathy for the communist rejection of private property; but no scriptural basis exists for this arbitrary alternative. The Judaeo-Christian revelation is clearly on the side of private property. While it provides no *carte blanche* for a secular capitalistic civilization, the biblical view does not assail private property per se, but assumes its legitimacy and reinforces its propriety as a social institution.

1. Jehovah gave the promised land to the Hebrews and their right thereto was not forfeited either by poverty or by slavery. This assignment of a land to the Hebrews implies the propriety of private property. The universal right of private property cannot be deduced from this fact alone, in view of the temporary nature of the Old Testament economy. The New Testament Church is not assigned possession of one sector of land as was Israel, but is set as a light among all nations; by its practice of justice and benevolence the church is to demonstrate that the community of faith waits for unlimited possession of the earth in righteousness and mercy.

2. The Mosaic Law implies that private property is legitimate and not sinful. *It confers the highest sanctity on the principle of private ownership and reinforces the inviolability of property.* The Eighth Commandment teaches that it is sinful to take what belongs to another, and the Tenth Commandment teaches that it is sinful even to covet what belongs to another. This right of ownership is presupposed in the details as well as in the broad outlines of the whole Mosiac legislation and by its application throughout Scripture.[2]

3. The teaching of Jesus and of the apostles does not condemn private property but *presupposes and reinforces its legitimacy.* The New Testament reaffirms the Decalogue (Matt. 19:18 f., Rom. 13:9 ff.), and the teaching and practice of the New Testament Christians assume the legitimacy of private property. Jesus and his disciples had a common fund for the meeting of their expenses (John 13:14), but the disciples retained ownership of boats and nets to which they returned after the crucifixion (John 21:3 ff.). Jesus' headquarters at Capernaum seems to have been the house which Peter retained as a private dwelling (Mark 1:29, 2:1), even as Mary, Martha and Lazarus whom Jesus loved had their own home in Bethany (Luke 10:38 ff., John 12:1 ff.). The assumption that private ownership is wrong makes havoc of Jesus' appeal to men's rights over their property to illustrate their duty to God (cf. Luke 19:12, Matt. 21:33).

The so-called communist passages of the New Testament are misnamed, for they disclose no kinship with Marxian dogma. That some of the early Christian believers in special circumstances voluntarily shared their possessions is clear enough (Acts 2:44 f., 4:32 ff.). But the notion that wealth is sinful and poverty meritorious is no more to be found in the Gospels than elsewhere in the Bible. Although Jesus' sayings about the rich and poor appear in Luke's Gospel in their most uncompromising form (cf. Luke 6:20, Matt. 5:3), these passages cannot be fairly considered to be hostile to wealth and partial to poverty as some interpreters consider them. But Andrew N. Bogle long ago stressed that in the Acts of the Apostles, which also comes from the pen of Luke, no inference about so-called communist activities of the primitive church is permissible beyond Luke's explicit statements ("Property," in Hastings' *Dictionary of the Gospels*). The facts remain that the practice of community of goods by the Jerusalem church did not survive perpetually; that it was not observed universally; that the Apostle Paul neither instructed churches he founded to practice such community of goods, nor condemned them for their failure to do so; that even believers who shared possessions *sold* their houses and lands; and that in the local situation where community of goods was observed, the Apostle Peter specifically reinforced the right of private property in his rebuke to Ananias: "While it remained, was it not thine own? And after it was sold, was it not in thine own power?" (Acts 5:4). The scriptural criticism of the use of property and wealth affords no license for the drawing of socialist or communist conclusions.

Yet, while the Judaeo-Christian revelation does not repudiate private property, it does not therefore endorse every exposition of private property. The Bible associates ownership with conditions of righteousness that confer moral goodness upon man's holding and use of possessions; it does not approach the subject of private property from a merely legal point of view. The Bible has an eye to ownership that is both legally right and morally good. Against any derivation and protection of property rights based exclusively on political or economic positions, whether conservative or liberal, Christian theology has a dual responsibility. It must show that the communist rejection of private property misunderstands God's purpose for human society, and it must show that God's ordination of things can be equally dimmed and distorted where human rights are promoted strictly in a secular manner. Although some expositors of the pagan Roman view also appeal to rational and moral principles to reinforce a constructive use of property, the Judaeo-Christian view holds man spiritually accountable to God for the use of his possessions.[3] In view of the modern temptation to perpetuate the tradition of private property solely on a nontheological basis, it is especially imperative to emphasize that capitalism just as much as communism or socialism can minimize the will of God in respect to property.

Insofar as civil law is concerned, however, the biblical view presupposes and reinforces man's legal right of ownership which, in respect to human society, is only virtually absolute.[4] Private property is a legal right and when acquired has, as President James Madison put it, "a right to protection as a social right."[5] Although man is not sovereign owner, the use of his possessions hangs on his personal decision. When the Roman emphasis on sovereign individual possession is viewed in the context of the state rather than in the context of the supernatural world, it has much in common with the biblical view. The Old Testament narrative of King Ahab's effort to acquire Naboth's vineyard near the royal palace (I Kings 21:1 ff.) is pointedly relevant. When Naboth declined the king's proposals for purchase or exchange of land, Jezebel had Naboth falsely accused and stoned to death. The prophet Elijah pronounced doom upon the tyrant, and Jezebel's death was viewed as a divine punishment (II Kings 9:25 f.). Private property implies man's formal right to use and enjoy his possessions as he pleases subject only to restrictions imposed by agreement or covenant or by law. The scriptural view of man's spiritual accountability presupposes his formal legal freedom to use possessions as he determines.

This distinction between what is legally right on the one hand, and what is spiritually and ethically good on the other, is inherent in any view that preserves the realities of moral freedom. While a man has no spiritual ground for not believing in God, he does have the legal right to be an atheist; while he has no moral basis for selfish use of private property, he has a legal right to use his possessions that way. Man's property right in respect to God is never absolute or indefeasible but always derivative and conditional. In respect to the state and society, however, man's property right has formal divine sanction even if his use of property subverts God's spiritual intention. The moral use of property confers goodness upon its possessor, but it does not confer the legal right of ownership. It is not man's legal and moral right to properly acquired property that is to be questioned but rather his moral use of it.

Today, therefore, when communism attacks the morality of private property as an institution, it is important not to contrast legal right and moral right absolutely, but to emphasize their partial coincidence. Christian theology distinguishes both the order that the state requires as justice and the benevolence that the Church spiritually demands from the order. The Church has no mandate to impose spiritual imperatives upon an unregenerate society. But the Church is obliged to proclaim those revealed principles which government must promote and men must observe for the sake of a just society. Social custom, tending to assign finality to the mood of the masses, needs always to be challenged by revealed morality. The state has no rightful authority to modify the divine principles of social justice, including individual freedom to do the will of God. From the viewpoint of biblical ethics the rejection of private property involves the rejection of a divinely sanctioned ideal, an arbitrary restriction of human freedom, and an ideological frustration of the possibilities of a just social order. Justice in respect to the possession of property is found neither through the Church's ordering of society or the state's ordering of society in a manner that dissolves individual freedom and moral responsibility; it is found, rather, in promoting and preserving the divine order of work, ownership and possessions that God has ordained for mankind.

Yet a Christian ethic of property must not be divorced from biblical teaching as a whole. Scripture nowhere approves private property as a possession that stands wholly at man's free disposition independent of moral and spiritual obligations.[6] Always and everywhere ownership implies responsible possession under God and subjection to the just claim of one's neighbors.

As Alfred de Quervain has noted, the Bible discloses an "order" of ownership,[7] an order whose implications strike deeply into the contemporary debate over property rights:

1. Man's possessions have their origin in the spiritual world as the creation of a gift-bestowing God. Hence they include from the outset a precedent of sensitivity to the survival needs of creatures—that is, to neighbor-needs.

2. Every man is to share God's world as a personal possession—the order and beauty of nature in which God declares his glory, the invigorating air and refreshing rain, the sun which shines upon just and unjust alike. Hence even apart from private property every person is to share abundantly in God's created universe.

3. The right of private property is connected with several things: with God's program of work and ownership, with individual freedom and well-being, with a peaceful life in society, with the power of the individual to resist the encroachments of the state,[8] and with spiritual development through generosity and benevolence. The solution of social problems therefore is not found, as Marxism asserts, in severing work from the aspiration for private property, but in promoting property rights and responsibilities within the orbit of God's will.

4. Private property confers upon each person a province of liberty that promotes human discipline and maturity. As a ruler of nature man may exercise dominion either by "keeping and dressing" it (Gen. 2:15), that is, by subsuming it under the spiritual purpose of the Creator, or by exploiting it for selfish and evil ends.[9] Individual ownership is the presupposition of an individual life and a means of character development. In the free use of his property, man as a bearer of God's image himself becomes a maker, a creator, with the responsible opportunity of shaping what is relatively "without form and void" (to borrow the words of the creation narrative). But this realm of liberty also provides a means of individual free service to others.[10]

5. Since God as Creator-Redeemer always remains the ultimate owner of life and things, man must seek always

the will of his sovereign Lord. Property no less than man is God's creation, and man was created for a specific purpose in relation to it. It is "the gift of God, to be held before all else in trust for the Giver's own uses, for the realization of His Kingdom or manifested sovereignty on earth."[11]

6. As a property holder, man stands always between two neighbors, the divine and human, and in the use of possessions is called not merely to gratify his personal desires but to serve God and mankind. This biblical concept of stewardship presupposes the right and responsibility of private property. Ownership is a loan whereby man remains forever indebted to the Lord of his possessions and is morally and spiritually responsible for their use. The Old Testament establishes the spiritual obligation of tithes, offerings, and a life of justice and mercy. The New Testament holds man's possessions as a whole, property included, in harmony between the Eighth Commandment and the New Commandment (or Love Commandment). The divine "Overlandlord" protests any misuse of property that violates the welfare of all and oppresses the poor. Where there are prevalent food and job shortages, property should be used for productive purposes.

7. How a man uses his property and possessions shows how he answers the fundamental question: "To whom do I belong? Whose possession am I?" As the Protestant reformers put it, since the Christian belongs to God and must serve him, his use of property and possessions will reflect the reality of this divine relationship and disclose whether he is possessed by God or by his possessions.[12]

8. God, and not material possessions, must remain the source of man's confidence. We must at one and the same time hear Moses' word on the ownership of property and Jesus' word about the peril of serving mammon.

9. Only possession under the rule of God protects both the individual and society from the baneful consequences of sin and confers goodness upon rightful ownership. Possessions gain their spiritual justification in the service they render the possessor (as a means of spiritual growth) and the community (as an instrument of justice and of benevo-

lence). Hence property has both an anthropological and social function;[13] it provides an arena of spiritual decision wherein Christian duty is performed and wherein Christian faith and love exercise their vitality.

10. The perversion of human rights, implicit in an unjust and immoral use of property, threatens human freedom as surely as the denial of human rights in respect to ownership.

11. The goal of good government is to promote justice and order in the community. This includes the preservation of what is right in the realm of ownership. The just state will protect rather than destroy property rights. A society in which these rights are preserved will be more stable than one in which they are jeopardized. Private property, in turn, remains one of the necessary foundations of durable government.

12. The equal dignity and worth of all human beings are basic biblical emphases. The Bible does not, however, identify justice or the good of the community with equality of possessions. Every man has, as Charles Gore once said, "the divine and equal right" to make the best of himself, but this does not imply the elimination of inequalities among men. If cosmic fiat were to level all economic status tonight, inequalities would reappear tomorrow through differences of intellect and opportunity. And if political fiat removes inequalities, they will reappear *ipso facto* in the removers. Nowhere does the Old Testament view disproportionate wealth as essentially sinful; in some cases it considers such wealth a sign of special divine blessing. The Christian concept of justice is not that justice is a matter of absolute equality. Equal distribution of property does not follow from the fact that property rights are equally human. The Protestant reformers advocated no such doctrine of equality of possessions. The industrious are to get more than the lazy; those who refuse work opportunities are to be rewarded proportionately. This subordination of the problem of ownership to the problem of work still has relevance for contemporary society.

13. A basic minimum of ownership is necessary for indi-

vidual survival and on this basic minimum no one else has the right to infringe. This minimum differs for different persons. Such private possessions as food, clothing, housing, furniture, and weapons are indispensable to human survival; ornaments, books, and other articles beyond mere biological utility are indispensable to human dignity. In a capitalistic society it is incorrect to identify property simply with land; multitudes now rent rather than own their homes, and money has a value equivalent to property.

14. Over against the recent tendency to contrast human rights and property rights, biblical teaching presents private property as one of the several human rights.[14] The weekly publication of the Religion and Labor Council of America, *Walking Together,* misrepresents the Bible when it states that "both religion and labor view individual rights as having moral priority over property rights" (Issue No. 422, July 16, 1964). This emphasis merely downgrades the right of property, for the Bible views property rights among human rights rather than as inferior to them.

15. The values of property are not to be isolated and exalted to the neglect of other human rights, and thus assigned priority over human dignity. The pagan Roman conception of man's sovereign control over property was reflected also in the attitude toward slaves, or the neglect of the value and dignity of persons, despite an acknowledgment that man is differently related to persons than to property.[15] The slave was classed as property in ancient pagan society and considered much as a domestic animal wholly at the disposal of his master.[16] Christianity doomed this perversion first in principle and then in practice.[17] Under Christian influence the Roman law of property underwent notable changes in respect to the law of property in persons (slaves, wives, and children), reflected in its later Justinian codification. Where this spiritual influence is lost, property rights may remain a prized possession while other human rights become a matter of indifference, although spiritual indifference will sooner or later undermine the whole range of human rights, property rights included. "We stand for the maintenance of private property. . . .We

shall protect free enterprise as the most expedient or rather the sole possible economic order." The words were Hitler's.[18] Yet Hitler was a socialist, not a champion of "free enterprise"; only the communists were to his left. And his warped devotion to private property was soon apparent. On the night of November 9, 1938, Nazi authorities in a systematic pogrom destroyed 815 Jewish shops, burned down 119 synagogues and 171 homes, and demolished another 76 synagogues. Hermann Goering told representatives of German insurance companies how to elude payment of casualty claims.[19] Jewish properties were to be destroyed when this involved no "danger to German life or property." It is noteworthy that race riots in the United States, presumably in the interest of civil rights, involve an increasing range of damage to white-owned property, just as the resistance movement manifested itself in the destruction of Negro-owned premises, churches included. A philosophy of liberty which thus fragments freedom and does not preserve an identity between human rights and property rights is not serviceable to social justice.

16. In respect to politico-economic philosophy the Bible establishes no approved code of detailed legislation, but instead supplies principles by which to resolve particular problems. The Bible, for example, proposes no ideal "regulation" of property by governmental control of human affairs, nor does it dictate quantitative limits in respect to ownership. But it does stipulate principles for the moral use of property, so that ownership is both protected and limited by divine commandment.

a. All land is intended for appropriate use, primarily that of meeting man's common needs. It is intended first of all for those who work it, not for those who do not work it. The normal pattern of existence in the Old Testament is that of the peasant farmer family united by the soil and its care. But today only a fraction of the populace could be supported by agricultural pursuits. A fundamental fact of capitalism is the dependence of great masses of people on land and assets that belong to others. Hence one must distinguish an order of priority between property that is necessary for survival, property that is necessary for true freedom, property that is held as a service, and property that is accumulated for profit, from property that is aggrandized for power, and property that cancels the liberty of others. In the latter area there exists a special responsibility for protecting the possibility of regular industry, meaningful labor, and personal freedom for dependent workers. The worst of all solutions is state control of power in a planned society; less objectionable is legislative constraint on the free use of power in a democratic society; preferable is voluntary use of economic power in a morally responsible way in a spiritually sensitive society.

b. The inheritance of possessions is a socially cohesive factor. Where inheritance ceases, the family ceases. Since all possession comes by attainment or gift, inheritance is not wrong but desirable. What is wrong is its misuse to promote a serviceless life.

c. The Old Testament both guaranteed and restricted permanent ownership (Lev. 25:23) by invoking the Year of Jubilee or fiftieth year (after "seven sabbaths of years"), which was binding upon every man in the Hebrew theocracy. The land was not to be sold "in perpetuity" because God is its ultimate owner and because the people are "strangers and sojourners" (Lev. 25:8 ff.). In the Jubilee year property reverted to its original owners (Lev. 25:10) and all slaves were to be set free (even as God has rescued the entire community from slavery in Egypt); it was a time of recovery of "liberty throughout the land." In addition, the land was to lie fallow as in the sabbatical year. Today some of the objectives of Jubilee are attained in other ways. Since the Industrial Revolution, scientific farming, for example, has achieved renewal of the land without sabbatical rest. An agricultural society, whose possessions are mainly in the form of land, could implement an actual return to possessions in a fixed year only with great difficulty. In an age of trade, commerce and capitalistic enterprise, when property is diversified, it could hardly be carried out at all. But its spirit and intention—to protect the poor from enslavement—are not wholly out of reach.

The Old Testament prophets denounced unlimited acquisition, retention, and perpetuation of property holdings as choking the vitality and depressing the life of others who were thereby precluded from acquiring property (Isa. 5:8). Today the amassing of properties is discouraged by estate taxes which in effect return a part of their value to the common pool. Modern economic theory often tends wrongly to think of wealth as a fixed quantity, like land; its problem, then, is to keep wealth divided among a great number of people. But this notion is naive: a generation ago there was no property, as there is today, in television, jet planes, space missiles, and so on. There is a striking difference, moreover, between the Old Testament restrictions, which had a divine sanction in the life of the community, and modern legal restrictions, which differ from country to country and which often seem intended to abridge rather than to preserve the right of property and fail to promote individual sensitivity and responsibility.

d. When it comes to determining the most appropriate use of the land, the only answer (short of a planned society which operates on the basis of objectionable criteria) must be sought in the purposes for which the land is utilized, including that of economic return.

e. Since God wills government, the state may be a property holder. But the state is not to be The Property Holder, since only God is sovereign owner and lord of all. Insofar as civic legislation does not conflict with divine authority, the lawful authority of government is to be supported. In the absence of voluntary discipline and as an expression of the corporate conscience of the community, government may be called upon to legislate restraints on undesirable uses of property. But the state dare not insulate itself against criticism aiming to limit the state to preserving universal justice and to restrict it from legislating the special interests of any one class to the detriment of another. The penalties of government limitation of human rights are greater than is generally assumed and are not worth the risk.[20] The exercise of freedom without moral and spiritual maturity soon sets up a demand for legal restraints, including restrictions upon rights and liberty. Preventing the misuse of private property contrary to public order and the general welfare is indeed the duty of the state, but that is not its first duty; acknowledging and maintaining private property are the state's prior responsibility. Private property, moreover, is not an institution to be authorized by the state but an inalienable right divinely conferred upon mankind. "It is much better," wrote Cecil DeBoer, "to practice Christian stewardship and to practice it on time, than when it is too late."[21] Their refusal to be stewards of God seems in our day to destine people to enslavement to false gods, whether mammon or government.

f. In early times a segment of the apostolic community practiced the sharing of possessions in compassionate responsiveness to each other's needs. Thus these people demonstrated their belief both in the value of persons amid property and in the priority of stewardship over selfishness in the life of faith. Their voluntary detachment from possessions misled some early church fathers into the theory that private property resulted from avarice.

However, legal ownership from the biblical point of view is spiritually and morally vindicated by the use of possessions in the service of God and man. There is no basis for the viewpoint of the religious socialists, that when ownership stands under God's judgment it becomes a matter of legal indifference. While the Bible approves government preservation of justice and restraint of injustice, it does not encourage such government manipulation of human life and property that compulsion replaces liberty. The error of the socialist thesis is twofold: first, its "acceleration of the eschatological" (that is, its ambition to establish a utopian society in the present) fails to recognize that human life in the present fallen age exists under political and economic systems that are not identical with the Kingdom of God; and second, it arbitrarily ascribes socialistic features to this kingdom. That Christianity is to challenge the social order creatively is true enough; there is, however, no biblical basis for defining that challenge in terms of an attack on either the private right or form of ownership.

In the present social crisis nothing is gained by intangible notions of private property. At the same time the concept of private ownership cannot rest simply on secondary sanctions which, legitimate as they are, will not carry the full weight of the case for private property in the face of modern counterattack. There are those who view property only in terms of character development or free enterprise economics, and certainly private ownership is integral to these concerns. But in a day when the totalitarian state arrogates to itself the whole determination of human life, no appeal lower than the divine source, sanction and stipulation of human rights will bear the weight of the edifice of human rights. Private property thus gains status not simply in the tradition of civil law but also in the realm of divine purpose and moral law. This theistic vindication of private ownership demands also that man live to God's praise in all facets of his existence including the realms of work and ownership. Even the declaration of capitalism in terms of its moral resources, while considering ownership in terms of strict duty as well as of human right and the use of possessions as a high service, must be raised to the higher vision of the purpose and goodness of God.

The secular capitalistic concept of private property is weak because it is detached from external supports; it is weak also because the neglect of external sanctions leads to ready compromise of its inner premises. In capitalistic countries the decline of respect for private property gives striking evidence of this fact. This decline may be measured by two trends. First, there is the increase of serious offenses against property, despite their condemnation by all civilized codes of law, and the lenient treatment of such criminals (which implies that such offenses are no longer regarded as seriously as in the past). Of all prisoners in state penitentiaries in 1950, 73 percent had been convicted of property offenses. The F.B.I. *Uniform Crime Reports* indicate that apart from organized crime, American society is battling increased highway robberies, burglaries in residential and commercial buildings, thefts of automobiles and car accessories and bicycles, purse snatching, petty larceny by employees, theft by shoppers, misrepresentation of facts in property sales, and outright swindling. These latter crimes, moreover, are justified by the cliché, *caveat emptor!*

The second trend in secular capitalism that attests to the decline of sensitivity in respect to property rights is the lack of concern for those who are nonpossessors of property. If private property is a human right, if it is a necessary instrument of character development, if it affords the means for the external exercise of power and stewardship, if it contributes to the security of existence and the stability of society, then those who possess private property must contemplate how the nonpossessors may participate in this realm—a realm not merely of privilege but of right. Without the right of property the pursuit of happiness soon becomes vain, and without property itself man's sense of self-worth deteriorates. Remember Arthur Young's comment in *Travels in France* (1787): "The magic of property turns sand into gold." Every economic philosophy that promotes private property must therefore offer a bold critique of the misuse of private property. Otherwise the antagonists of this social institution will undermine confidence in the right of property itself by exploiting the borderline illustrations. Every person with rights simultaneously has duties, and no duty is more urgent in the free world today than that of protecting rather than frustrating the rights of others.

If there is to be renewed respect for private property, it must come through the conviction and example of the free world, where Christian principle only will restore moral sensitivity to the realm of property. Our defection from the recognition of property rights—not in respect to the propertyless only, but in respect to our neighbors too—casts doubt over the moral earnestness of our commitment to private property. In an article "Rome on Two Wheels" (*Italviews*, January 1964), Thomas Sterling characterizes Rome's truck driver as one who "would dent the fender of an ordinary car as easily as he would step on a roach." America offers its own examples of day-to-day disregard for private property. The weekend tourist who tosses his empty beer cans on my lawn, the freight line that handles my fragile parcel as if it were a concrete block, the hotel clerk who snatches the foreign stamps from my mail, the person who always walks his dog on others' property—there are countless little ways in which Americans violate their professed belief in the sanctity of private property.

In summary, let it be said that the individual's right to private property needs to be stoutly reaffirmed today. Further, the strongest vindication of private property must include its biblical supports, for the Judaeo-Christian view sets all human rights, the right of property included, in the arena of moral and spiritual responsibility. Finally, the central problem of economics—considered from any angle—is one of stewardship, a fact that the Christian religion recognizes as extremely critical. When an atheistic philosophy attacks private property simply as the result of avarice, it is not sufficient to reply that private property is justified by its social consequences, by its value for character development, or even by its basis in the laws of nature. When adversaries argue that private property is a creation of convention and a travesty on justice, the soundest reply is to point out its creation by God who is the definer of justice and the source of human rights and duties.

NOTES

1. F.C. Grant, *The Background of the New Testament and Its Eschatology,* ed. by W.D. Davies and D. Daube (Cambridge, 1956) p. 101.

2. The commandment "Thou shalt not steal" prohibits the removal of another's property, and its fraudulent retention or injury to it through indifference or carelessness. One must pay in full for neglect that results in the loss of another's livestock (Exod. 21:33 ff.), and restitution twofold, fourfold and fivefold is stipulated as compensation for stolen animals (21:37 ff.). The Mosaic Law had, as part of its educational purpose, to reinforce respect for property rights and penalized the thief progressively according to whether he retained stolen property in his possession (and had the capacity to restore it) or had sold or destroyed it. If a thief is apprehended but cannot make restitution, he must earn compensation by labor (22:4). Injury to another's property through neglect is also to be compensated (22:5 f.).

3. In the pagan Roman view unless man's control of property is sovereign, its possession is not private. This theory is tenable if man is part of God (as classic Roman philosophy assumed) or if no God exists (as modern secularism presupposes). But if God is sovereign and man is His subject, the Creator may allow man certain rights over against other men in respect to some property, while simultaneously asserting His own right over all men and all property.

4. Absolute ownership is in fact today largely a myth. While many modern limitations on property do not spring directly from biblical considerations, one may often detect behind the restrictions a concern to protect the rights of others, and hence an extension of scriptural sensitivities. This application is obvious when the owner of a plot of ground in a residential zone is prevented from building a commercial structure or at any rate is required to conform any building to zoning regulations. But when, for example, all electric wiring must be done by a union electrician, and the completed project remain open to continual inspection by tax assessors, the limitations seem to be grounded rather in special interest and mere political considerations.

5. *Letters and Other Writings of James Madison* (Philadelphia: J.B. Lippincott & Co., 1865) Vol. IV, p. 51.

6. H.G. Wood remarks that the Evangelical Revival renewed the lagging sense of the stewardship of possession: "It viewed property not so much in the light of the Decalogue as in the far more searching light of the Gospel of the Cross, and of the sacred obligations it imposes on the Christian conscience." *Property: Its Duties and Rights,* essays by L.T. Hobhouse and others. (London: Macmillan and Co. Limited, 1913) p. 165.

7. Alfred de Quervain, *Ruhe und Arbeit, Lohn und Eigentum,* Ethik II, 3 Band, (Zollikon-Zurich: Evangelischer Verlag, 1956) pp. 113 ff.

8. Confiscation of gold in 1933 weakened the power to resist government.

9. G.K. Chesterton once described property as "merely the art of democracy," since the possession of property assures every man something that he can "shape in his own image."

10. Paul Althaus, *Grundriss der Ethik,* Gutersloh, C., (Bertelsmann, 1931).

11. Vernon Bartlet, in *Property: Its Duties and Rights,* essays by L.T. Hobhouse and others, p. 88.

12. Gottfried W. Locher, *Der Eigentumsbergriff als Problem evangelischer Theologie* (Zurich: Zwingli Verlag, 1962) p. 42.

13. Emil Brunner has stressed more than other recent theologians the fact that the individual and the social nature of man are not to be viewed as opposing elements but as necessarily dual principles rising from the *imago Dei.* The individual is by creation and redemption an in-

dividual in social relations (*Das Gebot und Die Ordnungen: Entwurf einer protestantisch-theologischen Ethik,* Tubingen: J.C.B. Mohr (Paul Siebeck), 1932, pp. 389 f., 633).

14. In recent years, as John Chamberlain notes, "fashionably smart people have fallen into the habit of opposing 'human rights' to 'property rights.' . . . But despite the fashionable notion, the property right is just as much a human right as any other. Where there is no property right, human beings are invariably kicked around—by the politicians, as in Soviet Russia; by the military, as in any War Lord system; or by a priestcraft, as in Peru of the Incas" (*The Roots of Capitalism*, New York, D. Van Nostrand Co., Inc., 1959, pp. 26 f.). Some social revisionists have said that Thoreau and Garrison respected human dignity while others promoted property rights, even as it later became popular among certain politicians to characterize Herbert Hoover as a champion of property and Franklin D. Roosevelt as a champion of persons.

15. W.E. Hocking comments similarly that this factor of complete control "is why human beings cannot be property" (*Strength of Men and Nations,* New York: Harper and Bros., 1959, p. 52). But if property rights are human rights they are no less answerable to human obligation to the claims of justice and neighbor love.

16. Vernon Bartlet has called this reverse twist of human/property rights as "the greatest of abuses of property rights" (*op. cit.*).

17. "While accepting the institution of private property as a condition of social life, Christianity changed," as Vernon Bartlet notes, "the whole perspective and emphasis of men's thoughts about it, and, what is still more difficult, their instinctive feelings toward it, by teaching the incomparable value of manhood" (*ibid.*, p. 95).

18. *Der Fuehrer*, 1926 (U.S. edition), p. 287.

19. William L. Shirer, *The Rise and Fall of the Third Reich* (New York: Simon and Schuster, 1960) pp. 431 ff.

20. Since by New Testament command Christians are required to submit to a great amount of bad government, it is all the more imperative that they try to limit civil power. Others may feel free to riot or revolt; Christians at best should prevent the need of revolt.

21. Cecil DeBoer, *Responsible Protestantism* (Grand Rapids: Wm. B. Eerdmans Publishing Co., 1957) p. 105.

3

Leopold Kohr

PROPERTY AND FREEDOM

THE THEORY of property deals with problems that can be summarized by the following set of questions: Is property natural? Is it conventional? Is it necessary? Is it just? What determines the legal title to property—possession, conquest, grant, contract, work? What determines the proper size of property—ability to acquire it, to exercise control over it, function? And lastly, what is the function of property? Is it the source of livelihood, of wealth, of power, of sovereignty, of freedom?

These are the principal questions answered by the theory of property. None, however, concerns the subject of this essay, which deals not with the theory of property, but with the relationship property has with other principles. Of these there are particularly four that have engaged the curiosity of philosophers from antiquity to our own time: the relationship between property and evil, between property and equality, between property and responsibility, and between property and freedom. Though I shall have to fall back here and there on the theory of property and discuss in a marginal way the first three relationships in which property is tied up with dimensions other than its own, the main objective is to explore the last of these relationships: the connection between property and freedom.

In the beginning was the Word, and the Word was God. I was always tempted to write a little play around this opening passage of John. The curtain would rise on a scene of swirling mists. Out of it would materialize the first Word: "I." And with it would emerge the figure of the first Speaker, the Lord, self-created by sound assuming shape.

Then, in quick succession, would follow the necessary stage props enabling life to unfold itself—the sun, the moon, the earth, water, land, vegetation, fish, birds, mammals, man, woman, people, cities, nations, tools, machines, bombs. All would spring into existence through the utterance of the creative, the defining Word. In the end I thought I might reverse the process, undoing creation not by exploding the bomb, but by blotting out word after word until even the "I" dissolves back into the limitless, formless infinity of swirling mists. However, the main point of the play would be to show the positive aspects of the Word, its supreme power to give content by encasing it in form, by putting limits to the limitless, by substituting the definite for the infinite. In other words, what I meant to dramatize is creation as an exercise in definition, picturing the Lord as a Super Samuel Johnson, as the Supreme Definer, and the universe as the Great Dictionary. For, to paraphrase Protagoras, the beginning, the measure, of all things, of those that are and of those that are not, is the Word, the definition.

So, beginning with the beginning, let me define the first of the two concepts that form the subject, and, like the Lord, let me then spin much of the rest from the Word that is in the beginning. But let me also stress that the definitions are mine, or adopted by me. One is nowadays told that this is not proper. One must adhere to accepted usages, to definitions laid down by Webster or Samuel Johnson. But whose definitions did Samuel Johnson or Webster accept? They did not accept definitions. They made them. And so should every scholar. For definitions are not so much statements as to what things are, but of what a person talking about them thinks them to be. They are declarations of intent, clarifying one's position, the platform from which one makes one's observations, and the tools with which one operates. They circumscribe not things perceived but, in the creator's sense, things conceived. I believe therefore strongly in the academic freedom of definition. But once a definition is set, *rien ne va plus.* It ties one down. Hence the reluctance of so many to get entangled in definitions. They might incriminate one.

Let me then take the plunge and define property as I see it, as I shall use the term, as the Romans seem to have used it, and as one of my law professors at the University of Innsbruck phrased it in what I still consider its most pungent presentation. Property, he said in quite un-Teutonic brevity, is the *Vollrecht an einer Sache*, the full right over a thing. Enlarging it a little, I usually render it as the *exclusive right of a person over a thing.* Property is thus not the thing itself, though by transference we frequently use it in this sense when we speak of a car, or a house, as our property. But legally, it is not the car that is our property, but our exclusive right over it. And it is a majestic right, a right so vast in scope that no other comes even remotely close to it. It is indeed so total, so absolute, that it alone of all rights survives death. Even those who think the soul ends with the owner's body accept the idea that his will lives on in his property, particularly if they have been made heirs through it.

Property being the exclusive right of a person over things must not be confused with possession, which is a person's physical power over things. Those of us who have our friends' books in our library are not the owners of these books. But to the distress of our friends, we have the physical power over them which, while it confers no right, is rather a compelling argument in favor of our honesty even if we are thieves. So much so, in fact, that the brute power of physical possession actually creates a legal link with the lofty right of ownership. For one thing, the exercise of prolonged physical power produces ultimately the title to retain by right what one has held in fact. This is why Rockefeller Center bars its private road to its possessors, its users, at least once a year to demonstrate that it has no intention of letting its exclusive right over it fall into disuse. For similar to the principle underlying the statutes of limitation, property rights atrophy if they are not constantly asserted and exercised. And secondly, possession establishes the *presumption* of ownership. We know of course that our friends' books in our libraries are not ours. But legally, they are presumed to be ours, so that the burden of proof to the contrary falls on our friends, the owners, not on us, the possessors, even if the owners' names are written in them. With their felicity of expression, the Romans spoke therefore of the *beatus possidens*, the happy possessor. But, as I said, this does still not alter the fact that physical power does not constitute a right. In contrast to the possessor, however happy, it is the owner in whom alone the vast, majestic, exclusive right of property is vested.

Property, then, means that its owner alone has legal command over it. He can give it away. He can throw it away. He can let it rot. He can destroy it. He can bequeath it. He can dispose over it by contract and rent or sell it. He is free to do with it as he sees fit. In other words, within the limits of his property, and only within the limits of his property, he is able to assert his freedom.

So we have insensibly arrived at the concept of freedom merely by keeping on talking about property, just as an earthbound caterpillar ends up being a winged butterfly merely by keeping on developing as a caterpillar. But just as this does not mean that a butterfly is a caterpillar, so it does not mean that property is freedom. It is the source of freedom, and it is its only source by the strength of its very definition. For a person can be free only within the limits of a right that excludes the rights of all others. If he cannot exclude all others when it comes to making a decision, he cannot be free. He depends on those who exercise this exclusive right, and freedom then belongs to them, not to him. It makes no difference whether these other persons are natural persons, or corporate and public persons in whom he may himself have a share in his capacity as stockholder or citizen. For the concept of both natural and corporate person adheres not to its cells, its stock, its shares, its parts, but to its organic totality. The only exclusive right a stockholder has is therefore over his stock, not over the corporation, which has a personality and an existence entirely separate from his own and whose property is of course its own, not his. And the only exclusive right he has as a citizen is over his personal property, not over public property which belongs to the community or the state whose personality is likewise wholly independent and radically different from that of its citizens.

The close connection between property and freedom is also reflected in the affinity of definition. For if property is the exclusive right of a person over things, freedom is the exclusive right of a person over his actions. In the material universe in which we live, it is obvious that this freedom of action—of speaking as we please, of doing as we please, of abstaining as we please, of changing dispositions as we please—can be exercised only on the ground and with regard to the things we own. Even in London's famous Hyde Park, I cannot do as I please. I cannot proclaim everything under the sun, chop down trees, or walk around naked. Its owner's tolerance is not my right. Only on my own property can I do all these things to the exclusion of anyone presuming to deny them to me, be it another individual, the people, or the state.

At this juncture one may object that even property does not insure complete freedom of action, and that what I have just said is not completely correct. For though I may throw my rubbish away, I cannot unload it in my neighbor's backyard. I can destroy a basket full of ripe tomatoes, but not by plastering the head of Richard Nixon or George McGovern. I can burn my house down, but not if it stands in a city street. So, property is not such an exclusive right after all, considering that even property must bow to certain claims of others.

This is quite true, but only because others also have property, and what goes for them, also goes for me. Just as they must not violate my property, I must not violate theirs. The freedoms derived from property are therefore of the same nature as the sovereignty adhering to the area of neighboring states. They are contained in their horizontal sway by the property of other owners, curling back on both sides in a narrow boundary district created by the touch of mutually exclusive forces. But geographic containment does not imply functional limitation. Hence vertically towards the sky, where it meets nothing but its own extension, freedom, like sovereignty, reigns supreme—a right unlimited and unlimitable. There is therefore no need to qualify the earlier definition and suggest with subtle sophistry that property makes free, but not quite. It makes me quite free. But so it does everyone else, and what contains us is not public concern, neighborliness, or moral principle but the physical limitation of things that can be owned, coupled with the fact that space, occupied by one thing, cannot at the same time be occupied by another. Nor can things located in one part of space at the same time be located in another.

But now another objection may be raised. So far I have maintained that, to be free, one must have property. Yet, one often hears that the opposite is true: that property is a chain. It burdens us. It enslaves us. It does not give us freedom, but deprives us of it. Hence the numerous stories suggesting that the only way of becoming truly free is not by acquiring but by giving up property. One of the most engaging of these stories tells of the troubled individual who is told that, if he wants to be happy, he must wear the shirt of a happy man. So he asks in succession a prince, a bishop, a banker, a millionaire, a merchant, an industrialist, a farmer, whether he is happy. But none is. Just as he is about to abandon his search he stumbles on a happy man in the most unexpected quarter. He is a penniless beggar. But when he asks him with rekindled hope to let him wear his shirt, the beggar answers: "I don't have one." The first happy man he meets—and he owns not even a shirt.

Now I do not mean to suggest that one must own property to be happy. What I suggest is that one must own property to be free—a vastly different proposition. Happiness is relief from misery. It is wonderful. But it is not freedom. Freedom is an active, not a passive, concept. It means freedom of, not relief from. Freedom means freedom of will, freedom of disposition, freedom of inclusion, and freedom of exclusion. And by definition, this cannot be had without property. I may give my house away, walk off relieved and happy as a bird, and bed myself down for an unworried, dreamless sleep in one of God's glorious fragrant pastures. But am I free? Next thing I feel is a boot in my ribs, and a farmer growls: "This is not God's pasture but mine. I have the exclusive right over this property. Get the hell out of here." So I bed myself down under God's infinite star-spangled roof in a public park, of which I fancy myself a part owner, only to be kicked by a policeman and told: "This property is neither God's nor yours. It belongs to the public which wants no part of private individuals. Beat it." And when I protest that I am myself the public, he asks me to produce my incorporation certificate establishing that I, like Louis XIV, am the state. Which, of course, I cannot do. So he arrests me for trespassing. For even public property belongs to someone with an identity and personality other than my own, justifying my exclusion in spite of my ownership of stock in it. And as I tramp on and on, I may still be happy if I have the hide of an elephant and the insensitivity of an ox. But I cannot ignore the fact that I may be driven away from every spot on the surface of the earth except from the plot I own myself. And from that, *I* can drive everybody away, the farmer, the policeman, the public, the government, the state, the king. For property makes me not only free; it also makes me sovereign, and anyone exercising sovereignty over me, such as the state, can do so only through my delegation, not by intrinsic right.

But again, this does not mean that property, as it confers freedom, necessarily also confers happiness. It does so only for those who *love* freedom, just as marriage bestows happiness not at random but only on those who love each other. As a result, the happiness derived from freedom is radically different from the carefree joys that may be extracted from tramping across the land or sleeping on a public beach. It entails in fact the very opposite of freedom from worry and care. In marriage, it means responsibility, not relief from bother. And in freedom it means hardship, not relief from work or responsibility which the tramp cherishes so much. For property, to convey pride, contentment, and happiness, must be maintained, kept in repair, and constantly inspected, surveyed, and defended. As Schiller said: "Nur der verdient sich Freiheit und das Leben, der taeglich sie erobern muss." Only those are entitled to freedom and to life who are willing to battle for it every day.

So the happiness of freedom arises not from ease but from struggle. It is different from that of the beggar without a shirt. But it, too, gives unbeclouded bliss, as we can see from the farmer who has been in harness from dawn to dusk and, before turning in, takes his wife or son on a last round over the scene of his daily struggle to see what is his—his garden, his fields, his barn, his stable, his cows munching contentedly through the night—and to retrace with the Creator's mind all the rest to which he has given shape in a day's hard work. But which true farmer would consider the hardship of his work a burden, a source of enslavement, rather than the prelude to his supreme happiness, the enjoyment of what to him is the greatest of goods: to be his own master; to be independent; to be free; to be subject to nobody's will but his own?

Whatever our attitude towards happiness, there can be therefore only one answer as far as freedom is concerned. What deprives us of it, what enslaves us, is not property but the absence of it. Even Marxists seem to concur with this. Otherwise one would have difficulty understanding why they should pour such venom over the bourgeoisie whom they accuse of being a class not so much of appropriators but of expropriators, depriving the workers of freedom not by burdening them with the "chains" of property but by taking property off their hands. Only old fashioned defenders of property can take this position. Also when Marxists speak of the propertyless class, they imply by their commiseration that it is *absence* of ownership rather than ownership of the means of production that is the cause of its misfortune, depriving, as it does, the victims, along with their freedom of action, also of their freedom of gaining a livelihood in any way except by selling themselves into the servitude of propertied employers. In other words, if their program were consistent with their rage, Marxists, instead of making things worse by a final act of expropriation of what is still left in private hands, would have to advocate the restoration of personal property to everybody.

Actually, however, Marxists are quite consistent. They agree that property is the exclusive right of a person over a thing, that freedom is the exclusive right of a person over his actions, and that in a universe that acts through things the latter cannot be had without the former. The only point in which they differ is in the question of the entity to which adheres the concept of personality. And this is, of course, a fundamental question. For only a *person* can wield the majestic right of property. Who then is who? Is everyone a person, as individualists are inclined to think? Or are all of us merely parts of a higher entity in which alone the concept of personality is fully materialized, as collectivists seem to believe? In the one case, every human and corporate being can be an owner, in the other, only the higher entity of which we are part.

Now Marxists tend to be collectivists. They believe that the supreme concept of personality is concentrated in the group, the people, the nation, in society as a whole. Hence the term socialist, though I should like to stress that neither a socialist nor even a communist needs necessarily be a collectivist. Members of the British and Scandinavian labor parties are still in their majority individualists, and so are the monks of Catholic monasteries whose *vita communis* has indeed furnished the awe-inspiring term communism. But generally, Marxists tend to be collectivists. Nor does this mean that they deny the value of the individual human person, not any more than the human body would deny the value of the individual cell. All a collectivist maintains is that society comes first and the individual second; that society is the master and man merely a serving particle whose action is not free but circumscribed by the purposes of the superior entity of which he is part.

Once we accept this philosophy, the position of Marxists toward property becomes completely consistent. It then makes sense that they should rage against private expropriators and yet refuse to hand over to the proletarians what they propose to take away from the bourgeoisie. For in the eyes of the collectivist, the proletarian has no more personality than the bourgeois. Neither of them has an independent purpose of existence, and neither of them is therefore entitled to hold property through which he can, by definition, exclude and frustrate the purpose of the community. Hence their advocacy of vesting all property not in the propertyless, whom they pity, but in the only element that has ego, personality, sovereignty—in society, the public, the people, the state. But they do not dispute the nature of property which the state must have for the same reason for which an individual aspires to it: to exclude all others from interference; to be free. There is therefore no difference in meaning between public and private property. As Ford property is the private property of the Ford Motor Company, so public property is the private property of the public. But there is a vast difference in implication. Both are the source of unlimited freedom to their owners. But a public property system knows only a single owner endowed with sovereignty-conferring personality—the state, while in a private property system the state is merely one amongst many of equal importance. The former implies indisputably a free society, an attribute that adheres even to communist states. But it is the latter that matters for those who are interested in a society of the free.

If we are interested in the survival of a society of free citizens rather than merely a free society, it is therefore not enough to advocate a private property system. We must justify it. Just as Marxists do with their system, we must reason it philosophically. And the only social philosophy justifying private property and the individual freedom it confers is the philosophy of individualism which, in contrast to collectivism, is based on the assumption that it is not the group that precedes man, but man the group; that the culmination of human existence is reached not in the nation but in the individual; that the essence of freedom is not that the citizen has only one master, the people, but that he has no master, least of all the people; that the opinion that must be obeyed is not public opinion reflecting the pleasure of the group, even if this means poisoning Socrates or crucifying Christ, but private opinion reflecting the conscience of the individual person; and that, finally, the primary duty of government is not to be of, for, and by the people, but of, for, and by the individual. In sum, everyone owning property is able to be free. But only an individualist is entitled to be free.

This means that in contrast to the relationship between the *two* institutions, the case in favor of property and freedom is not terminological, legal or political, but philosophical; and the question arising at this juncture is consequently no longer one of definition of what property is and what property does but one of argumentation. How can the idea be defended that man does indeed stand in the center of the social universe, and that sovereignty-conferring property ought therefore indeed be vested in man rather than society?

Before discussing the arguments in favor of individualism, however, let us have a look at those that make collectivism so seductive that not only captive Marxists but also a majority of free Americans seem to have fallen under its spell. For only collectivists can be taken in by such popular ideas that, for example, democratic government should be for rather than against the people, considering that the only force other than government powerful enough to crush the individual citizen is precisely the people. Far from handing us over to the people, democratic constitutions therefore actually protect us from it by putting the government on its neck, not by making it subordinate to it. Yet which senator will not again and again move himself to the verge of tears by feelingly expressing the hope that government by the people will not perish in a country in which fortunately it does not exist. For what we have in America is, of course, government by government, not government by the people. But it does show the power collectivism exerts over the mind even in the United States—a point I like to bring home by asking my students to test their reactions to the following categories of arguments that defend the case of collectivism:

—Beginning with a biological argument, there seems hardly any doubt about society preceding man. In a hundred years we shall all be dead. But Puerto Rico will still exist. America will still flourish. Humanity will still be around. Is it not reasonable, then, to assume that what is blessed with such longevity should come first, while the impermanent individual should devote his fleeting passage through life to the service of the community which, akin to God, is practically eternal? Are not the individual citizens in the same position in relation to the social body in which the individual cells are to the human body, meant to be replaced every generation to give vigor to the superior system that rejuvenates itself by feeding on their death?

—Physically, the nonentity of the individual person is even more obvious. What are we in the face of the tremendous, crushing weight of the group? What chance would we have were we to pit our 150 to 200 pounds against the collective power emanating from the mass? And where would we stand culturally? Do we not owe everything we cherish—our language, our customs, our literature, our art—to our national environment, to the uniquely creative power of the community, the people? Without it, we would be beasts. Instinctively realizing this, do we therefore not justly speak of Greek, German, English, American rather than of Homeric or Shakespearean civilization?

—Finally, by adding up the biological, physical, and cultural case for collectivism, we can argue it even from a theological point of view. For if such attributes of divinity as biological longevity, physical superiority, and cultural fertility have been granted to the community, must it not obviously have been dearer to the Lord than the insignificant human person? President Eisenhower seems to have implied exactly this when he coined the term "citizen-minister" in praise of clergymen rendering to the Lord apparently superior service by serving him through the nation. Which is of course quite reasonable, but only if we assume that, in its semidivine capacity as Hobbes' "mortal god," the nation is closer to the Lord's heart than are its components, or that it is at least a more representative image of His nature than we, endowed with a precious soul of its own, and a reserved seat waiting for it in heaven.

By this time my students are usually convinced that this is exactly what they have been made to believe, with the only difference that, what they considered the identifying features of proud American individualism, turn out to be the hallmarks of anti-individualist collectivism. It also suggests that the real danger to the concept of a society of the free, a free-enterprise system, arises not so much from communist as from our own habits of thought. This is why Khrushchev should never have been taken to task for offering to bury capitalism. He merely meant to be kind. He did not propose to kill capitalism. This it threatens to do itself by swallowing a heavier dose of collectivist philosophy than its system can stand. He simply suggested, with no surviving capitalist around to do the job, to perform the last rites for an antagonist whose company was much enjoyed.

Does this mean individualism is knocked out? And with it, the system of personal freedom which it alone is able to defend? Maybe. Yet, the picture is not as bleak as it appears. For individualism can also draw on a reserve of compelling arguments. From a biological point of view, it can challenge the collectivist position by stressing with Bernard Shaw that longevity is an argument not for superiority but for imbecility. It is a quality gracing the brainless. The lower the organism, the longer it lives until we come to the primitive primeval one-cell structure which is practically imperishable. Does this make it divine, the end rather than the tool of creation? Precisely because imbecile society cannot die anyway, it would seem that the purpose to be served by life is that of the short-lived individual. From a physical point of view, the individualist can point to the fact that, far from being crushed by the mass of the group, man has forever outwitted it singlehandedly, not in spite of but because of his mobile small bulk. All history is the history of men riding, using, abusing, bewitching, molding, dominating groups; not of groups squashing men except on the rare occasions of revolution.

But what about culture? Well, what about it? The only thing society, the divine people, has generally seen in it is an affrontery to its prejudice. It has poisoned Socrates. It has called the Lyceum of Aristotle "the peripatetic nest of traitors." It suffered Cicero and Seneca to be liquidated. It condemned to death Dante. It hounded Brunelleschi. It tortured Galileo. It starved Mozart and Schubert. It guillotined Lavoisier. It destroyed pictures. It toppled monuments of art. Its main cultural function has always been to stimulate intellectual development by impeding it, jumping on the bandwagon when individual creators had gained immortality, not with the help of their nations but in opposition to them. It is therefore not England's plays which we admire, but those of Shakespeare, who was not a people but an individual; and not Austrian music but the music of Mozart, who was not a people either. Indeed so illiterate are society and people, and so devoid of intellectual capacity, that after millions of years of somnolence Dr. Gallup succeeded at last to endow it with a vocabulary of two words: "yes" and "no." The medieval German prankster Till Eulenspiegel achieved that much with a donkey.

And theologically, the individualist can point to the fact that though religions have deified people, state, and nation, none has ever suggested that anyone but the individual soul, the ego, reflects the image of creation's will. But this is a matter of faith. Theologically more convincing is the physical fact that, had nature willed it otherwise, we could have been created as fused parts of million-eyed and legged creatures. Instead, each of us has been created in total separation, a solitary universe from birth to death, with everything we are able to grasp beginning and ending with our private existence. *Cogito, ergo sum.* I think, therefore I am. This is the only thing we know for certain. We can say it of nothing else and of no one else. The rest is gray theory.

Thus, as collectivism can be powerfully argued, so can individualism. But this does not mean that it has a stronger case. If I have argued it with a little more fervor, it is merely because I have an individualist taste. And, as Luther has said, about taste one cannot really argue.

Yet, the ability to argue one's philosophic preference for freedom—or for whatever else it may be—is as important as one's ability to argue one's architectural preference for, let us say, a medieval stone house such as I acquired in the Cotswolds two years ago. We can safely indulge in it only if a majority of those with whom we live either share our taste or, if not, can be persuaded to share it through the strength of our argument. This is why I have elaborated in the foregoing somewhat on the intellectual ingredients that hold our social philosophies together. For we can make our argument compelling only if we have ourselves a crystal clear picture of what we really want. If we confuse natural quarried stone with artificially reconstructed stone which every builder wants to palm off on us, we shall soon find that, after repairing a house, it may still look like a medieval stone cottage but no longer have the charm and soul for which we loved it. And if we mistake collectivist concepts for hallmarks of individualism, as many of our propagandists have begun to do, we shall soon find that what we are cultivating is no longer a philosophy of freedom but one of serfdom disguising itself in the language of liberty.

But the power of argument is not everything. It is only one of two factors necessary for widening the base of our individualist preference among our fellow citizens in a manner that will insure our continued ability to indulge in it. The other is the existence of a practical down-to-earth interest that makes our taste for freedom not only philosophically but also materially convincing to others. And this brings me back to the role property plays in all this. For only where a large majority of citizens hold freedom-conferring property, will the social philosophy justifying it be able to maintain itself and arouse the popular enthusiasm without which no system can survive.

But if this is the case, how can we explain that collectivist patterns of thought should have made such inroads in America where, after all, a majority of citizens still do own private property? And why, on the other hand, is there no evidence of a return to individualist concepts of freedom in collectivist countries such as the Soviet Union, whose citizens are likewise the owners of all sorts of private property, considering that even cells, though they may have no private purpose, have a private existence? Does it mean that the relationship between property and freedom is more tenuous than we have heretofore assumed?

All it means is that a few distinctions must now be introduced, not with regard to the concept of property which has only one definition, but with regard to the things over which property rights can be extended. Thus, Soviet citizens cannot own property in land or in means of production the operation of which requires more than the owner's own labor. But constitutionally, if not philosophically, they are entitled to own their incomes, savings, houses, cars, furniture, and any other consumer goods under the sun. However, though the ownership of consumer goods entails by definition freedom of action, its very nature limits the range of action which their owners are free to exploit. They are free to sleep in their houses, accommodate guests, or have parties in them. They can sell them. But they cannot lease them. They cannot draw income from them. They are free to eat their apples, let them rot, give them away, sell a basket of them to friends. But they are not free to make a living by going into the apple selling *business*, presuming that this would require the employment of labor other than their own. In other words, ownership in consumer goods constitutes property all right. But it is passive property; a property that restricts freedom of action to a single exercise—consumption. It does not entail the freedom to use it for making a living, so that, however pleasantly the individual Soviet citizen may be set up, his only way of earning an income is still by selling his labor and spending most of his day performing actions in conformity with the whims and wishes of his employer, the state, not his own. This is not freedom.

To be truly free, one must own active property, that is property in the means of production through which a majority of individuals can gain their livelihood in their own fashion, by employing their labor themselves, not by selling it; and by employing it in any way they please, in farming, carpentering, innkeeping, shoemaking, writing poetry, organizing enterprises, not just in the service of the communal design. Thus, freedom being an active principle, it is not enough merely to own property. Only active property, property that works, property in producer goods, can give us the full range of sovereign independence. And insofar as we have assumed freedom to be the original attribute of every individual rather than of society, it is not enough that active property is held only by a few. In Benthamite fashion it must be held by the greatest number of people. Which means the safeguard of positive freedom lies not only in active property but in an active-property system; not only in freedom of enterprise but in a free-enterprise system. And the free-enterprise system that is best is the one in which active property is held by most. For only then will a majority of citizens have a direct interest in maintaining an individualist philosophy.

Now this explains the absence of an individualist revival in the Soviet Union. But how does it explain the erosion of individualism in the United States, where a majority of citizens seems to hold not only passive but active property? The reason for this is that individual, though not private, ownership of active property has in fact been rapidly dwindling under the impact of large-scale industrialization even in the United States. For each major business in both agriculture and industry requires nowadays the employment of such large quantities of capital and such large units of land that they have long outgrown the reach of individual accumulation. Hence the need of either bringing the public personality of the state into the picture, whose command over means of production is unlimited, or of concentrating the required blocks of active property in the hands of giant corporations. But giant corporations can by nature be only relatively few in number, with the result that the same has happened with active property among corporate persons which Pareto discerned in his famous law as likely to happen in uncontrolled societies among individual persons: something like 90 percent of it has become concentrated in the hands of perhaps 5 or 6 percent of the corporate population—a base much too narrow to preserve the philosophical interest of a compelling majority not just in a private but in an individual free-enterprise system.

Now one may say that, while it is true that relatively few large corporations own the bulk of freedom-conferring active property, a majority of individuals are, in turn, the owners of corporations. So they are bound to retain a vested interest in the survival of the system that protects their holdings. But as I have pointed out earlier, individuals do not own corporations. Corporations have sovereign personality in their own right, and no person can be owner of another person. What individuals do own is stock. And stock in large complex corporations creates as a rule no more interest in the operation, the work, the hardships and problems of a company than the voting rights in large nations create in the running of government. What it tends to create is in fact the opposite: an interest not in freedom-asserting work but in income *without* work, *without* the need of engaging the mind in bothersome entrepreneurial decisions resulting from putting active property to use.

Unlike the ownership of a farm or a factory, the ownership of stock thus establishes a wholly impersonal relationship. It fosters no attachment. It encourages unpatriotic desertion whenever there is a chance for a greater yield elsewhere. *Ubi bene ibi patria,* as the Romans said. It creates no loyalty to stick by a company in times of crisis. Nor for that matter does it create loyalty to stick by a free-enterprise system in times of depression. For the freedom of enterprise enjoyed by large corporations conveys no direct experience of the exercise of freedom to the stockholders. Viewed from their perspective, it is enterprise by delegation, which is as self-defeating as the experience gained from charging someone to make love by delegation.

This means that the primary element keeping the interest in private enterprise alive in an economy which, such as ours, is dominated by corporations vying in size with the government itself, is no longer its appeal to freedom and independence, for which private property is essential, but its appeal to security, which can be satisfied also by the state. And since security is precisely also the chief selling point of a public property system, it is not surprising that, in a society of stockholders looking passively on while others operate their active property, the boundaries between the individualist and collectivist way of viewing our social relationships should become blurred to the point that one may change into the other without anybody noticing it except Khrushchev standing by with his shovel.

And this answers the first question: Why the individualist interest in a society of free men rather than merely in free society seems to recede also in the United States in spite of the fact that a majority of Americans own not only an amplitude of passive property but also stock in active property. But stock in active property is not in itself active property. It is sitting in a car owned and driven by someone else. To appreciate what freedom really means in all its hardship and all its bliss, one must not just own but operate one's property. In other words, if the true spirit of freedom known to the pioneers is to be rekindled, the United States must once again turn from a nation of owners of property into a nation of *operators* of property or, as Hitler said in referring to the English with the contempt befitting a philosophical collectivist, into a nation of shopkeepers. And as far as the system is concerned with insuring the spirit of freedom, emphasis must be placed not so much on a private as on an individual enterprise system. A private-enterprise system is also one of feudal barons.

This does not mean however that, to preserve our individualistic philosophy, without which neither private property nor freedom nor free enterprise makes sense, we must all become small farmers again considering that the only total freedom-conferring property is property in a bit of land large enough to give us our daily bread. This is why the torch of freedom has never burned so fiercely as in the communities of small land-owning peasants such as in Switzerland and the Austrian Tyrol, in agricultural states such as France, or in the communities of American pioneers which were so individualistic that many of them were hardly communities. Nor does it mean that those who cannot become farmers should become operator-owners of the next best thing: modestly sized subsistence shops. Nor does it mean that corporations should be abolished or, particularly, all large-scale enterprise dissolved. For even giant corporations have their place in the relatively few fields where only large-scale organization can handle the job.

What it does mean is that a system should be restored in which the giant concern does not predominate and that, where industrial realism requires the corporate form of business, it should be organized on a relatively small scale. For what I have said of stock in large corporations does not apply to stock in small ones. It, too, removes the owner from operation, but not so far as to destroy his understanding, his interest, his personal connection, and his loyalty to the firm in which he has invested. As a result, even though such stock does not represent active property, it strengthens the owner's active interest in a private property system. And this is nearly as good a safeguard of the ideology of freedom as the interest derived from operating property directly. So all that is suggested is a return to the Greek ideal of harmony through moderation, permitting a greater range of human unevenness while avoiding excess.

But this again does not mean that my general emphasis on personal rather than corporate enterprise as the best guarantor of an individualist philosophy of freedom, or that my emphasis on small rather than large corporations where the corporate form suggests itself, is but a rationalization of an admitted romantic fascination with the personal dimensions of the Middle Ages, of which many of my friends like to accuse me. Apart from the fact that I see indeed nothing wrong with such a fascination considering that only an inveterate romantic can face the rational nonsense imposed on us by social existence, small operational-unit systems have actually proved most valuable also from the naked rationalist point of view of economic efficiency. The most successful laissez-faire systems have been those of the earlier stages of capitalist development when the giant concern was a rare phenomenon. And one of the most flourishing economies even today is that of Switzerland, whose largest business employs twelve thousand workers, and the second largest nine thousand, while 82 percent of her industrial enterprises employ fewer than fifty. Yet Switzerland, with 53.6 percent of industrialization compared with 40 percent in the United States, has not a medieval but one of the most advanced of modern economies. Its small-unit pattern has not prevented it from becoming in fact the most highly industrialized country on earth, while at the same time remaining the most tenacious defender of individualist freedom.

Summing up, my position, then, is this: No one can be free without property, neither the state, nor a corporation, nor an individual person. Property implies freedom by definition. But while everyone holding property is thus able to be free, the question is: is everyone *entitled* to be free? And, by implication, is everyone *entitled* to own property?

The answer to this question depends on our social philosophy. A collectivist is inclined to think that the fullness of personality is materialized only in society as a whole, the citizens being merely interchangeable and individually inessential parts. With only society being capable of sovereign freedom, only society is entitled to own freedom-conferring property. The citizens can own property only by grant, not by right. An individualist thinks that the fullness of personality is materialized in every individual. He is sovereign in his own right, a universe passing through existence to fulfill his own purpose, society being merely his tool. Everyone is therefore entitled to be free and own the property that, by definition, confers this freedom. But persons can be both natural and legal persons, the latter, such as the state or corporations, being created by the will and for the purposes of natural persons. Hence individualism concedes that also legal persons are entitled to own property. But they are merely a number in a great multitude of coequals.

A society based on the concept of free citizens rather than a free society can thus maintain itself only if the philosophy of individualism is shared by a great majority of its people. To insure that this is the case, one needs more than the institution of individual property. One needs an individual-property system, a system in which most individuals are actually holding property. But not every property confers a full measure of freedom of action. Passive property, such as property in consumer goods, exhausts itself in a single action: consumption, which, by definition, is destruction of utility. And so does property in stock, whose freedom of action exhausts itself in the act of selling. Only active property, property that is operated by oneself in the task of gaining one's livelihood, is capable of preserving a live interest in the philosophy of individualism by making the exercise of freedom a daily experience. What is needed is therefore an individual *active* property system or, as we call it normally, an individual free-enterprise system.

What we have in the United States is essentially a corporate free-enterprise system, with most individuals being content with the ownership of stock in private enterprise rather than of private enterprise itself. This does not in itself undermine the vital active interest in free enterprise and the philosophy of individual freedom as long as a majority of corporations retain an easily surveyable human scale, enabling the stockholders to participate, if not physically, at least emotionally in the exercise of free decision. But if an excessive part of the free-enterprise system becomes dominated by a relatively small number of nation-like large corporations, vying with the state itself not only in size but even in function, the boundaries between private and public purposes tend to become so blurred that the gate is opened to the insensible infiltration of collectivist patterns of thought, ending in veneration no longer of a society of the free but of a free society.

The only way of rekindling the spirit of individualist freedom with all it entails in hardship and glory would therefore seem to lie in making once again the concept of free enterprise more equal to the concept of individual enterprise and placing once more emphasis not just on property, but active property.

There are many other vital aspects of the problem of property and freedom which should be discussed. One of these concerns the role played by giant organization on the side not only of business but also of labor in the disruption of the self-balancing mechanism of the dynamic mobile of free-enterprise capitalism. As long as business units are both numerous and small, the unavoidable clashes amongst them in an uncontrolled, free, competitive system tend to be self-correcting. For then their collisions themselves release the forces restoring balance and equilibrium within the system as a whole. But if they are few and large, the unavoidable collisions resulting from their uncontrolled freedom of movement produce such dislocations that, instead of invigorating the free-enterprise system, they threaten to annihilate it, forcing a return of government control also on sheer physical grounds that have nothing to do with the ideology of collectivism. This is why the first piece of massive control legislation in the United States, the Sherman Anti-Trust Act, was passed in response not to Marxist agitation but to the hurricane effect produced by large business, and long since also by large labor organizing as a reflex reaction to business likewise on a giant scale.

But elaboration of this would require another paper. And so would another aspect which has occupied my main interest during the past twenty years and is indeed the *leitmotiv* running through most of my writings. This is the role played in the destruction of freedom not only by giant enterprise but by the unnecessarily large social size of nations resulting either from immense territorial holdings or from the excessive integration and centralization of all their activities. For the most fertile soil for both giant economic organization and the appropriate philosophy of giantism, massism, and collectivism to develop is precisely the excessively large society. But, as I said, this too would require another paper.

4

James W. Wiggins

THE DECLINE OF PRIVATE PROPERTY AND THE DIMINISHED PERSON

MY INTENT HERE is to demonstrate that private property is an extension of the person, and thus a part of the person. As an extension of the person, private property may be attacked in indirect aggression against the person. Successful aggression against private property diminishes, dehumanizes the person.

While the recognition of this relationship furnishes a basis for personally satisfying action by all levellers, the failure to recognize it leads other men, without intention and for the highest motives, to equally effective reduction of persons. Some of the immediate and long-term consequences of person-diminution are described. And, finally, some of the characteristics of possible solutions are presented.

As a first step, it is helpful to review the kinds of evidence which may be adduced or examined in relation to the propositions. Man's knowledge is based initially on his own perceptions, feelings, pleasures and pains. When stored away, subject to anamnesis, these perceptions become experience. But if this were all, man could neither communicate, nor form social groups, nor test his unique experience against the experience of others. So, going beyond this schizoid or monadic state, man seeks confirmation by his fellows.

This search for confirmation and support first involves man's contemporaries. This is not necessarily in the sense of Reisman's "other-directed" person, who completely distrusts his own experience. It is rather a discriminating testing against the reports of selected others of the same generation or cohort. This kind of behavior offends many American parents and teachers, who deplore adolescent testing against other adolescents rather than against the elders. The practice may be wise occasionally, even among adolescents. This "horizontal" testing of experience emphasizes purely contemporary standards.

The experience of ancestral fellows is also examined. Both the living and the dead are included. If it does not confirm individual experience, it may be disregarded. Since ancestral circumstances may be different in detail from the contemporary, it may be necessary to discard some of this experience. Nevertheless, the totality of the distilled experience of mankind, selected and transmitted over many generations, may be ignored only at man's grave peril. In the whole sweep of human existence as we are able to know it, ancestral ("vertical") testing has tended to take precedence over other types. Only in a few times and places has "temperocentrism" (Robert Bierstedt's word)—the conviction held by contemporary Chicken Littles that all events are unprecedented—been a dominant faith.

All of these bases of knowledge may be misleading, or just wrong. Since this is true, man—especially modern man—may further evaluate his experiences against those of other societies. Knowledge which comes through the kaleidoscopic cultural haze, through the multidimensions of languages, has a claim to full acceptance. Such testing may not produce absolutes, but it at least uncovers universals. The problem arises from the insignificance of much which filters through. Cross-cultural testing of experience may, like committee decisions, produce merely a lowest common denominator.

Man sometimes recognizes that Bacon's Idols obscure greater knowledge than can be confirmed by sources outside the individual. When the individual expresses this awareness and insists on the validity of his unique experience, he is taken to be odd, at the very least. He may even be removed from society as a troublemaker—which he is.

Man is also able to seek validation for some of his experience in the observation of lower animals. Since man occasionally becomes an extremist, he may, at this level, take similarity for equivalence. Both animals and plants exhibit response behavior which tends to maintain the integrity of the organism, and even a casual knowledge of biology strongly suggests the ubiquity of something like private property. Man may be the only genuine creator or secretor of private property, but he also seems to be the only living creature who does not consistently fight to the death to protect it.

What ever happened to a fate worse than death?

As we examine the contemporary scene, we find considerable confusion and uncertainty over private property. It is therefore appropriate to examine the evidence for the integration of private property into the person.

It is clear, initially, that private property does not exist except in its relationship to persons. While its material existence, if it is material, is unquestioned both before and after its becoming private property, this is not what gives it a special nature. As property, it becomes significant both as part of the person and as an element in relationships between persons.

As Charles Cooley and others have shown, the development of the conception of the self involves both awareness of limits and of extensions to the person. The identification of oneself with objects, people, and ideas seems to be a standard process. The involvement of the ego with extensions of the self, whether material, animal, human, or ideational, is a matter of common experience. It has also been a matter of both common and systematic, that is, scientific, observation. As identification becomes firm, threats to extensions of the ego produce reactions as vigorous as threats to the central ego itself.

The identity of private property with the self is taken for granted in language. If there are required discriminations in a social group, the language must reflect them. It is unnecessary to accept all of the implications of Benjamin Whorf's hypothesis that language carries a "hidden metaphysics" to recognize that while language may impose structure on experience it must also reflect the understandings of those who use it. In these terms, then, it is enlightening to examine the use of the possessive adjective and the possessive pronoun. The distinction among various categories of private property is one based in some degree on the qualities of the property. The possessive form which indicates relationship does not vary. It is "my house," "my heart," "my wife," "my son," "my right arm," or *Mein Kampf.* There is no suggestion of variation in *relationship.* I am assured by my linguist friend, Louis Ghisletti, that this nondiscriminating possessive is common to at least the Indo-European languages.

The reciprocal of "my" or "mine" exhibits a nearly universal tendency of mutual support. "You" and "you and yours" are often used interchangeably. And in a sense too little recognized, the maintenance of one's own ego depends on a reciprocal support of the ego of the other.

While the analysis has, up to this point, emphasized the involvement of the owner with his property, it is clear that he is culturally "mad" unless others agree with his conception. When the owner is treated *as if* he were coextensive with his property, his thinking is confirmed. And he *is* so treated. With the supposed decline of superstition, much remains. The child holds to his father's cigarette lighter *as if* it were a part of the father. The golfer cherishes Nicklaus' ball *as if* it were part of Jack's person. And many indeed cherish keepsakes because they are "part of" the original owner. Such pervasive positive assurance to the owner confirms his self-concept and our basic proposition.

Not all is positive, however supporting. In the general context of awareness of identity of thing and person, from childhood to death, what has been called displaced aggression involves action *as if.* The child who cannot attack a larger child or an inviolable brother, may, without explicit philosophy, attack or destroy the private property of the other. He knows that this diminishes the person. The muckraker who cannot physically attack the "big man" substitutes attacks on reputation or destroys the "name" of the inviolate person. And even the niggling gossip makes a career of confirming an identity of person and private property. Envy, about which Helmut Schoeck has made important observations, is from this point of view a validation of this argument.

As we move to a cursory examination of ancestral experience, the origins of private property as person disappear in mists. Nevertheless, the Old Testament story of creation reports that woman was "born" of man, and the primordial treatment of woman as private property has a sound base in the Judaeo-Christian tradition. The Ten Commandments, viewed in context, furnish strong support of the relationship between the person and private property. The commandments were given to men; women were treated as property. Three commands identify the Person of God with His property. But five forbid aggression against the person-property of other men. Adultery, in a context of polygamy and concubinage, is theft of private property, and few would deny that a cuckold is a diminished person. The other four in this group are more direct. It is interesting to note, for later purposes, that the final commandment indifferently forbids coveting house, wife, slaves, or animals "that is thy neighbor's."

To a member of other traditions, the Bible is merely a collection of folklore. Anthropologists have collected details of many systems, and we may profitably examine some conclusions. Weston LaBarre has emphasized the *alloplastic* nature of man's evolution. Pointing to the stability of the biological characteristics of the human being, he shows that man's adaptations have been made, and some limitations overcome, through the production of tools. Perhaps the best illustration of the extension of the person through tool-making is the spear thrower. A narrow wooden cradle, nesting a spear, held along the throwing arm, it literally extends the arm to double its length or much more. Without the spear-thrower, the aborigine is diminished as a person.

Except for a few determined ideologues, anthropologists seem to agree that private personal property is universal. Primitive communism has few supporters, and the evidence for it is indeed flimsy. Some primitive bands have apparently failed to conceive of land as private property, except as modified by human action. The modifier gains a special relationship to his creation, which is typically supported by the other members of the band. The writer has long been convinced that the Indians' sale of Manhattan Island was, from *their* standpoint, a swindle. Any price at all, for nonproperty, is too great.

Other traditions include faith in magic. The magical manipulation of the person through his private property approaches universality. The Voodoo use of locks of hair, nail parings, and teeth as the direct object of attack assumes identity of person and property. Even the spells themselves are part of the person, and in many societies may be stolen, bartered, or sold. The Dobu, glamorized by Ruth Benedict, identified themselves with their private yam lines. They were as conscious of person-property connections as any people known. For their trouble they were given the paranoid label.

Names, incantations, and ideas have widely been treated as part of the person and as private property. To canvass the varieties of attitudes and definitions of person-property identity is a task far beyond present purposes, but this brief treatment is suggestive, at least.

The proposition that private property is both an extension and part of the person is shown to have strong support from contemporaries, from ancestral experience, and from a variety of other cultural traditions. The evidence is not absolute, but few arguments are absolutely supported.

One form of private property deserves special attention here. This is property in persons. The person who *is* private property seems to identify reciprocally with, and find personal extension in attachment to, the owner. From the extension of the self through becoming a child (i.e., property) of the Divine, to the slave whose person expands to include his owner, to the wife who flowers as "part" of her husband, man seems to have a determination for ego expansion. While such complete ownership of persons is out of style, the basic character of man seems unlikely to allow extinction of either ownership or expansive response.

In the days of the old Hebrews as in many systems of slavery, considerable tenacity has been shown by the "property" in holding its owner. The Hebrews, required to free their slaves every seven years, found them returning to ownership when it was legitimate. The pride of Southern slaves in their property-relation to the owner is hardly comprehensible except in recognition of this pattern of self-extension as property.

Some observers may be convinced that the element of ownership in marriage has disappeared in such forward-looking times. Reduced in range it may be, but hardly in significance. We have tempered our treatment of the woman who is not property, who is ownerless. We have also softened our handling of the nameless, ownerless, child. No longer do we, like the Tasmanians, turn widows over to the men of the tribe or, like the earlier people of India, require the widow to commit suttee. Not to belabor the language, the "unattached" woman is in our day less a person than the attached. And the report of the facts does no indignity to woman. In some countries it has been suggested that women have a right to be wives, even if this requires a drastic change in systems of marriage.

While both spouses are diminished when marriage is terminated, the man is still man. The wife is no longer a wife, and her diminution is far greater.

When we come to consider the attacks on private property as indirect aggression against persons, one other point must be made. We not only find an apparent displacement of the object, but also understandable camouflage of the attackers. The clearest example may be found in state action, which uses excise taxes to diminish the person. The taxes are collected from persons as part of a price for goods, but the price of the goods is named and collected by the retailer, not the state. Then the state organizes crusades to convince persons that they are being diminished by producers and sellers, never the state. Consumers are told that selfish people are taking advantage of their ignorance. This is often true. Only the names of the selfish people have been changed to protect the guilty.

It is too easy to conclude that the state is the only or at least major source of attacks on private property. It deserves great credit for such aggression, but attention is commonly directed to it alone. Many writers have identified labor unions, others management, others bankers, as the real foes of private property. Karl Marx is a favorite whipping boy. There is justification in all of these identifications, but the disease seems endemic. In the following pages we shall identify other culprits, which are not so commonly marked.

A substantial contribution to the diminution of the person is made by organized education in the United States. The first major step was the separation of the parent from his child. Nothing could be more clearly private, or property, or extension of the self than a child. The removal of the child from the parent, for most of childhood, almost makes breeding stock of fathers and brood mares of mothers. The result is typical: having taken private property, many teachers and much of society are still determined to point at the parents when the property does not function properly. The schools are expected to supplant the parent in ownership, and the property—the child—is required to identify with the school (school spirit) as the school struggles to become the focus of human life.

Not very surprisingly, we hear many complaints about the collapse of the American family—from many of the same people whose determination has doubtless helped produce it. Here is an interesting similarity to the pediatrician of a generation ago who assured mothers that he could design better milk than they. With the best of intentions, the school has gone further. When the school furnishes the textbooks, all children are pauperized. When the school furnishes his food, *it* makes his choices, not his parents. When the school teaches manners, parents are discredited. When the school teaches morality, parents are obsolete. And, of course, the school cannot teach religion.

But let us look higher. The brain-child is a direct secretion of the person, private property of the order of a child. Higher education has apparently been frustrated by the treatment of this kind of private property as private property. In its frustration it now seeks to use the arm of the state to deprive the creator of his creation. A case in point is at hand.

For some years the laws of copyright have been under discussion. Creators of original material have been inclined to seek extension of the time during which the copyright protects the creation. The present maximum protection of this private property is for 56 years, although there is no clear basis for limiting this ownership while other property is owned indefinitely. The general practice in major publishing countries around the world is to grant a copyright for the life of the author plus fifty years. But there have been and are some interesting people who wish to either reduce the life of the copyright, or to use this private property under special exemptions.

Hayward Cirker, president of Dover Publications, has urged a reduction of the period of copyright protection in a letter to *Science* (9 August 1963). As a publisher, he would quite naturally like to acquire at no cost manuscripts which have been bought and promoted by other publishers. His letter was compellingly rebutted by Curtis G. Benjamin, of McGraw-Hill Book Company. As a preliminary to a detailed rebuttal, Benjamin wrote, " . . . Cirker . . . makes a number of erroneous statements and observations—so many, in fact, that a mere cataloging of them is an embarrassment."

To Cirker's argument that the availability of books is of such public interest that the property rights of authors should be limited for the common good, Brendan A. Maher responded:

> But even if books *were* more important than bread, we move into an Alice-in-Wonderland kind of logic when we maintain that the more

valuable something is to society, the less right there is for the man who produces it to receive his reward!

Thus far we have viewed the marketplace and found what we are supposed to expect. Let us look for a moment at the world of higher education, which serves as custodian of the best in our culture.

From *Higher Education and National Affairs* (Vol. XIII, No. 5) we learn:

> Nonprofit educational organizations should be allowed to use copyrighted works—free and without permission—for noncommercial educational purposes, according to testimony by a representative of twenty-five such organizations, including the American Council on Education. The educational organizations, which have formed an ad hoc committee on copyright law revision, include such other national groups as the American Association of School Administrators, Council of Chief State School Officers, American Association of University Women, National Education Association, National Educational Television and its affiliated stations, National Catholic Welfare Conference, National Association of Educational Broadcasters, National Council of Teachers of English, National Science Teachers Association, and a number of associations for foreign language teachers.

A short time after the presentation of this testimony to the Consultants Panel to the Register of Copyrights, a complete revision of the copyright laws was proposed in identical bills introduced to the Senate and House. HR11947 and S3008 placed several limitations on exclusive rights, particularly in cases of performance by instructors or pupils, broadcasts in "nonprofit" educational institutions, and performance in the course of services at a place of worship, performance by "unpaid actors" for no admission charge if proceeds go to educational, religious, or charitable purposes.

It is not clear why religious groups, which usually view stealing rather dimly, are included among those with a license to steal. Such an action is clearly outside the tradition of voluntarism in American religions. If this religious provision is a result of organized pressure such as that of the educators, it not only violates tradition and doctrines, but also furnishes another example of the tragic tendency of religion to use the coercion of the state to achieve its own ends. The communicant may, without let, give his creations to his Creator. But it is difficult to say how the unwilling pawn of the state achieves grace through the forced contribution of his private property for the church.

Unfortunately, the matter is more complicated. The confiscation of private property for educational use not only diminishes the person. Regardless of how we define profit, the professor is paid, both directly and indirectly, for the use of another's creation. If the actors in a college play are not paid for their performances, what of the faculty director?

The attorney for the educational organizations, finding some property rights left in the creator, is urging that royalty-free dramatic performances be legalized over educational television channels available to the general public. If this change is made in the proposed law, we will no doubt be faced with a choice of "educational" or "commercial" performances of the same drama. And the dramatist's income will necessarily be reduced, in competition with himself! What would happen to royalty rates under such conditions is hardly a matter for speculation.

Parts of school and church, then, with the best of intentions, not only join Mr. Cirker, but also go far beyond what even he would recommend.

Since some educators and some clergymen produce material which now qualifies for copyright, these men may become suddenly and sharply aware of the double-bitted edge of this axe. Only a few educators and clergymen produce such material, however, while all use it. So the public good, i.e., the good of the unproductive, in the democratic process, merely leads to honing the edge of the axe. Procrustes must be served.

Further analyses of person-diminution could be aimed at welfare activities, public and private, at the preemption of the worker's private property by his unions, or the failures in "land reform." Most, if not all such analyses, will bring to light the basic contempt for the person held by the attackers of private property. However tempting the opportunity, we move to a consideration of counterfeit ownership and the spurious ego, while the foregoing struggle continues.

With apologies to Thomas Robert Malthus and C. Northcote Parkinson, we may examine Wiggins' First Law: *"Genuine private property expands the real ego arithmetically: counterfeit ownership expands the spurious ego exponentially."* All such scientific laws can be tested only if terms are defined. By genuine private property is meant property added to the person through the use of his own energies and thus subject to his ultimate legitimate control. The *real* ego expands legitimately on the basis of expansion of *genuine* private property. Counterfeit ownership involves the agency function, which, since it is not directly correlated with effort or "production," may lead the agent's ego to unfounded, spurious expansion. (This is not to suggest that the agency function is "worthless." It is rather that the modest reward of the agent may seem to allow inadequate ego-expansion and support a tendency to incorporate that which is managed also as a part of the person.)

We may identify at least four significant settings in which agents may confuse their functions with ownership. Many individuals, happily, are able to resist the temptation, even in settings which offer unusual opportunities. Here we are interested in those who find the opportunities irresistible.

One setting in which counterfeit ownership often leads to spurious ego is religious. Some religious leaders have, in becoming the agent of the Divine, apparently reached the conclusion that God's property is really their own. And if God's property is their own, He may be invoked for convenience, as the spear-thrower is used by the savage. Having reached this point, it is easy to "make" God a puppet—speaking the words of the agent. With the support of earthly property, the *ex cathedra* pronouncement becomes *ex cathedral.* This may be a partial explanation for such abominations as the Social Gospel.

More commonly recognized as the ideal setting for the operation of Wiggins' First Law is the bureaucracy. The bureaucrat is typically devoid of ownership of the property he administers. Too nearly typically, he is inclined to conceive of his relationship as ownership. In the "predicted" pattern, the spurious ego expands at a furious rate. With proper respect for the ill, we draw a curtain before the patient.

Surely few groups seek to do good more than professional social workers. Many individual social workers, because of personal qualities, respect for fellow man, humility, and firmness, do great good. The professional setting makes control of the spurious ego difficult indeed, and two particular dangers are chronic. The first of these involves grants of money, other people's money, to the needy. Those who furnish the money are the truly beneficent, but the hand that delivers it may become the extension of an inflated ego. The agent, through coercion based on property of others, may go far beyond the desires of the real givers. It has been noted, further, that on occasion organized welfare workers seek to prohibit the distribution of largesse by its owners. If this is successful, and it has been to some extent, the social worker gains a monopoly on benevolence—with a somewhat limited investment. Nothing could be worse, we are told, than for the giver to make the gift.[1]

As a final case, we have the oft-buffeted businessman. In particular, we refer to the management level in corporate enterprise. They have been urged to accept something called "social responsibility," sometimes by muddy thinkers, more often by men and institutions who expect their own agent-egos to expand with success. . .as they do.

Like other men, the management man occupies many statuses, and "social responsibility" urges him to confuse two of them. As a person, he has private property, sometimes a great deal. He may be invited to give his private property to any good, indifferent, or bad cause, and he may legitimately contribute his private property. The corporate property, owned by stockholders, is normally far greater than the private property of management. If the executive can be convinced that his *personal* gifts of money are no different from his gifts of corporate money—he is always the same man—the mother-lode is tapped.

The executive who is convinced of his "social responsibility" is likely to be further rewarded. His ego may be extended spuriously through the granting of a variety of honors, including an occasional doctoral degree. It is difficult to see a basic difference in this course of action and other types of larceny after trust.

It is unfair to leave the executive thus exposed. He may, of course, administer the decisions of duly elected directors to distribute as gifts a portion of a corporation's profits. He may also, as agent of the stockholders, appropriately accept such gratitude as these gifts may evoke. Just as may any just man.

My thoughts can be summed up in the commandment THOU SHALT NOT STEAL:—that which *is* thy neighbor.

NOTES

1. For a further development of a related analysis, see Alan Keith-Lucas, "Psychoanalytic Thinking and the Relief of the Poor," in Helmut Schoeck and James W. Wiggins (Eds.) *Psychiatry and Responsibility* (D. Van Nostrand, 1962).

5

James A. Sadowsky

PRIVATE PROPERTY AND COLLECTIVE OWNERSHIP

I PROPOSE to attempt a justification of private ownership and then analyze the term "collective ownership." I hope to show that this latter term is without any meaning. Unfortunately, it is often assumed to have meaning and the existence of such a thing in reality is frequently taken for granted, even by would-be defenders of individual ownership. I shall conclude by pointing up a number of cases where this occurs—to the great detriment of economic debate.

We shall begin by stating our fundamental thesis concerning private property. *Any man has the right to acquire previously unowned goods, keep or give them away at his pleasure, use or not use them at his pleasure.* We shall now attempt to justify this proposition.

Lest there be any confusion, it would be well to define exactly the manner in which we are employing the term "right." When we say that one has the right to do certain things we mean this and only this: that it would be immoral for another, alone or in combination, to stop him from doing this by the use of physical force or the threat thereof. We do *not* mean that any use a man makes of his property within the limits set forth is necessarily a *moral* use. We do not deny, therefore, that one may in many instances have an obligation to share his property with various of his fellows. It does not follow that one may with propriety produce and sell addictive drugs to whomsoever desires them. What is wrong, however, is the use of physical force to stop these things from happening.

We mention this to point up the fact that we do not give

automatic approval to whatever occurs on the free market. Not only this, but the market itself provides suitable punishments to what we may regard as undesirable forms of conduct. As an example, let us mention the Legion of Decency. In the early thirties there was widespread disapproval of many of the films being turned out in Hollywood. The Legion was extremely active in organizing a boycott of such films. Now whether we approve of the particular effort or not, we should note that it did not rely on physical force and that it was effective to a considerable degree. It relied on voluntary activity and relied entirely on the right of free speech. There is also the old remedy of the raised eyebrow. Most of us do not like to be known as skinflints; on the contrary, we like to be known as great benefactors of mankind, and some of us even want to *be* that way. Doubtless, factors such as these had considerable influence on much of the philanthropy during this and the last century. We may say that a man's right to property tells us not so much what *he* may properly do but rather what *others* may not properly do to him. It is fundamentally a right not to be interfered with.

We may now ask ourselves on what this right rests. It derives, we would say, from the prior right of self-ownership. Each of us owns himself and his activities. This means that we may not *initiate* violence against others. We say "initiate" because we may certainly employ violence against those who have initiated it against us. In other words, we may repel violence. Now let us suppose that in various manners I deploy my activity upon material nonhuman goods that are previously unowned. By what right does anyone stop me? There are but two possible justifications: either he has the right to direct my activities by using violence (in other words he owns me) or else he owns the material goods in question. But this contradicts the assumptions we have already made: that each human being is self-owned and that the material goods in question are not *previously* owned. This man is claiming either to own me or the property I think I have acquired. The only factor open to question is whether the other man had peacefully acquired the land before me. But to raise this question is to concede the right of private property which is the thing we are trying to establish. Now, if no one man has the right to do this, it follows that no greater number may do so, for the same question that was asked of A may be asked concerning C, and so of all the others. Surely, if this is true of any of them taken singly, there is no reason to suppose that they could properly do this if they banded together.

There is, then, an unlimited right of acquisition. This applies, however, only to what others have not already acquired. This sounds obvious, but apparently it is not for many. One frequently hears the claim that there should be a redistribution of property on the ground that its present division does not enable everyone to be a land owner and each one has the right to be a property owner. The equivocation should be clear: each one has the right to appropriate what no one else has appropriated. The right to appropriate is without content unless he who does so may keep what he has taken. And if one may keep what has been taken, it follows that nobody has the authority to wrest it from him.

The right of self-ownership implies the right to give away property either *gratis* or in exchange for something else. By what right could one force an individual to retain ownership of his property? Likewise, if an individual may give away his property then by the same token a person may receive it. One is the corollary of the other. All the objection to inherited wealth is an attack on the right of a man to give away his property. Where do we derive the authority to force a man to give his property to the individuals whom *we* designate? Surely their income is just as much unearned as the one to whom the original owner desires to bequeath his goods.

There appears to be an extremely powerful prejudice against unearned wealth. But it is as selective as it is powerful. The "liberals" object to it when the recipients are wealthy and favor it when they are poor. Some "conservatives" select in the opposite direction. These latter will object to the guaranteed annual income on the grounds that it is unearned by the recipient and it removes from him the stimulus to produce. Neither of these reasons is valid. The mere fact that an income is unearned is totally irrelevant, and although the fact that a person is not productive may be bad for the rest of us, we do not have the authority to force him to be productive. The true answer to the advocates of such subsidies is that they involve stealing from legitimate owners. This has nothing to do with whether we favor the Protestant Ethic. By using this type of argument "conservatives" fall into the hands of their opponents who have a field day in raising all the difficulties against that ethic. The unearned income of the rich is justified because it belongs to them; whereas that of the man on government relief is not because it is stolen from its rightful owner. It is certainly proper to point out to those who favor a guaranteed annual income that most of the people whom this kind of income would motivate not to produce would eventually become poorer than they already are—this because they are unaware of long-range economic effects. But the primary issue still remains ethical. Suppose that even without welfare payments the leisure preferences of most people increased enormously. All of us would then be poorer because of their failure to produce. This fact would not justify our forcing them to produce. The only legitimate alternative would be to move elsewhere.

Man also has the right to use or not to use his property as he sees fit. By use we mean any alteration in the physical constitution of the thing owned. Once the property has been appropriated the owner may either leave it alone or alter it any manner whatsoever. Many object to the continued ownership of "unimproved" land on the grounds that the owner has done nothing to increase its value. Were he later to sell it he would be obtaining something without any effort on his part.

Here again is implicit the fallacy that gain is justified only to the extent that it is the result of previous misery—a doctrine that Marx and others inherited from the Schoolmen, of all people. But more basically, it relies on a totally false supposition: that by transforming an object we can increase its value. There is no such thing as value in the object. Objects are valued by people: what is valued by people is the physical reality. People do not value values! The only way to increase another's valuation of what I have is by hypnotism.

True, we may so change the physical constitution of objects that they correspond to the future values of people. But note that there is no absolute certainty as to what their values will be. It may very well be the case that what people will value will be the object in its *original* form. If this happens then all my efforts will have been in vain. I would have benefited him and myself far more by doing nothing. In other words, the owner of property performs an entrepreneurial function. He must predict the future valuations that he and others will make and act or *not act* accordingly. He is "rewarded" primarily not for his work but for his good judgment.

This is a simple lesson the learning of which would have spared the world a tremendous amount of misery. Unfortunately the world seems as far from accepting it as always. The view that one should be rewarded for one's efforts is part of the conventional wisdom and one finds it on the tongue of both the liberal and the conservative. One of the reasons why Marxism always finds such a ready ear is the fact that before hearing about it people already hold its basic theory of value. And it is an easy matter for the Marxist to show such a person that the way in which wages are paid accord very poorly with commonly accepted ideas of justice. Far from retarding the acceptance of socialistic ideas, a person's religious convictions will tend to accelerate the process. Witness the numbers of clergymen who have been caught in this trap.

So much, then, for the basic principles connected with the notion of private property. The sad reality at the end of the eighteenth and the beginning of the nineteenth centuries was rather different from the ideal situation. Undoubtedly the extent of the misery that prevailed after the introduction of more or less free economies has been grossly exaggerated. Indeed there would have been even greater misery had this system not been introduced. This leads us to believe that there was something radically wrong before the change that was never given the proper attention. While most of the frightful restrictions on economic action were removed, the enormous feudal landholdings were left untouched in the name of respect for private property.

As we know, these holdings were mostly the result either of conquest or state land-grants. It is highly dubious that these holdings could ever have attained their size on the free market. Justice would have dictated the division of these lands among those who lived and worked on them. Unfortunately this was not done. The result was that a few individuals had votes in the market far beyond their due and were thereby enabled to determine the course of events. These were responsible for the spectacular amount of investment and consequent economic growth of the area. There is no doubt but that we have more goods at our disposal now because of what happened then.

Suppose the land had been divided up. Probably agriculture would have been a much more important industry in England. It is also likely that the rate of consumption would have been higher. This would have meant less investment, less "growth." We would not be where we are today. Supposing all this to be true: What of it? The primary question is the one of justice. Where does a man get the authority to require that someone else use his property in the manner that the outsider judge to be the most economic? It is his property and he has the right to use it in the way which satisfies him. If he does not want to "grow," that is his business.

The fact that a future generation may be better off because of a forced rate of growth during the previous generations excuses nothing. This would be tantamount to allowing future generations to impose taxes on their ancestors. The forced abstinence from consumption is constantly being justified on the grounds that "we will be better off in a hundred years." Just who is "we"? In a hundred years we will all be dead. Even if we were not, suppose we want to be better off now. Should not individuals be allowed to function in accordance with their own time-preferences?

The unwillingness of some to remedy an unjust distribution of holdings on the ground that to do so would be uneconomic is positively scandalous. After all, if not to remedy such an iniquitous distribution is justifiable in the name of economics, then would it not also be legitimate to create an unjust system for the same reason? Why not seize small holdings and give them to those men who would choose to save rather than to consume? But this would be unjust. True, but so it is if people are allowed to retain holdings that really do not belong to them.

We can go even further, however, and challenge the thesis that the system of holdings that obtained at the time the free market was instituted was the most economic one. How can anyone tell? On the supposition that a free market had obtained from the beginning, we say that the distribution of wealth is the most economic one. The size of anyone's holdings will tend to reflect the extent to which he satisfied the desires of those with whom he engaged in business. Since, ex hypothesi, there never was coercion, everybody benefited by the exchanges. Certainly no such claims can be made in behalf of a system that preexisted the unhampered market. All we can say is that if the holdings are left untouched and if free exchange is introduced, then eventually a satisfactory system will develop. Here, however, the long run may be long indeed, and what about the rights of the people in the meanwhile? They will prefer to consume the smaller pie that is theirs by rights. That people who possess what is rightfully yours are busy making a larger pie which can be consumed only by your descendents is cold comfort indeed.

These considerations surely raise numerous questions about the situations in the undeveloped areas of the world. Obviously one of the big problems is what to do with the vast holdings of land. There is little doubt but that these were not acquired by legitimate means. Because these exist, large numbers of individuals are doomed to a life of misery even by their own standards. One can sympathize with the misguided concern of the Marxist reformer. On the other hand, we must deplore his forked-tongued approach to the propaganda problem. Interestingly he will appeal to the peasant by his proposals to divide the land—an effective appeal because by instinct the peasant firmly believes in private property and feels he has been defrauded of it. To the factory worker, however, he has an entirely different story to tell. He gives them to understand that the capitalistic mentality of the peasant is his real enemy and promises that the land will be taken over by the state, so that the kulaks will not be able to charge the workers in the city exorbitant prices.

Anybody who understands the workings of the free market can see that the policies advocated by collectivists are doomed to failure. For the most part, those who pay lip service to the market show little desire to question the property arrangements in these areas. This is why they have little to say that would interest the poor and downtrodden in these countries. These people have come to associate the free-market system with the approval of the status quo. They will not be greatly helped by the fact that from now on their oppressors will be able to exchange with each other on an unhampered basis. All this means is that for the foreseeable future a few more crumbs may fall from the tables of those who profit by facilitated exchange.

Here again the spirit of growthmanship is operative. "These countries will never become industrialized unless the vast holdings are allowed to continue or the land will not be well used if divided up." Could a Marxist be more critical of the free market than these people? Is it not the right of the real owners to decide to what extent their area shall be industrialized?

Also operative are certain special interests who want justice here but not abroad. Some of them have bought land from people who had no right to it in the first place. Others have been given land by governments who had previously expropriated it. This makes them a party to the injustice. Obviously much of the justified complaining in these areas is misdirected. Just as these foreign companies will object to any expropriation by appealing to the sanctity of property, so the natives will blame their troubles on the system of private property itself, or they will attack foreign investment as something which is evil in itself. As in so many instances people are unable to locate their real enemy. Surely if these people blame their troubles on free enterprise, the defenders of this system are partly responsible for their error.

We have given a general analysis of what is involved in the notion of private, individual property. We have attempted to prove that this system is justified by the more basic right of self-ownership. We then pointed out that the only ground on which others could prevent a person from acquiring ownership is an implicit claim to previous ownership by somebody else. But to concede that somebody else owned the property is to admit that there is such a thing as the right to property. Then we establish that no one has the authority to interfere with the nonaggressive use of that property. It is finally important to realize that those goods that have been illegitimately acquired do not become lawful property in virtue of the mere passing of time.

We have put off until now reckoning with one final notion: that the goods of the earth belong to no individuals, but rather are vested in an entity called "society." Somehow, this entity is a whole of which each one is a part. It is conceived as having rights and also duties. The actions of the parts may be permitted only to the extent to which they aid the whole. The organ through which society expresses itself can be either a king, a parliament, or simply the majority of its members. Supposedly, whatever these organs want "we" want. Pervasive as it is, this theory is quite difficult to formulate, and for good reason. It is often enough used as the ultimate justification of government.

The question we should ask is not so much whether society has the rights attributed to it, as whether such an entity can be meaningfully said to exist at all. When, however, you ask what kind of entity this could possibly be, you are referred to various analogies. Just as we are made up of cells, so society is made up of individuals. "If you claim that the notion of 'society' is unintelligible, you must also claim that the notion of a whole is meaningless." It is, indeed, difficult to admit that the one could exist and not the other. If, therefore, the notion of "society" derives its plausibility from these analogies, it might pay us to inquire a bit into these analogies. Are they really, anywhere, entities that are made up of entities, or are we the victims of a linguistic trick? If nowhere are such entities to be found, then automatically this notion of "society" will fall to the ground.

Perhaps the best approach to the matter would be through an examination of what is meant by a collective noun. As an example, let us take "baseball team." We use this term to designate many things that are united in some particular respect. In the case at hand each man acts in conjunction with others in order to bring about a certain pattern of activities. Do we literally have a new being which did not exist before these people joined forces? Certainly not. We do as a matter of fact speak *as if* there were now a single entity. We use the word "team" as the subject of a sentence, we replace the word "team" by "it." But we are conscious that in so doing we are simply using a convenient manner of speaking which is designed to save time. The proof of this is that we could simply eliminate the word "team" from our language and substitute a more prolix language that referred "those men who are united for the purpose of playing baseball." This is quite a complicated formula and it is well we have discovered more convenient fashions of expressing ourselves. Nor does this cause any problem as long as we realize exactly what we are doing.

Note that in the example given there is no "ego" over and above that of the individuals who have pooled their activities. Nor, strictly speaking, is there a collective activity; there are only individual activities directed by individual persons towards a mutually agreed-upon end. The "whole" is nothing but the individual players insofar as they cooperate. The only real entities are the individuals or the "parts." This suggests that we could in principle eliminate "whole" sentences from our language and replace them by more complicated sentences whose subject is "parts" or "individuals."

In what sense can we speak of these organizations or societies as owning property? These groups vary considerably from one another but there are a few general remarks that should apply to all. The first thing to realize is that no matter what else may be true of the arrangements, these groups own what they do because of the free choice of the individuals who have entered into this type of cooperation. Indeed, the very existence of the organization presupposes the willingness of individuals to join together, and its continuance requires new decisions on the part of those willing to collaborate with the already existing members. It is certain that the organization cannot have preceded its first members. The financial arrangements will be those decided upon by the original members, for even if changes are later to be made, the procedure for introducing them will have been set up by the founders. So, from first to last the social ownership presupposes individual ownership. And as long as the society continues, the ownership is ultimately that of its individual members.

Let us now return to the contention that the original owner of property is not the individual but "society." We have seen that the only real entities are individuals so that nothing can be true of this society which is not true of the individuals that make it up. Consider first the ownership of the individuals. In so doing we shall suppose a society made up of two individuals, A and B. There are but two possibilities: A owns A, B owns B; or A owns B, or B owns A. There is no third entity that can own them both. But there must be a third if both of them are to be owned; that is, for them to belong in the literal sense to society. If we suppose that A owns B or the opposite, we still do not have societal ownership but individual ownership. Now since the appropriation of nonhuman goods takes place via the activities of people, it follows that what is appropriated by the individuals will belong to the owners of the individuals. Since it is impossible that society owns the individuals, it cannot own what they appropriate.

It is true that the two members of our little society can agree jointly to appropriate land of which they will be co-owners. But in this case the initial decision is entirely voluntary, and each one is an individual owner of that property and may abandon his share of ownership at his own pleasure.

Thus we see that the thesis that society is the original owner of land cannot stand up under analysis. This is not simply a question of historical fact. In the very nature of the case, the individual precedes society and this includes the ownership of the individual. All the rest must be the result of a contractual relationship, itself dependent on the free decisions of individuals.

Though the concept that there are goods that belong to society is unacceptable, there are many occasions where it is taken for granted that society is an entity in its own right and that it automatically does own things. It constitutes the unspoken major premise of many political proposals. We would like briefly to examine a number of cases where this assumption is made.

"It is necessary to conserve society's valuable resources." This is the famous problem of waste. As we have already seen, these resources are either unowned or else their ownership is distributed among various individuals. There is no third possibility. The first alternative presents little difficulty. How come nobody owns these resources? Surely if it were in the interest of the economy, you would have various individuals appropriating such resources. Why do they fail to do so? Why is it not to their interest to acquire them? The fundamental reason appears to be the fact that such goods are not sufficiently scarce to justify the cost (and there is one) of appropriating them. In other words the very fact that there are goods which no one sees fit to acquire for his exclusive use is of itself a sign that no problem exists concerning their conservation. Surely, if there were some, entrepreneurs would notice the fact and do something about it. It is surely suspicious when the only one who can see that it is worthwhile to acquire resources is the government.

The other possibility is that the resources are already distributed among individual owners. In which case the only ones who have the right to speak about wasting "our" resources are the owners themselves. Each owner will make use of his resources in the way he sees fit. He can be said to have wasted his resources only when he makes mistaken predictions, and the more resources he has the ability to acquire, the less likely he is to be the kind of person who makes the wrong predictions. The same may be said concerning those who make eccentric use of their resources, as for example setting their oil fields afire in order to produce spectacles. Here we cannot say that the man is wasting something. He may be so constituted that he gets more out of doing this than from other uses to which he might put his property. All we can say is that in a free society people of this type are unable to acquire any considerable amount of property unless someone makes a gift of it to them. In an unhampered market the entire tendency is that one grows wealthy only by serving in large measure the interest of his fellows. If the wealth were given to someone of this nature, again, he would not be able for any length of time to preserve his position. So we can say that full freedom to perform nonaggressive actions tends to prevent any large scale use of resources that is not *mutually* beneficial. Not only is it meaningless to speak of society's resources; it is not even helpful.

"Our country is importing too much." Here is another statement which, given a free society, is without content. Countries do not import. Only people do. How can an individual import too much except by failing properly to predict his future wants? If he is that poor a guesser he will not be around for long, and the less wealthy he is the more quickly he will cease importing. In any area some people will import a great deal, others much less. But no one can go on importing too much for his own good for any long time. But perhaps some people are importing too much for the good of others in the sense that they are failing to help the others. We must not assume, first of all, that their importing is not the reason why those around them are not helped. Suppose they were to cease importing and not buy the goods from those near them. Are they any better off because they stopped importing? We may also add that to the extent the importer had extensive relationships with those near him, his imports from elsewhere will positively benefit them because these extensive relationships can continue only because what he imports is of greater benefit to them. Obviously, the fewer economic ties he has with his neighbors, the less they will be helped by his imports. But then to complain about this is to say in effect that because X lives within a certain radius of Y, he should be forced to help Y.

One of the common complaints against an unmanaged currency is that the people are unable to control their money. The ambiguity lies in the concept "the peoples' money." Does it mean that there is collective ownership of the medium of exchange? If so, the phrase is unintelligible. Given the free economy, each individual owns whatever money he is able to acquire. He values it as he sees fit, controls it as he sees fit, and manages it as he sees fit. The people control their money in the same way they control their television sets. Of course, the last thing that advocates of government planning want is for people to have control of their money. What they want is for the government to control it. What they mean by "uncontrolled" is precisely that it *is* controlled, but not by those whom they would like to see control it. One of the great problems of the world is the fact that money is not controlled by its rightful owners.

Then there is the old chestnut that has it that our country is losing gold. Supposing that each individual owns whatever gold he has, it is obviously impossible for a country to lose gold. The "country" doesn't have it in the first place. Only the individuals who have the gold can lose it—not a very likely contingency. Normally people do not lose gold. They exchange it for things that they would rather have. We would be somewhat astonished to hear someone maintain in all seriousness that he lost two dollars because he went to the movies. The real truth behind such claims is that the government which has expropriated the people's gold is being called upon by other governments to redeem its currency. But this would never have happened had not the government engaged in an inflationary policy.

I will end with a very weird example from Robert Heilbroner's *The Making of Economic Society*, pp. 96-97:

> Yet England experienced difficulties enough in launching the Great Transformation. As we can now see, many of these difficulties were the direct consequences of the problems which our model highlighted for us. The industrialization process of the eighteenth and nineteenth centuries did, indeed, necessitate a great amount of saving—that is, of the releasing of consumption—and much of the social hardship of the time can be traced to this source.
>
> For who did the saving? Who abstained from consumption? The manufacturers themselves (for all their ostentatious ways) were among those who plowed back a substantial portion of their profits into more investment. Yet the real savers were not the manufacturers so much as another class—the industrial workers. Here, in the low level of industrial wages, the great sacrifice was made—not voluntarily, by any matter of means, but made just the same. From the resources they could have consumed was built the industrial foundation for the future.

We have already referred to what we believe were the great injustices of the period of the "Great Transformation." Had there been a more equal distribution of property individuals would have been consuming more of what they produced, simply because each of them would have been producing a smaller quantity and, therefore, would have had less to save. Since Heilbroner's reasoning does not depend on any prior unjust distribution of property, let us take for granted the justice of the arrangement and see if his analysis makes any sense.

It is true that nonconsumption is a necessary condition for saving. But the nonconsumption in question concerns *one's own* resources, not those of other people. It can hardly be said that I am saving for you when I fail to consume your resources. This is not the place to discuss the problem of wages. Suffice it to say that had less been produced, real wages would not have been as high as they were at any given time. The increased production was mutually beneficial to the owners and the workers. The fact that the owners saved rather than consumed made the workers' condition much better than otherwise. They were perhaps victimized by the fact that the producers had the money that rightly belonged to them. But not by the fact that the money was *saved.* It is absolutely ridiculous to assert that the workers actually did the saving since they did not have the resources to save. Even if someone takes my money away from me and saves it, it is hardly enlightening for me to claim that I am doing the saving. It is only because Heilbroner indulges in this type of collective thinking that he was able to write such nonsense. Its plausibility can only rest on the analogy of a family where some members, anxious to increase the total wealth, deliberately abstain from consuming their earnings in order to contribute them to the investments of the more productive individuals of the group.

In the next paragraph we are told that "England *had* to hold down the level of its working class consumption in order to free its productive effort for the accumulation of capital goods." What on earth is the entity that ever made such a decision? Practically the only entities making decisions in nineteenth century England were those who owned resources. There were many decisions on the part of many *people*, but none by *England.* And I am quite sure that no one thought himself capable of "holding down the consumption of the working class" or desired to do so "in order to free its productive effort for the accumulation of capital goods." Decisions of this kind are made today, however. But they are made, not by property owners, but by dictators.

If there is a lesson to be learned from this it is that the only enlightening way of analyzing economic and property problems is by always returning to the individual who, alone, is real. People are ill served by the manufacture of spurious entities.

6

Murray N. Rothbard

JUSTICE AND PROPERTY RIGHTS

I. *The Failure of Utilitarianism*

UNTIL very recently, free-market economists paid little attention to the entities actually being exchanged on the very market they have advocated so strongly. Wrapped up in the workings and advantages of freedom of trade, enterprise, investment, and the price system, economists tended to lose sight of the things being exchanged on that market. Namely, they lost sight of the fact that when $10,000 is being exchanged for a machine, or $1 for a hula hoop, what is actually being exchanged is the *title of ownership* to each of these goods. In short, when I buy a hula hoop for a dollar, what I am actually doing is exchanging my title of ownership to the dollar in exchange for the ownership title to the hula hoop; the retailer is doing the exact opposite.[1] But this means that economists' habitual attempts to be *Wertfrei*, or at the least to confine their advocacy to the processes of trade and exchange, cannot be maintained; for if I and the retailer are indeed to be free to trade the dollar for the hula hoop without coercive interference by third parties, then this can only be done if these economists will proclaim the justice and the propriety of my original ownership of the dollar and the retailer's ownership of the hula hoop.

In short, for an economist to say that X and Y should be free to trade Good A for Good B unmolested by third parties, he must *also* say that X legitimately and properly owns Good A and that Y legitimately owns Good B. But this means that the free-market economist must have some sort of theory of justice in property rights; he can scarcely say that X properly owns Good A without asserting some sort of theory of justice on behalf of such ownership.

Suppose, for example, that as I am about to purchase the hula hoop, the information arrives that the retailer had really stolen the hoop from Z. Surely not even the supposedly *Wertfrei* economist can continue to endorse blithely the proposed exchange of ownership titles between myself and the retailer. For now we find that retailer Y's title of ownership is improper and unjust and that he must be forced to return the hoop to Z, the original owner. The economist can then only endorse the proposed exchange between myself and Z, rather than Y, for the hula hoop, since he has to acknowledge Z as the proper owner of title to the hoop.

In short, we have two mutually exclusive claimants to the ownership of the hoop. If the economist agrees to endorse only Z's sale of the hoop, then he is implicitly agreeing that Z has the just, and Y the unjust, claim to the hoop. And even if he continues to endorse the sale by Y, then he is implicitly maintaining *another* theory of property titles: namely, that theft is justified. Whichever way he decides, the economist cannot escape a judgment, a theory of justice in the ownership of property. Furthermore, the economist is not really finished when he proclaims the injustice of theft and endorses Z's proper title. For what is the justification for Z's title to the hoop? Is it only because he is a nonthief?

In recent years, free-market economists Ronald Coase and Harold Demsetz have begun to redress the balance and to focus on the importance of a clear and precise demarcation of property rights for the market economy. They have demonstrated the importance of such demarcation in the allocation of resources and in preventing or compensating for unwanted imposition of "external costs" from the actions of individuals. But Coase and Demsetz have failed to develop any theory of justice in these property rights; or rather, they have advanced two theories: one, that it "doesn't matter" *how* the property titles are allocated, so long as they are allocated precisely; and, two, that the titles should be allocated to minimize "total social transaction costs," since a minimization of costs is supposed to be a *Wertfrei* way of benefiting all of society.

There is no space here for a detailed critique of the Coase-Demsetz criteria. Suffice it to say that even if, say, in a conflict over property titles between a rancher and a farmer for the same piece of land, even if the allocation of title "doesn't matter" for the allocation of resources (a point which itself could be challenged), it certainly matters from the point of view of the rancher and the farmer. And secondly, that it is impossible to weigh "total social costs" if we fully realize that all costs are subjective to the individual and therefore cannot be compared interpersonally.[2] Here the important point is that Coase and Demsetz, along with all other utilitarian free-market economists, implicitly or explicitly leave it to the hands of government to define and allocate the titles to private property.

It is a curious fact that utilitarian economists, generally so skeptical of the virtues of government intervention, are so content to leave the fundamental underpinning of the market process—the definition of property rights and the allocation of property titles—wholly in the hands of government. Presumably they do so because they themselves have no theory of justice in property rights and therefore place the burden of allocating property titles in the hands of government. Thus, if Smith, Jones, and Doe each own property and are about to exchange their titles, utilitarians simply assert that if these titles are *legal* (i.e., if the government puts the stamp of approval upon them), then they consider those titles to be justified; it is only if someone violates the government's definition of legality (e.g., in the case of Y, the thieving retailer) that utilitarians are willing to agree with the general and the governmental view of the injustice of such action. But this means, of course, that, once again, the utilitarians have failed in their wish to escape having a theory of justice in property; actually they *do* have such a theory, and it is the surely simplistic one that *whatever government defines as legal is right.*

As in so many other areas of social philosophy, then, we see that utilitarians, in pursuing their vain goal of being *Wertfrei,* of "scientifically" abjuring any theory of justice, actually *have* such a theory, namely, putting their stamp of approval on whatever the process by which the government arrives at its allocation of property titles. Furthermore, we find that, as on many similar occasions, utilitarians in their vain quest for the *Wertfrei,* really conclude by endorsing as right and just whatever the government happens to decide, that is, by blindly apologizing for the *status quo.*[3]

Let us consider the utilitarian stamp of approval on government allocation of property titles. Can this approval possibly achieve even the limited utilitarian goal of certain and precise allocation of property titles? Suppose that the government endorses the existing titles to their property held by Smith, Jones, and Doe. Suppose then that a faction of government calls for the confiscation of these titles and redistribution of that property to Roe, Brown, and Robinson. The reasons for this program may stem from any number of social theories or even from the brute fact that Roe, Brown, and Robinson have greater political power than the original trio of owners. The reaction to this proposal by free-market economists and other utilitarians is predictable: they will oppose this proposal on the ground that definite and certain property rights, so socially beneficial, are being endangered. But suppose that the government, ignoring the protests of our utilitarians, proceeds anyway and redistributes these titles to property. Roe, Brown, and Robinson are *now* defined by the government as the proper and legal owners, while any claims to that property by the original trio of Smith, Jones, and Doe are considered improper and illegitimate, if not subversive. What now will be the reaction of our utilitarians?

It should be clear that since the utilitarians base their theory of justice in property only on *whatever the government defines* as legal, they can have no groundwork whatever for any call for restoring the property in question to its original owners. They can only, willy-nilly, and despite any emotional reluctance on their part, simply endorse the *new* allocation of property titles as defined and endorsed by government. Not only must utilitarians endorse the *sta-*

tus quo of property titles, they must endorse whatever *status quo* exists and however rapidly the government decides to shift and redistribute such titles. Furthermore, considering the historical record, we may indeed say that relying upon government to be the guardian of property rights is like placing the proverbial fox on guard over the chicken coop.

We see, therefore, that the supposed defense of the free market and of property rights by utilitarians and free-market economists is a very weak reed indeed. Lacking a theory of justice that goes beyond the existing *imprimatur* of government, utilitarians can only go along with every change and shift of government allocation after they occur, no matter how arbitrary, rapid, or politically motivated such shifts might be. And since they provide no firm roadblock for governmental reallocations of property, the utilitarians, in the final analysis, can offer no real defense of property rights themselves. Since governmental redefinitions can and will be rapid and arbitrary, they cannot provide long-run certainty for property rights, and therefore they cannot even ensure the very social and economic efficiency which they themselves seek.[4] All this is implied in the pronouncements of utilitarians that any future free society must confine itself to whatever definitions of property titles the government may happen to be endorsing at that moment.

Let us consider a hypothetical example of the failure of utilitarian defense of private property. Suppose that somehow government becomes persuaded of the necessity to yield to a clamor for a free-market, *laissez-faire* society. Before dissolving itself, however, it redistributes property titles: granting the ownership of the entire territory of New York to the Rockefeller family, of Massachusetts to the Kennedy family, etc. It then dissolves, ending taxation and all other forms of government intervention in the economy. However, while taxation has been abolished, the Rockefeller, Kennedy, etc., families proceed to dictate to all the residents in what is now "their" territory, exacting what are now called "rents" over all the inhabitants.[5] It seems clear that our utilitarians could have no intellectual armor with which to challenge this new dispensation; indeed, they would have to endorse the Rockefeller, Kennedy, etc., holdings as "private property" equally deserving of support as the ordinary property titles which they had endorsed only a few months previously. All this because the utilitarians have no theory of justice in property beyond endorsement of whatever *status quo* happens to exist.

Consider, furthermore, the grotesque box in which the utilitarian proponent of freedom places himself in relation to the institution of human slavery. Contemplating that institution and the "free" market that once existed in buying, selling, and renting slaves, the utilitarian who must rely on the legal definition of property can only endorse slavery on the ground that the slave masters had purchased their slave titles legally and in good faith. Surely, any endorsement of a "free" market in slaves indicates the inadequacy of utilitarian concepts of property and the need for a theory of justice to provide a groundwork for property rights and a critique of existing official titles to property.

II. *Toward a Theory of Justice in Property*

We conclude that utilitarianism cannot be supported as a groundwork for property rights or, *a fortiori,* for the free-market economy. A theory of justice must be arrived at which goes beyond government allocations of property titles and which can therefore serve as a basis for criticizing such allocations. Obviously, in this space I can only outline what I consider to be the correct theory of justice in property rights. This theory has two fundamental premises: (a) the absolute property right of each individual in his own person, his own body: this may be called the *right of self-ownership;* and (b) the absolute right in material property of the person who first finds an unused material resource and then in some way occupies or transforms that resource by the use of his personal energy. This might be called the *homestead principle*—the case in which someone, in the phrase of John Locke, has "mixed his labour" with an unused resource. Let Locke summarize these principles:

> ...every man has a *property* in his own *person*. This nobody has any right to but himself. The *labour* of his body and the *work* of his hands, we may say, are properly his. Whatsoever, then, he removes out of the state that nature hath provided and left it in, he hath mixed his labour with it, and joined to it something that is his own, and thereby makes it his property. It being by him removed from the common state nature placed it in, it hath by this labour something annexed to it that excludes the common right of other men.[6]

Let us consider the first principle: the right to self-ownership. This principle asserts the absolute right of each man, by virtue of his (or her) being a human being, to "own" his own body; that is, to control that body free of coercive interference. Since the nature of man is such that each individual must use his mind to learn about himself and the world, to select values, and to choose ends and means in order to survive and flourish, the right to self-ownership gives each man the right to perform these vital activities without being hampered and restricted by coercive molestation.

Consider, then, the alternatives—the consequences of *denying* each man the right to own his own person. There are only two alternatives: either (1) a certain class of people, A, have the right to own another class, B; or (2) everyone has the right to own his equal quotal share of everyone else. The first alternative implies that while Class A deserves the rights of being human, Class B is in reality subhuman and therefore deserves no such rights. But since they *are* indeed human beings, the first alternative contradicts itself in denying natural human rights to one set of humans. Moreover, allowing Class A to own Class B means that the former is allowed to exploit, and therefore to live parasitically, at the expense of the latter; but, as economics can tell us, this parasitism itself violates the basic economic requirement for human survival: production and exchange.

The second alternative, which we might call "participatory communalism" or "communism," holds that every man should have the right to own his equal quotal share of everyone else. If there are three billion people in the world, then everyone has the right to own a three-billionth of every other person. In the first place, this ideal itself rests upon an absurdity: proclaiming that every man is entitled to own a part of everyone else and yet is not entitled to *own himself*. Secondly, we can picture the viability of such a world: a world in which *no* man is free to take *any* action whatever without prior approval or indeed command by *everyone else* in society. It should be clear that in that sort of "communist" world, no one would be able to do anything, and the human race would quickly perish. But if a world of zero self-ownership and 100 percent other-ownership spells death for the human race, then any steps in that direction also contravene the natural law of what is best for man and his life on earth.

Finally, however, the participatory communist world *cannot* be put into practice. For it is physically impossible for everyone to keep continual tabs on everyone else and thereby to exercise his equal quotal share of partial ownership over every other man. In practice, then, any attempt to institute universal and equal other-ownership is utopian and impossible, and supervision, and therefore control and ownership of others, would necessarily devolve upon a specialized group of people, who would thereby become a "ruling class." Hence, in practice, any attempt at communist society will automatically become class rule, and we would be back at our rejected first alternative.

We conclude, then, with the premise of absolute universal right of self-ownership as our first principle of justice in property. This principle, of course, automatically rejects slavery as totally incompatible with our primary right.[7]

Let us now turn to the more complex case of property in material objects. For even if every man has the right to self-ownership, people are not floating wraiths; they are not self-subsistent entities; they can only survive and flourish by grappling with the earth around them. They must, for example, *stand* on land areas; they must also, in order to survive, transform the resources given by nature into "consumer goods," into objects more suitable for their use and consumption. Food must be grown and eaten; minerals must be mined and then transformed into capital and finally into useful consumer goods, etc. Man, in other words, must own not only his own person, but also material objects for his control and use. How, then, should property titles in these objects be allocated?

Let us consider, as our first example, the case of a sculptor fashioning a work of art out of clay and other materials; and let us simply assume for the moment that he owns these materials while waiving the question of the justification for their ownership. Let us examine the question: *who* should own the work of art, as it emerges from the sculptor's fashioning? The sculpture is, in fact, the sculptor's "creation," not in the sense that he has created matter *de novo,* but in the sense that he has transformed nature-given matter—the clay—into another form dictated by his own ideas and fashioned by his own hands and energy. Surely, it is a rare person who, with the case put thus, would say that the sculptor does *not* have the property right in his own product. For if every man has the right to own his own body, and if he must grapple with the material objects of the world in order to survive, then the sculptor has the right to own the product which he has made, by his energy and effort, a veritable *extension* of his own personality. He has placed the stamp of his person upon the raw material, by "mixing his labor" with the clay.

As in the case of the ownership of people's bodies, we again have three logical alternatives: (1) either the transformer, the "creator," has the property right in his creation; or (2) another man or set of men have the right to appropriate it by force without the sculptor's consent; or (3) the "communal" solution—every individual in the world has an equal, quotal share in the ownership of the sculpture. Again, put baldly, there are very few who would not concede the monstrous injustice of confiscating the sculptor's property, either by one or more others, or by the world as a whole. For by what right do they do so? By what right do they appropriate to themselves the product of the creator's mind and energy? (Again, as in the case of bodies, any confiscation in the supposed name of the world as a whole would in practice devolve into an oligarchy of confiscators.)

But the case of the sculptor is not qualitatively different from *all* cases of "production." The man or men who extracted the clay from the ground and sold it to the sculptor were *also* "producers"; they too mixed their ideas and their energy and their technological knowhow with the nature-given material to emerge with a useful product. As producers, the sellers of the clay and of the sculptor's tools also mixed their labor with natural materials to transform them into more useful goods and services. All the producers are therefore entitled to the ownership of their product.

The chain of material production logically reduces back, then, back from consumer goods and works of art to the first producers who gathered or mined the nature-given soil and resources to use and transform them by means of their personal energy. And use of the soil logically reduces back to the legitimate ownership by first users of previously unowned, unused, virginal, nature-given resources. Let us again quote Locke:

> He that is nourished by the acorns he picked up under an oak, or the apples he gathered from the trees in the wood, has certainly appropriated them to himself. Nobody can deny but the nourishment is his. I ask then, when did they begin to be his? When he digested? or when he ate? or when he boiled? or when he brought them home? or when he picked them up? And 'tis plain, if the first gathering made them not his, nothing else could. That labour put the distinction between them and common. That added something to them more than Nature, the common mother of all, had done, and so they became his private right. And will any one say he had no right to those acorns or apples he thus appropriated because he had not the consent of all mankind to make them his? Was it a robbery thus to assume to himself what belonged to all in common? If such a consent as that was necessary, man had starved, notwithstanding the plenty God had given him.... Thus, the grass my horse has bit, the turfs my servant has cut, and the ore I have digged in my place, where I have a right to them in common with others, become my property without the assignation or consent of any body. The labour that was mine, removing them out of that common state they were in, hath fixed my property in them.[8]

If every man owns his own person and therefore his own labor, and if by extension he owns whatever material property he has "created" or gathered out of the previously unused, unowned "state of nature," then what of the logically final question: who has the right to own or control the earth *itself*? In short, if the gatherer has the right to own the acorns or berries he picks, or the farmer the right to own his crop of wheat or peaches, *who* has the right to own the land on which these things have grown? It is at this point that Henry George and his followers, who would have gone all the way so far with our analysis, leave the track and deny the individual's right to own the piece of land itself, the ground on which these activities have taken place. The Georgists argue that, while every man should own the goods which he produces or creates, since Nature or God created the land itself, no individual has the right to assume ownership of that land. Yet again we are faced with our three logical alternatives: either the land itself belongs to the pioneer, the first user, the man who first brings it into production; *or* it belongs to a group of others; *or* it belongs to the world as a whole, with every individual owning an equal quotal part of every acre of land. George's option for the last solution hardly solves his moral problem: for if the land itself should belong to God or Nature, then why is it more moral for every acre in the world to be owned by the world as a whole, than to concede individual ownership? In practice, again, it is obviously impossible for every person in the world to exercise his ownership of his three-billionth portion of every acre of the world's surface; in practice a small oligarchy would do the controlling and owning rather than the world as a whole.

But apart from those difficulties in the Georgist position, our proposed justification for the ownership of ground land is the same as the justification for the original ownership of all other property. For, as we have indicated, no producer *really* "creates" matter; he takes nature-given matter and transforms it by his personal energy in accordance with his ideas and his vision. But *this* is precisely what the pioneer—the "homesteader"—does when he brings previously unused land into his private ownership. Just as the man who makes steel out of iron and transforms that ore out of his knowhow and with his energy, and just as the man who takes the iron out of the ground does the same, so too does the homesteader who clears, fences, cultivates or builds upon the land. The homesteader, too, has transformed the character and usefulness of the nature-given soil by his labor and his personality. The homesteader is just as legitimately the owner of the property as the sculptor or the manufacturer; he is just as much a "producer" as the others.

Moreover, if a producer is *not* entitled to the fruits of his labor, who is? It is difficult to see why a newborn Pakistani baby should have a moral claim to a quotal share of ownership of a piece of Iowa land that someone has just transformed into a wheatfield—and vice versa of course for an Iowan baby and a Pakistani farm. Land in its original state is unused and unowned. Georgists and other land communalists may claim that the entire world population "really" owns it, but if no one has yet used it, it is in the real sense owned and controlled by no one. The pioneer, the homesteader, the first user and transformer of this land, is the man who first brings this simple valueless thing into production and use. It is difficult to see the justice of depriving him of ownership in favor of people who have never gotten within a thousand miles of the land and who may not even know of the existence of the property over which they are supposed to have a claim. It is even more difficult to see the justice of a group of outside oligarchs owning the property, and at the expense of expropriating the creator or the homesteader who had originally brought the product into existence.

Finally, no one can produce *anything* without the cooperation of ground land, if only to be used as standing room. No man can produce or create anything by his labor alone; he must have the cooperation of land and other natural raw materials. Man comes into the world with just himself and the world around him—the land and natural resources given him by nature. He takes these resources and transforms them by his labor and mind and energy into goods more useful to man. Therefore, if an individual cannot own original ground land, neither can he in the full sense own any of the fruits of his labor. Now that this labor has been inextricably mixed with the land, he cannot be deprived of one without being deprived of the other.

The moral issue involved here is even clearer if we consider the case of animals. Animals are "economic land," since they are original nature-given resources. Yet will anyone deny full title to a horse to the man who finds and domesticates it? This is no different from the acorns and berries which are generally conceded to the gatherer. Yet in land, too, the homesteader takes the previously wild, undomesticated land, and tames it by putting it to productive use. Mixing his labor with land sites should give him just as clear a title as in the case of animals.

From our two basic axioms: the right of every man to self-ownership; and the right of every man to own previously unused natural resources that he first appropriates or transforms by his labor—the entire system of justification for property rights can be deduced. For if anyone justly owns the land himself and the property which he finds and creates, then he of course has the right to exchange that property for the similarly acquired just property of someone else. This establishes the right of free exchange of property, as well as the right to give one's property away to someone who agrees to receive it. Thus, X may own his person and labor and the farm he clears on which he grows wheat; Y owns the fish he catches; Z owns the cabbages he grows and the land under it. But then X has the right to exchange some of his wheat for some of Y's fish (if Y agrees) or Z's cabbages. And when X and Y make a voluntary agreement to exchange wheat for fish, then that fish becomes X's justly acquired property to do with what he wishes, and the wheat becomes Y's just property in precisely the same way. Further, a man may of course exchange not only the tangible objects he owns but also his own labor, which of course he owns as well. Thus,

Z may sell his labor services of teaching farmer X's children in return for some of the farmer's produce.

We have thus established the property-right justification for the free-market process. For the free-market economy, as complex as the system appears to be on the surface, is yet nothing more than a vast network of voluntary and mutually agreed upon two-person or two-party exchanges of property titles, such as we have seen occurs between wheat and cabbage farmers, or between the farmer and the teacher. In the developed free-market economy, the farmer exchanges his wheat for money; the wheat is bought by the miller who processes and transforms the wheat into flour; the baker sells the bread to the wholesaler, who in turn sells it to the retailer, who finally sells it to the consumer. In the case of the sculptor, he buys the clay and the tools from the producers who dug the clay out of the ground or those who bought the clay from the original miners; and he bought his tools from the manufacturers who in turn purchased the raw material from the miners of iron ore.

How "money" enters the equation is a complex process; but it should be clear here that conceptually the use of money is equivalent to any useful commodity that is exchanged for wheat, flour, etc. Instead of money, the commodity exchanged could be cloth, iron or whatever. At each step of the way, mutually beneficial exchanges of property titles—to goods, services, or money—are agreed upon and transacted.

And what of the capital-labor relationship? Here, too, as in the case of the teacher selling his services to the farmer, the laborer sells his services to the manufacturer who has purchased the iron ore or to the shipper who has bought logs from the loggers. The capitalist performs the function of saving money to buy the raw material, and then pays the laborers in advance of sale of the product to the eventual customers.

Many people, including such utilitarian free-market advocates as John Stuart Mill, have been willing to concede the propriety and the justice (if they are not utilitarians) of the producer owning and earning the fruits of his labor. But they balk at one point: inheritance. If Roberto Clemente is ten times as good and "productive" a ballplayer as Joe Smith, they are willing to concede the justice of Clemente's earning ten times the amount; but what, they ask, is the justification for someone whose only merit is being born a Rockefeller inheriting far more wealth than someone born a Rothbard?

There are several answers that could be given to this question: for example, the natural fact that every individual must, of necessity, be born into a different condition, at a different time or place, and to different parents. Equality of birth or rearing, therefore, is an impossible chimera. But in the context of our theory of justice in property rights, the answer is to focus *not* on the recipient, not on the child Rockefeller or the child Rothbard, but to concentrate on the *giver,* the man who bestows the inheritance. For if Smith and Jones and Clemente have the right to their labor and their property and to exchange the titles to this property for the similarly obtained property of others, then they *also* have the right to *give* their property to whomever they wish. The point is not the right of "inheritance" but the right of *bequest,* a right which derives from the title to property itself. If Roberto Clemente owns his labor and the money he earns from it, then he has the right to give that money to the baby Clemente.

Armed with a theory of justice in property rights, let us now apply it to the often vexing question of how we should regard existing titles to property.

III. *Toward a Critique of Existing Property Titles*

Among those who call for the adoption of a free market and a free society, the utilitarians, as might be expected, wish to validate all existing property titles, as so defined by the government. But we have seen the inadequacy of this position, most clearly in the case of slavery, but similarly in the validation that it gives to *any* acts of governmental confiscation or redistribution, including our hypothetical Kennedy and Rockefeller "private" ownership of the territorial area of a state. But how much of a redistribution from existing titles would be implied by the adoption of our theory of justice in property, or of any attempt to put that theory into practice? Isn't it true, as some people charge, that all existing property titles, or at least all land titles, were the result of government grants and coercive redistribution? Would *all* property titles therefore be confiscated in the name of justice? And who would be granted these titles?

Let us first take the easiest case: where existing property has been stolen, as acknowledged by the government (and therefore by utilitarians) as well as by our theory of justice. In short, suppose that Smith has stolen a watch from Jones; in that case, there is no difficulty in calling upon Smith to relinquish the watch and to give it back to the true owner, Jones. But what of more difficult cases—in short, where existing property titles are ratified by state confiscation of a previous victim? This could apply either to money or especially to land titles, since land is a constant, identifiable, fixed quotal share of the earth's surface.

Suppose, first, for example, that the government has either taken land or money from Jones by coercion (either by taxation or its imposed redefinition of property) and has granted the land to Smith, or alternatively, has ratified Smith's direct act of confiscation. What would our policy of justice say then? We would say, along with the general view of crime, that the aggressor and unjust owner, Smith, must be made to disgorge the property title (either land or money) and give it over to its true owner, Jones. Thus, in the case of an identifiable unjust owner and the identifiable victim or just owner, the case is clear: a restoration to the victim of his rightful property. Smith, of course, must not be compensated for this restitution, since compensation would either be enforced unjustly on the victim himself or on the general body of taxpayers. Indeed, there is a far better case for the additional punishment of Smith, but there is no space here to develop the theory or punishment for crime or aggression.

Suppose, next, a second case, in which Smith has stolen a piece of land from Jones but that Jones has died; he leaves, however, an heir, Jones II. In that case, we proceed as before; there is still the identifiable aggressor, Smith, and the identifiable heir of the victim, Jones II, who now is the inherited just owner of the title. Again, Smith must be made to disgorge the land and turn it over to Jones II.

But suppose, a third, more difficult case; Smith is still the thief, but Jones and his entire family and heirs have been wiped out, either by Smith himself or in the natural course of events. Jones is intestate; what then should happen to the property? The first principle is that Smith, being the thief, cannot keep the fruits of his aggression; but in that case, the property becomes unowned and becomes up for grabs in the same way as any piece of unowned property. The "homestead principle" becomes applicable, in the sense that the first user or occupier of the newly declared unowned property becomes the just and proper owner. The only stipulation is that Smith himself, being the thief, is not eligible for this homesteading.[9]

Suppose now a fourth case, and one generally more relevant to problems of land title in the modern world. Smith is not a thief, nor has he directly received the land by government grant; but his *title* is derived from his ancestor who *did* so unjustly appropriate title to the property; the ancestor, Smith I, let us say, stole the property from Jones I, the rightful owner. What should be the disposition of the property now? The answer, in our view, completely depends on whether or not Jones' heirs, the surrogates of the identifiable victims, still exist. Suppose, for example, that Smith VI legally "owns" the land, but that Jones VI is still extant and identifiable. Then we would have to say that, while Smith VI himself is not a thief and not punishable as such, his *title* to the land, being solely derived from inheritance passed down from Smith I, does not give him true ownership, and that he too must disgorge the land—without compensation—and yield it into the hands of Jones VI.

But, it might be protested, what of the improvements

that Smiths II-VI may have added to the land? Doesn't Smith VI deserve compensation for these legitimately owned additions to the original land received from Jones I? The answer depends on the moveability or separability of these improvements. Suppose, for example, that Smith steals a car from Jones and sells it to Robinson. When the car is apprehended, then Robinson, though he purchased it in good faith from Jones, has no title better than Smith's which was nil, and therefore he must yield up the car to Jones without compensation. (He has been defrauded by Smith and must try to extract compensation out of Smith, *not* out of the victim Jones.) But suppose that Robinson, in the meantime, has improved the car? The answer depends on whether these improvements are separable from the car itself. If, for example, Robinson has installed a new radio which did not exist before, then he should certainly have the right to take it out before handing the car back to Jones. Similarly, in the case of land, to the extent that Smith VI has simply improved the land itself and mixed his resources inextricably with it, there is nothing he can do; but if, for example, Smith VI or his ancestors built new buildings upon the land, then he should have the right to demolish or cart away these buildings before handing the land over to Jones VI.

But what if Smith I did indeed steal the land from Jones I, but that all of Jones' descendants or heirs are lost in antiquity and cannot be found? What should be the status of the land then? In that case, since Smith VI is not himself a thief, he becomes the *legitimate* owner of the land on the basis of our homestead principle. For if the land is "unowned" and up for grabs, then Smith VI himself has been occupying and using it, and therefore he becomes the just and rightful owner on the homestead basis. Furthermore, all of his descendants have clear and proper title on the basis of being his heirs.

It is clear, then, that *even if* we can show that the origin of most existing land titles are in coercion and theft, the existing owners are still just and legitimate owners if (a) they themselves did not engage in aggression, and (b) if no identifiable heirs of the original victims can be found. In most cases of current land title this will probably be the case. *A fortiori,* of course, if we simply *don't know* whether the original land titles were acquired by coercion, then our homestead principle gives the current property owners the benefit of the doubt and establishes them as just and proper owners as well. Thus, the establishment of our theory of justice in property titles will not usually lead to a wholesale turnover of landed property.

In the United States, we have been fortunate enough to have largely escaped continuing aggression in land titles. It is true that originally the English Crown gave land titles unjustly to favored persons (e.g., the territory roughly of New York State to the ownership of the Duke of York), but fortunately these grantees were interested enough in quick returns to subdivide and sell their lands to the actual settlers. As soon as the settlers purchased their land, their titles were legitimate, and so were the titles of all those who inherited or purchased them. Later on, the U.S. government unfortunately laid claim to all virgin land as the "public domain," and then unjustly sold the land to speculators who had not earned a homestead title. But eventually these speculators sold the land to the actual settlers, and from then on the land title was proper and legitimate.[10]

In South America and much of the undeveloped world, however, matters are considerably different. For here, in many areas, an invading state conquered the lands of peasants and then parcelled out such lands to various warlords as their private fiefs, from then on to extract rent from the hapless peasantry. The descendants of the *conquistadores* still presume to own the land tilled by the descendants of the original peasants, people with a clearly just claim to ownership of the land. In this situation, justice requires the vacating of the land titles by these feudal or coercive landholders, (who are in a position equivalent to our hypothetical Rockefellers and Kennedys) and the turning over of the property titles without compensation to the individual peasants who are the true owners of their land.

Much of the drive for "land reform" by the peasantry of

the undeveloped world is precisely motivated by an instinctive application of our theory of justice: by the apprehension of the peasants that the land they have tilled for generations is *their* land and that the landlord's claim is coercive and unjust. It is ironic that, in these numerous cases, the only response of utilitarian free-market advocates is to defend existing land titles, regardless of their injustice, and to tell the peasants to keep quiet and "respect private property." Since the peasants are convinced that the property is *their* private title, it is no wonder that they fail to be impressed; but since they find the supposed champions of property rights and free-market capitalism to be their staunch enemies, they generally are forced to turn to the only organized groups that at least rhetorically champion their claims and are willing to carry out the required rectification of property titles—the socialists and communists. In short, from simply a utilitarian consideration of consequences, the utilitarian free-marketeers have done very badly in the undeveloped world, the result of their ignoring the fact that others than themselves, however inconveniently, *do* have a passion for justice. Of course, after socialists or communists take power, they do their best to collectivize peasant land, and one of the prime struggles of socialist society is that of the state *versus* the peasantry. But even those peasants who are aware of socialist duplicity on the land question may still feel that with the socialists and communists they *at least* have a fighting chance. And sometimes, of course, the peasants have been able to win and to force communist regimes to keep hands off their newly gained private property: notably in the cases of Poland and Yugoslavia.

The utilitarian defense of the *status quo* will then be *least* viable—and therefore the least utilitarian—in those situations where the *status quo* is the most glaringly unjust. As often happens, far more than utilitarians will admit, justice and genuine utility are here linked together.

To sum up: all existing property titles may be considered just under the homestead principle, *provided* (a) that there may never be any property *in people;* (b) that the existing property owner did not himself steal the property; and particularly (c) that any identifiable just owner (the original victim of theft or his heir) must be accorded his property.

It might be charged that our theory of justice in property titles is deficient because in the real world most landed (and even other) property has a past history so tangled that it becomes *impossible* to identify who or what has committed coercion and therefore who the current just owner may be. But the point of the "homestead principle" is that if we *don't know* what crimes have been committed in acquiring the property in the past, or if we don't know the victims or their heirs, then the current owner becomes the legitimate and just owner on homestead grounds. In short, if Jones owns a piece of land at the present time, and we don't know what crimes were committed to arrive at the current title, then Jones, as the current owner, becomes as fully legitimate a property owner of this land as he does over his own person. Overthrow of existing property title only becomes legitimate if the victims or their heirs can present an authenticated, demonstrable, and specific claim to the property. Failing such conditions, existing landowners possess a fully moral right to their property.

NOTES

1. Economists failed to heed the emphasis on titles of ownership underlying exchange stressed by the social philosopher Spencer Heath. Thus: "Only those things which are *owned* can be exchanged or used as instruments of service or exchange. This exchange is not transportation; it is the transfer of ownership or title. This is a social and not a physical process." Spencer Heath, *Citadel, Market and Altar* (Baltimore: Science of Society Foundation, 1957), p. 48.

2. For a welcome recent emphasis on the subjectivity of cost, see James N. Buchanan, *Cost and Choice* (Chicago: Markham Pub. Co., 1969).

3. I do not mean to imply here that *no* social science of economic analysis can be *Wertfrei,* only that any attempt whatever to apply the analysis to the political arena, however remote, *must* involve and imply some sort of ethical position.

4. On the arbitrariness and uncertainty of all legislative law, see Bruno Leoni, *Freedom and the Law* (Los Angeles: Nash Pub. Co., 1972).

5. The point here is not, of course, to criticize all rents *per se,* but rather to call into question the legitimacy of property titles (here landed property) derived from the coercive actions of government.

6. John Locke, *An Essay Concerning the True, Original, Extent and End of Civil Government,* in E. Barker, ed., *Social Contract* (New York: Oxford University Press, 1948), pp. 17-18.

7. Equally to be rejected is a grotesque proposal by Professor Kenneth E. Boulding, which however is a typical suggestion of a market-oriented utilitarian economist. This is a scheme for the government to allow only a certain maximum number of baby-permits per mother, but then to allow a "free" market in the purchase and sale of these baby rights. This plan, of course, denies the right of every mother over her own body. Boulding's plan may be found in Kenneth E. Boulding, *The Meaning of the 20th Century* (New York: Harper & Row, 1964). For a discussion of the plan, see Edwin G. Dolan, *TANSTAAFL: The Economic Strategy for Environmental Crisis* (New York: Holt, Rinehart & Winston, 1971), p. 64.

8. Locke, *Civil Government,* p. 18.

9. Neither is the government eligible. There is no space here to elaborate our view that government can never be the just owner of property. Suffice it to say here that the government gains its revenue from tax appropriation from production rather than from production itself, and hence that the concept of just property can never apply to government.

10. This legitimacy, of course, does not apply to the vast amount of land in the West still owned by the federal government which it refuses to throw open to homesteading. Our response to this situation must be that the government should throw open all of its public domain to private homesteading without delay.

7

Arthur Kemp

LEGAL INSTITUTIONS AND PROPERTY RIGHTS

IT IS BEYOND dispute that different institutional arrangements affect and are affected by economic behavior. In considering differing forms of modern economic systems, what are the appropriate institutional factors upon which we should focus our attention in order to understand and to explain that economic behavior?

I shall argue here that there are two essential institutional factors: first, the system of property rights and, second, the monetary framework employed. Further, I shall argue that the interrelations of the two are significantly different under different systems and that these differences have an important bearing upon the objectives of these systems, on their economic functions, and are capable of being interpreted in terms of positive economic analysis.[1]

Some definitions are required, for the words "property" and "property rights" are employed in a variety of ways and for a variety of purposes. Indeed, beliefs as to whether the institution of private property is desirable or not and to what extent has constituted a major source of ideological dispute for several centuries. John Locke, for example, defined property with a decidely economic emphasis when he wrote:

> Every man has a "property" in his own person; this nobody has any right to but himself. The labour of his body and the work of his hands, we may say, are properly his. Whatsoever then he removes out of the state that nature hath provided and left it in, he hath mixed his labour with it, and joined to it something that is his own, and thereby makes it his property.[2]

Locke, of course, went much further than this. He proclaimed property to be a natural right, a moral law, superior to government, having the highest ethical justification. Indeed, the major governmental function, in Locke's view, is to protect property rights, and where government fails to do so, revolutionary overthrow is justifiable. Locke's ideas had considerable influence upon the framers of the Declaration of Independence and the Constitution of the United States, particularly in the formulation "life, liberty and the pursuit of happiness" (which could as well have been life, liberty and property) and in the "life, liberty and property without due process of law" clause expressed in Amendments V and XIV. Adam Smith, too, although he has been accused of being inconsistent at times, accepted Locke's position that government is instituted for the purpose of defending property rights: to protect the rich against the poor.[3] Similar ideas were expressed by practically all the advocates of limited government during the eighteenth century in England and France, as well as the United States. They also serve as the essential basis of Blackstone's evaluation of property.[4] Perhaps the notion of property as an ethical concept, a moral postulate, gave rise to attacks on property as an immoral concept in certain religious thought[5] as well as political thought, such as that of Marx, Engels and Laski. But this need not be of great concern to us here, nor need we be concerned with the highly technical treatises concerning the legal aspects of property rights in their various forms and complexities, at least not for the present. The particular quotation from Locke is useful because it suggested the possibility of defining property rights so as to emphasize principles while abandoning the ethical and normative aspects.

By property right I mean the right to use resources or abilities in any way that is not prohibited or in some way constrained. Nothing in the use of the word "right" should necessarily be interpreted to mean good or bad, desirable or undesirable. Property right in this definition is a more or less restricted choice of use. Choice of use may be restricted in a variety of ways: by force of law (statutes, common law, judicial decisions, decrees, orders, commands) or by social patterns (etiquette, custom, mores, tradition, etc.) or by some combination of the two. I do not use the term property right as indicating something within the thing itself—whether that thing be land, capital equipment, buildings, personal attributes or abilities or whatever—although for some purposes it is useful to refer to the thing as property in contradistinction to property right as the right to use. In this sense, property rights could be subdivided into rights to use land, labor, or capital similar to the familiar division of the factors of production of classical economic analysis. Nor is it important, for the purposes here, how property rights originated. For the comparison of economic systems it is merely necessary to recognize that such rights do exist and that there are both advantages and disadvantages to people who possess them.

It also follows from this that there can be no such thing as an *absolute* property right for several reasons: first, the right to use is limited by the physical nature of the thing (or property). It may not be possible, physically, to move land; or, at least, the possibility of certain physical alterations are strictly limited. Even if we speak of personal attributes, there are physical limitations in the use of these abilities. Time, for example, is scarce.

Second, the rights to use are restricted by the forces mentioned above—by the social factors and the legislative structure in their various forms.

Third, the enforcement of property rights implies costs of enforcing. If these rights are enforced by the formal exercise of police power and the courts, the costs are, in a sense, socialized. Perhaps more properly, the enforcing costs are paid for out of funds raised in some fashion by government. If these rights are enforced by custom and tradition, without formal exercise of police power, the costs are borne voluntarily by the members of that society by refraining from using their property so as to interfere with others' property and by their efforts employed in educating or ostracizing those who do not submit to tradition. Owners of property rights may be willing to pay the necessary costs of policing; on the other hand, they may not. But the policing costs are paid by someone, or property rights do not exist.

Fourth, ownership of property rights implies the assumption of a risk; indeed, one might describe ownership as the act of assuming the risks of loss for the possibility of gain. Under any form of economic system, changes will take place in the relative values of things and, therefore, gains and losses will occur. Consider an ideal (and therefore improbable) system in which all property is private and whatever restrictions exist are given and unchanging. The owner would receive all of the returns from the uses of the resources and abilities and, at the same time, would have placed upon him all the costs associated with the exercise of these property rights, including the policing costs. Would this result in a better or more desirable system than one in which the policing costs are borne by the state? Economics cannot provide an answer; it can only say that when the policing costs are borne by the state and not by the owner he will not take these costs into consideration when choosing among the uses for his property. If moreover, the gains to be obtained from certain uses of his property are denied to him or made very expensive by virtue of taxes, rules, statutes or custom (thus increasing costs or decreasing returns in these uses), he will employ his property less in these uses and more in others.

Fifth, the fact that these resources and abilities cannot function in multiple uses at the same time means that the opportunity costs of using property in one way is the foregone return of its alternative use or uses.

Anything reducing the policing costs or transactions costs will extend property rights: will extend the range of choice of use to which property may be put. Conversely, anything increasing policing costs or contracting costs will reduce the range of choice. The range of choice (and therefore property rights) is also extended by the discovery or invention of devices that permit the division of property rights (to the extent that they do not involve an offsetting increase in policing or transactions costs). If, to use a simple example, it is possible to sell the rights to oil or minerals in land separately from other rights (i.e., as a golf course or for locating an apartment house), the range of choice is extended and so is the range of possible satisfaction to the owner. Indeed, so is the overall possible social output through increasing specialization of labor in being able to employ the specialized talents of the building contractor and the oil driller.

Much of the body of both statute law and common law in Western civilization concerns the forms and functions of property rights and their transference within the institutional framework of private property. But how does private ownership of property rights differ from public ownership? Alchian suggests, and I think correctly so, that the potential gains and costs schedules differ, primarily because ownership is transferable when it is private and non-transferable when it is public.[6] A corollary or extension of this proposition is to regard public property as very difficult to divide or transfer and private property as very easy to divide and transfer. There are thousands of volumes of legal lore relating to stocks, bonds, trusts, estates, condominia, cooperatives, options, warrants, trademarks, copyrights, designs, licenses, water rights, mineral rights and so on, the purpose of which is to make possible the division and transfer of property rights. Two implications follow: first, under a private property system, the rewards and penalties of ownership are borne more directly by those who control the property than under a public ownership system; and, second, there are greater advantages to be achieved from specialization of labor (including specialization of knowledge and other personal talents such as management and risk-bearing) under private ownership than public.

The monetary framework is another factor of great importance. Without the convenience of money both the division and transfer of property rights would be greatly limited, although not destroyed. To put it in the terms used above, the existence of a suitable monetary framework can greatly reduce the transactions costs of exchange (of transferring property rights). Use of the word "suitable" or its equivalent raises a few questions. Suitable for what purpose? Suitable, one might say, to the ends and objectives of the economic system whatever these may be. It is not difficult to formulate monetary systems that decrease the transferability of property rights. Many of the more heretical suggestions in monetary theory have been of this sort, although not necessarily intended to be so. If the objective of the economic system is a centrally planned economy a "suitable" monetary framework ought logically to differ substantially from that "suitable" to a market system. If the objective is to bring about equality in wealth or incomes, the monetary structure may well be different from both. Some monetary systems could be devised to thwart or make more difficult the plans of the central planners; in short, the nature of the appropriate monetary system is dependent upon the nature of the politico-economic structure. Those who desire a planned or centrally directed economy should favor, if they are consistent, the use of a planned monetary system for social ends, or at least the ends desired by those in command. The monetary systems they propose, and the changes they suggest in existing systems, are and ought to be different from those who seek to attain an autonomous price system, political decentralization and limitations on the concentration of both political and economic power. But, even where there is the desire to promote a particular kind of system, it may not be possible to say, with precision, what is the best monetary system for the purpose.

Of one thing, however, I am almost certain. There is no natural, simple development either of property rights or monetary arrangements. Perhaps this is another way of saying that both the anarchy of pure communism (after the state has supposedly withered away) and the anarchy achieved by the absence of all state activity violate the principles of economic behavior. These are not attainable systems—at least, not in this world. Both property rights and the monetary arrangements are dependent upon legal systems. By this I do not mean that they are granted, in some fashion, by the state. The institutional framework, two aspects of which we are concerned with here, is not simply natural growth but a combination of evolutionary growth, spontaneous development, adaptation to changing circumstances and the conscious ordering of the framework to achieve desired ends. That there is conscious direction in a centralized, authoritarian system needs no particular emphasis. But for the market system, too, it is necessary. To quote Lionel Robbins:

> For cooperation to be effective it must be restrained within suitable limits by a framework of institutions. Neither property nor contract are in any sense natural. They are essentially the creation of law; and they are not simple creations.[7]

This may, of course, somewhat overstate the case. Property concepts appear in very primitive societies and even in animal behavior. The observed behavior of "one tiger to a hill" is an example, and certainly our house cat seems to have remarkably well developed property senses. But in modern society, in any society beyond the primitive, property rights involve complex legal arrangements.

Hayek suggests that if a reasonably free society is to be achieved there must be conscious planning for a suitable framework:

> Where traditional discussion becomes so unsatisfactory is where it is suggested that, with the recognition of the principles of private property and freedom of contract, which indeed every liberal must recognize, all the issues were settled. . . . It is only after we have agreed on these principles that the real problems begin.[8]

Similarly, although it is generally accepted that money originated from the voluntary actions of merchants to facilitate exchange (by lowering transactions costs), to promote the preservation of purchasing power over time and to aid in the formation of capital, this cannot truly be called a simple, natural order.[9]

Even if this evolutionary development is, in some sense, regarded as a natural origin, the state stepped into the picture at a very early stage. The first stage was probably for the purpose of supplying legal sanctions and setting standards for monetary practices the community had already accepted. Using monetary powers to further the purposes of the state probably came at the second stage—but it was not far behind. The legal certification of weight and fineness almost invariably became a governmental function, as did the specification of the means to be used in settling disputes in the courts—essentially property disputes—involving debt, trover, trespass, libel, and so forth. Like it or not, governments have asserted their responsibility for monetary affairs, virtually without exception, and without differentation as to the type of economic system. "Where money and credit are concerned," writes Lord Robbins, "the idea of a simple natural order is not only not plausible, it is also positively absurd."[10]

The appropriate legal and monetary framework of an economic system, therefore, must depend upon the ideological objectives of the system. A liberal market system requires "equality before the law" as the phrase goes so that individual differences in property rights, desires, talents and attributes may be coordinated. There may be, nay, must be, restrictions but these are intended to be equally applicable to all so that each individual may be able to choose within the range of choice open to him (that is to say within the necessarily restricted limits of his property rights) without being subject to the whims and caprice of arbitrary authority. Further, the restrictions that do exist are, preferably, the result of experience, of evolutionary development, of discovery, and are not the inventions of an authority designed to achieve specific ends above and beyond the intent of the individual.[11] Arbitrary rules, regulations and decrees are costly; in terms of economic analysis, they increase both the transactions costs and the policing costs. Uncertainties due to the vagaries of nature, changes in values, changes in tastes, all impose costs also. These no legal structure can eliminate. But an appropriate legal and monetary structure for a market system seeks to avoid adding further uncertainties.

It may be informative, occasionally, to look on money in ways differing somewhat from the customary emphasis on its function as a medium of exchange. We have already indicated that the use of money reduced the transaction costs of engaging in exchange; it serves to make information concerning alternative uses of resources and abilities available and calculable also. Being a sort of generalized purchasing power, it can and does serve as a motivator: inducing people to act on the basis of this information about alternative uses of resources. Are there property rights in money? Leaving out of consideration the particular thing of which money may be composed—such as gold, silver, copper, nickel, paper—money can be regarded as a way of avoiding some of the risks of property ownership over time and space. Ownership, as has been pointed out, is not necessarily advantageous; property may be a liability from the economic point of view if not from that of the accountant. Changes in the value of resources and abilities over time must take place. Holding money instead of the property avoids both the risks of loss and the possibilities of gain associated with the particular resource or ability.

In the case of personal services, the degree of risk is high since they cannot be stored conveniently over time. To a greater or lesser extent, the same is true of all property. Whatever risk is involved will be borne by the owner of property, but money enables him to avoid part of the risk by sale, hypothecation, and so on. Money, money markets and financial intermediaries permit property rights to be sold or borrowed against, including borrowing against personal services or selling personal services on a long-range basis. To the extent that holding money in some form is low in cost, it permits a much wider range of choice over time. It must be recognized, however, that all risk is not avoided. There are storage costs associated with holding money. Holding money in its simplest form, as cash, has a cost associated with the interest payment foregone from a more complicated promise to pay money. There are also policing costs associated with holding money, as any banker will testify, and there is the uncertainty and risk associated with changes in the prices of goods while holding money instead of goods.

Why should a market system wish to preserve a relatively stable price level? Surely part of the answer must be that this tends to reduce the unforeseeable risks involved in holding money. Why do we place restrictions, in a variety of ways, on the total quantity of money? Partly because variation in that quantity can increase unforeseeable risk. A market system can function more perfectly in the allocation of resources if the policing and transactions costs are low relative to the value of the resources and abilities being allocated. Private property rights and a stable monetary framework are thus important institutional factors promoting the functioning of a market system.

Simply to say this and no more begs several important questions. A market system's legal framework usually includes restrictions on many kinds of property rights. Those who attempt to exercise their range of choice by forms of violence—murder, theft, arson—are not only violating other persons' property rights but are also a threat to the government itself. Without exception, government tends to monopolize the power of physical coercion, not alone in private property rights systems but all kinds. Of course, theft of state-owned goods may be regarded as a more heinous act under a socialist system than the theft of private property, to whatever extent private property is permitted, and the punishment may be more severe. This is the result of value judgments, not economics. And a government may permit or even encourage violence for noneconomic reasons as many American ambassadors and their staffs can testify. But leaving aside the moral aspects, violence tends to be frowned upon by the state because it is jealous of its own prerogatives and, as one result, a large part of the policing costs guarding against violence are paid for by the state in the first instance.

But in many, probably all, market systems, nonviolent restrictions on property rights are permitted or even encouraged. Sometimes these are imposed by government itself in the form of minimum wage laws, conservation laws, zoning laws, pure food and drug acts, tariffs, professional licensing laws, immigration laws, usury acts, retail price laws—to mention only a few. Policing costs in these matters are also borne by the state, in the first instance, and not by those whose property rights gain in value as a result of the restrictions on others. These must be regarded as imperfections in the institutional framework undertaken because of nonmarket and probably noneconomic reasons. They may be justifiable on moral or political grounds; they are not explainable however, as part of the appropriate institutional framework of a market system.

Frequently it is said that one of the essential institutions of a market system is government enforcement of contracts voluntarily entered into, and the provision for judicial settlement of disputes arising out of conflicts between or among private parties. Until recently I have tended to accept the statement without much thought about its implications or the possible reasons for it. When translated into terms of costs and property rights, the statement seems to mean that, in a market system, the policing costs should be borne by society, acting through the state, rather than directly by property owners themselves. Ultimately, of course, *all* the property owners (domestic and foreign) bear *all* of the policing costs, but there is only a tenuous relationship, if any, between specific property and specific policing costs. One possible explanation for this may be that the alternative of placing the policing costs on the property owners themselves would involve private police forces, or some such device, thus forming centers of physical force possibly capable of challenging the state itself. One can also generalize the usual arguments for defense, fire protection, and so on by suggesting that centralized enforcement means lower total policing costs than if these costs were borne by the owners themselves. This ought to be subjected to empirical verification but, on the surface, it seems likely. Further, if these policing costs are not paid by the owner, he will not take them into consideration in choosing among alternative uses. Policing costs are thus made lower relative to the value of the resources, so far as the owner is concerned. Of course, policing costs can be and are economized; the property owner is not guaranteed absolute control of his property for the obvious reason that it would be too costly. Lastly, the enforcement of contracts also involves the judicial function. Not all contracts, voluntarily entered into, will be performed. The impossibility of performance, or simple nonfulfillment, is a not infrequent occurrence—sometimes in spite of the best intentions. Under these circumstances, enforcement carries with it the assessment of damages (usually in money) in favor of the damaged party. In short, to give to the state the function of enforcing contracts can be explained because it provides an appropriate framework for facilitating exchange in a market system.

On the face of it a market system suitably endowed with an appropriate institutional framework should promote a high degree of economic efficiency. Resources and abilities will be employed in such a manner as to achieve the highest known market value for the total output of goods. Again, this does not mean that a market system is good, bad, desirable or undesirable. It does mean, however, that if what is sought is a system giving to people *what they want,* a market system is the one most likely to achieve that end. What people want, of course, is continually changing, and a market system provides a prompt and continuous adjustment to change. This does not mean that any given market system will achieve, in fact, the ideal of perfect economic efficiency. Nor does it imply that a market system is one in which each individual must seek to maximize his monetary income. Nor should it be a surprise to find existing market systems with imperfections in the institutional framework; indeed, these may be necessary for the existence of such systems. Nor does it mean that a nonmarket system cannot be more efficient in performing particular activities or areas of activities—whether these be in certain particular lines of production (monuments, missiles and moon-shots?) or even in the overall organization of a war economy. But recognition of the tendency toward economic efficiency in a market system may permit the comparison of existing systems—whether centrally planned, partly planned, welfare state, or partly market—as to institutional framework, how the benefits and costs are distributed, what restrictions on property rights are imposed or permitted, what the effects of certain tax systems are, and how the systems function in the actual, as opposed to the intended, allocation of resources.

In summary, there are several reasons why an existing market system, although tending toward maximum efficiency as defined above, never reaches it. First, there may be restrictions on property rights and the access to market. Second, there may be deficiencies in the laws concerning property rights and the assessment of damages. Third, there may be instances in which the transactions costs and/or policing costs are too high to warrant a market solution for the allocation of some resources. Fourth, the monetary system may be employed for purposes other than the attainment of maximum economic efficiency. Fifth, external nonmarket forces are a continuing source of disequilibrium.

The intent of Marxian socialism today, and of all kinds of socialism in the past, was to eliminate private property rights. It is clear that this objective has been substantially altered in the countries of western Europe. In our sense of the words property rights, even the older socialists would not have attempted to do away with all forms of private property rights. I have defined labor, for example, in terms of property rights: the right to *use* one's abilities; others would certainly attempt to make a distinction between human rights or property rights on some kind of value judgment basis. From the standpoint of economic analysis rather than ideology, the distinction seems to me useless. In practice, when the Soviet Union came to deal with the question of private property, it tried to eliminate only nonpersonal property. State ownership of the means of production is the key principle. The Constitution of the U.S.S.R. provides for two kinds of state ownership: (1) state property and (2) property belonging to the collectives and cooperatives of the agricultural sector. Personal property rights continue to exist in money incomes and savings plus the hand tools of peasants and handicraftsmen and personal and household articles. These items can also be inherited. In agriculture, householders on collective farms are assigned small plots of land, not over about two and a half acres in size, on which they are permitted to raise crops and to own livestock and poultry of various kinds.[12] One authority estimates the amount of private ownership to be appreciable only in urban housing (37%) and livestock (28%). Cooperatives and collective farms are substantial owners of livestock (44%), agricultural land (42%) and retail outlets (29%). By the nature of the case, these are rough estimates and approximations.[13] But it seems clear that the possibility of dividing and transferring property rights is very limited in the Soviet Union, at least legally; whether and to what extent illegal transference takes place is difficult to determine. The individual worker, farmer or manager, by virtue of the limitations placed on his ability to sell, transfer and exercise his abilities (property rights), is in a very different position than in a market system. In other words, it is doubtful that the essential criterion for examining different economic systems is simple ownership. Rather it is the more complicated problem of the results of less divisibility and less transferability of property rights and the effects these have upon information, innovation, centralization, potential reforms, economic growth and a myriad of other factors.

If this is correct, we would expect to find central planning systems striving to find substitutes for the incentives provided by property rights in market systems. For exceeding the fulfillment of specified output goals, managers in the Soviet industrial system are given substantial bonuses; these latter are often more than the basic salary of the manager. In addition, there are other economic perquisites apart from the noneconomic ones of power, prestige, patriotism and the like. Further, there are apparently quite severe punishments for failure.[13]

The simple carrot and stick technique, when compared with the far more complex mechanism possible in a well-developed market system, sometimes carries within itself some counter-incentives. For example, one would expect that a system of incentives based on bonuses for physical output achievement would underplay questions of quality of product and would tend to prevent innovation by placing the main incentive upon continuing production. Indeed, this has been clearly shown to be a major problem in Soviet industry; the evidence consists in the amount of discussion devoted to it in Soviet literature. As one student observes:

> There is little reason for those involved in production, aside from sheer patriotism or professional pride (and these may be substantial) to introduce new products or technical methods, and there is often substantial personal material risk involved in doing so, not to say frustration in the face of the bureaucratic leviathan.[14]

One might at first suppose that centrally controlled economies might be able to supply better and more complete information to, say, industry in general or to particular industries. Certainly in the market structure a firm having a lower cost method may be reluctant to pass on precise information to competitors (and the cost of obtaining it through what is sometimes called industrial espionage may be substantial). But there are costs associated with information and its dissemination in all systems, and it is by no means clear that under the Soviet system, for example, those costs are lower; indeed, they may well be higher. First, there is the question of the quality of the information. Doubtless there is an enormous volume of statistical information available to the central planners, but its real value—its usability—may be very limited. Second, there is the question of motivating the use of the information. Where motivation is provided by the widening of choice to the individual in a market system, information and motivation go hand in hand—not without costs, of course, but it may well be at lower costs than in the centralized system. Professor Grossman has characterized the lack of effective communication between Soviet enterprises and other organs of the economy as a "malignant situation" contributing to the lack of motivation for innovation.[15] Whatever incentive there is to innovate or to change is provided in the Soviet system of central planning from above and not from below. But this is costly also. As the size of the economy increases, so does the number of communications and the complexities of planning inputs and outputs for thousands of enterprises. If this is correct it would seem to put the Soviet Union into the dilemma of choosing between, on the one hand, some degree of decentralization, with the attendant risk that this might reduce the political power of the Soviet Communist Party and, on the other, relying on the fond hope that technological improvements in computer techniques will permit a truly efficient and truly centralized command economy in the relatively near future.[16] From the amount of attention given to the suggestions made a few years ago by Soviet economist E. Liberman, there is little doubt that the Soviet planners are quite aware of the problem and are seeking to find solutions.

Perhaps the more fundamental question is not so much why the problem exists in a centrally planned economy but rather why, in the Soviet case, the centrally planned economy has lasted and accomplished as much as it has. One factor of course is the timing. The importance of appropriate information, incentives and motivation was less important at the earlier stages of development; to some extent the existence of data from more advanced industrial nations could provide a very important flow of knowledge; and the relative gains at the early stages could greatly offset the inherent disadvantages. Another part of the explanation is given by Professor Nutter:

> There is one important reason why the economy has managed to keep moving along: it has never worked the way it was intended and claimed to work. There has always been a complex network of extralegal markets of various shades of gray, tolerated by ruling authorities precisely because the system would not function otherwise. Without their "fixers" and "expediters" most plants would be strangled in red tape. Without their subsidiary shops for manufacture of needed supplies they would starve periodically and unpredictably when allocated supplies fail to arrive. Similarly, distribution to households would have broken down without collective farm markets, "speculators" and the like.[17]

Certainly there is enough evidence to suggest that tracing through the effects of property rights and their restrictions and attenuations under different systems can be useful. Professor Berliner, less than half facetiously, has suggested that the rewards going to entrepreneurs have been too small in the socialist countries and that the appropriate remedy might be to create a class of Soviet millionaires! But if this is true, why not an entire property rights system? He reports, in passing, that Czechoslovakia is said to have the most egalitarian income distribution in eastern Europe, and that "some managers regard demotion as a welcome relief from responsibility."[18] Perhaps it is too much to expect that the long-standing antiproperty bias in Marxism and other socialist thought can be consciously abandoned. But it can be useful to examine some of the evidence of the importance of property rights in other economic connotations—in the money and banking sector, in production and pricing, in welfare activities, in the distribution of wealth and income and in economic growth.

NOTES

1. The basic idea for attempting this form of presentation came from the papers presented at a similar conference on the humane economy held at The Institute of Paper Chemistry in 1964. I am particularly indebted to the papers presented by Harold Demsetz and Armen Alchian. The Demsetz paper, in revised form, appears in *The Journal of Law and Economics,* Vol. VII (October, 1964), titled "The Exchange and Enforcement of Property Rights," and much of Alchian's paper exists in slightly different form in Armen A. Alchian and William R. Allen, *University Economics* (Belmont, California: 1964), Chapters 3, 12, 20 and 25. I have been greatly influenced by Ronald H. Coase, "The Problem of Social Cost," *The Journal of Law and Economics,* Vol. III (October, 1960); by Lionel Robbins, *An Essay on the Nature and Significance of Economic Science* (London: 1935), esp. Chapters I and VI; and by F. A. Hayek in ways too numerous to mention.

2. John Locke, *On Civil Government,* Book II, Chapter V.

3. Cf. Jacob Viner, "Adam Smith and Laissez-Faire," *Journal of Political Economy,* Vol. XXXV, (April, 1927), pp. 198-232; reprinted in Spengler and Allen, *Essays in Economic Thought* (Chicago: 1960), pp. 305-329.

4. For an extended discussion, see Gottfried Dietze, *In Defense of Property* (Chicago, 1963).

5. Cf., for example, Bruno Leoni, *Freedom and the Law* (New York, 1961), pp. 52ff. One cannot say that the Decalogue is an attack on property, however.

6. Perhaps we should say property rights are substantially less able to be transferred when property is held publicly than when it is held privately. To rule out public property by definition as some writers have done, does not appear to be very helpful.

7. "Individual Action in the Environment of Capitalism," reprinted in W. A. Leeman, ed., *Capitalism, Market Socialism and Central Planning* (Boston: 1963), p. 7.

8. *Individualism and Economic Order* (London: 1949), p. 111.

9. Cf. W. W. Carlile, *The Evolution of Modern Money* (London: 1901); William Ridgway, *The Origin of Metallic Currency and Weight Standards* (Cambridge: 1892); A. R. Burns, *Money and Monetary Policy in Early Times* (New York: 1927).

10. *Politics and Economics* (London: 1963), p. 44.

11. This is intended as a brief summary. For an extended discussion see F. A. Hayek, *The Constitution of Liberty* (Chicago: 1960), Part II, "Freedom and the Law"; Bruno Leoni, *Freedom and the Law* (New York: 1961), *passim.*

12. Nicholas Spulber, *The Soviet Economy* (New York: 1962), p. 77.

13. For an excellent brief description of economic rewards and punishments in Soviet practice, see Robert W. Campbell, *Soviet Economic Power,* 2d ed., (New York: 1966), pp. 68ff.

14. Gregory Grossman, "Soviet Growth: Routine, Inertia, and Pressure," *American Economic Review,* Vol. L, No. 2 (May, 1960), p. 65.

15. Gregory Grossman, "Innovation and Information in the Soviet Economy," *American Economic Review,* Vol. LVI, No. 2 (May, 1966), pp. 120ff. The author estimates the obstacles to innovation as more than offsetting the effects of enterprise secrecy in a market economy.

16. Cf. Egon Neuberger, "Libermanism, Computopia, and Visible Hand: The Question of Informational Efficiency," *American Economic Review,* Vol. LVI, No. 2 (May, 1966), pp. 131-144.

17. G. Warren Nutter, "Trends and Prospects in Eastern Europe—Discussion," *American Economic Review,* Vol. LIII, No. 2 (May, 1963), p. 573.

18. Joseph S. Berliner, "Soviet Economy—Discussion," *American Economic Review,* Vol. LVI, No. 2 (May, 1966), p. 158.

8

Louis M. Spadaro

THE IMPACT OF INVASIONS OF PROPERTY ON FINANCIAL CRISES

THERE CAN be little doubt that the topic of the present book deals, so far as the participants are concerned, with approximately the same general set of practical economic problems. Since this is the case, I shall indulge the temerity to suggest turning the topic on its head, so to speak, without substantial danger of either being misunderstood or pulling the discussion from its intended path.

As stated, the topic, "Ownership and Private Property under the Impact of Financial Crisis," could be understood to convey the implication that the line of causality—or at least the order of occurrence—is from financial disturbances to certain effects on ownership and property. In the elegant terms of contemporary economics, this could be interpreted (though, I believe, incorrectly) as assuming that financial crises are the "independent" or "autonomous" variable and property the dependent. Now this is precisely the nexus which I propose to reverse; not only for the reason that analytical thoroughness would in any case recommend trying a different "fix" on the problem, but because, as I must now hasten to confess, I am strongly of the opinion that financial crises are themselves the result, though by no means the only result, of *attempts* to interfere with the proper exercise of property rights. I emphasize "attempts" because I think the stated result follows whether or not the interference is successful; indeed it may well be that the consequences of unsuccessful interference with property provide the analytically more interesting and more instructive case.

The suggestion to reverse reduces—let us face it at once—to insistence upon changes in the treatment of property as the independent variable or, more simply, the cause and financial stringency as the effect. In theory, this alternative formulation should not be terribly difficult to justify. The notion of property is admittedly deeply rooted in the nature of man, in his history and in his institutions—though it must be noted that not all who accept this as a fact are prepared to accept its implications. By comparison, not even the institution of money as a system of exchange, as old and as ubiquitous as it is, can be said to be fully coextensive with that of property, either historically or categorically. In contrast to money as a system, monetary disturbances are, in themselves and without reinforcing outside influences, relatively short-lived, particular, and not self-perpetuating. Their recurrence, though frequent and painful, can hardly be said to have seriously inhibited the spread or the refinement of the use of money in exchanges among men.

As between the money system and money disturbances there has been relatively little doubt, or even discussion, as to which is primary and abiding. There have been, it is true, the ever-recurring schemes of the "utopians" which appear to call for the abolition of money. But on closer examination, all such panaceas (a) really involve not the removal of money but rather supplanting the existing money by another set of counters—usually in terms of labor; (b) ultimately oppose property rather than money—a point not without relevance to the present discussion; and (c) have hardly ever been put to the test of practice. Two exceptions to this last should perhaps be noted briefly. One is the only substantial attempt to effect the abolition of money early in the Soviet experience, an attempt so notably and instructively disastrous that it needs no further comment in the present connection. The other case—more interesting and far more complex—is the largely unacknowledged connection between Keynesian monetary doctrine and the monetary panaceas, comprising a debt which the former is increasingly forced to pay through more explicit recognition of the inflationary effects of its advocacy. All in all, then, the appearance of monetary and banking difficulties has not convinced anyone that we can or ought to do without the technical services of a money system.

Now it would seem that if money disturbances cannot impugn the institution of money as such, then *a fortiori* they ought not to be able to call into question an even more basic and pervasive institution—that of property. But this, unfortunately, is not the position of a large segment of current orthodoxy. The same people who would hardly take the recurrence of money and credit crises as the signal to dismantle the money system are not averse to interpreting these same crises as some sort of mandate to tinker with property rights. It is precisely in this connection that it is important and relevant to inquire, as we did earlier, which of the components of our topic really revolves about the other. The modern formulation of a "mixed" economy implies an equally "mixed" economic astronomy. To hold that the money system is stable relative to property is analogous to postulating a solar system in which the moon revolves about the earth and the sun around the moon. It is hardly surprising that attempts to explain such a system require resort to models at least as "sophisticated" as the celebrated epicycles. It is, of course, to be hoped that in the fullness of time simpler and more general explanations of the economic process will emerge, and in the light of such new synthesis or insight all of us who precede will be classified as "pre-Copernicans." But if, as I think, any real progress toward more definitive explanation will be found to lie in the direction of the fundamentality and force of property rights, the members of the current orthodoxy will face the additional indignity of being pre-Copernicans who came *after* Copernicus.

Thus, while this paper considers the topic under discussion by inverting it, we should not fail to observe that the original phrasing of the question is more in line with the terms and concepts of contemporary discussion. In this form, it seems to include a rather crucial hidden premise: that the practice—and therefore the right—of private property is undergoing a sort of evolutionary change through a continuing series of modifications and qualifications made under the impact of the recurrence of financial crises. As a purely descriptive statement of historical fact there is little here with which to argue, though believers in the inviolability of property rights can deplore it and express some nostalgia and alarm. Conferences too often do little more than this, with the result that they take on the characteristics, in more than one sense, of an old-fashioned Irish wake.

But the statement is frequently understood as much more than the description of a *de facto* development; it is put forward also as explanation. In this sense it clearly implies that the occurrence of financial crises is proof of the invalidity or, at least, the inadequacy of the system of property rights as "conventionally" understood. It is precisely at this point that current analysis needs to be challenged, as I believe. The usual formulation counterposes two terms: a system of property rights on the one hand and some undesirable phenomenon on the other—in our present case the appearance of financial difficulties. The existence of the latter and the desirability of its elimination then makes it seem both possible and desirable to admit changes in the former; and if these were indeed the only forces at work, the conclusion would indeed appear to follow logically. But what if there is a third term? Then the set of possible relations between property and, say, financial crisis changes radically and interestingly. Now it is possible to suggest that, given the potent force and ultimate stability of property, the attempt to engage in some action (the third term) results in financial problems. The appearance of these financial problems is no longer logically indicative of some necessary deficiency in property institutions, since there is now the possibility of calling into question the wisdom and propriety of the attempted action. For the financial crisis can be the price paid for the economic invalidity of the action attempted—a price which will correspond the more closely to the invalidity the more inexorable and unyielding the force of property. Thus the occurrence of financial difficulties, far from proving the desirability of changes in the institution of property, may actually constitute evidence of the impossibility of such changes.

What sort of "model" does this suggest in terms of the economic process? It suggests that certain things we do, either individually or collectively, impinge on the property of others who then act forcefully in defense and that the result is quite different from what it would have been if the original action had met no substantial resistance. In this sense property forces in human nature are no more the "cause" of undesired results than the wall of a handball court is the cause of the speed and direction of the ball that has bounced from it. It is the task of the remainder of this paper to analyze some typical economic phenomena as possible instances of this sort of relationship.

The first step is to identify those meanings of major terms which are directly relevant to the analysis. A moment's reflection will reveal that the sort of relationship referred to in the preceding pages depends in an important way on at least the following: (a) the identification of property rights in their simplest and most irreducible sense; and (b) the extent to which financial transactions or, more broadly, the uses of money, involve property implications. Let us consider each of these in turn.

The essential nature of property rights would appear to be capable of being stated simply and unequivocally. Professor Kirzner does just this in discussing individual rights to private property:

> This means that each individual is free at each moment to employ the means available to him for the purpose of furthering his own ends, providing only that this should not invade the property rights of others. At the same time each individual can plan his activities with the assurance provided by the law, first *that the means available to him are secure against appropriation by others, and, then, that he will not be prevented by others from enjoying the fruits of his productive activities.*[1]

It is particularly important for us to note, in the present connection, that property involves *both* the unimpaired maintenance of existing means (subject to the qualification stated) *and* the fruit, or income, properly assignable to these means. The appropriation either of these, all or in part, therefore constitutes invasion of property—an invasion recognized as such under the law, in principle, if not always in practice. And it is reasonable to suppose that such invasions will be resisted by the individuals affected either directly by force, or defensively by attempts and arrangements which will offset or avoid or at least attenuate the effects of actual or foreseen invasions of this sort. It is crucial to our argument to recognize that individuals, by their very nature, will not willingly and knowingly submit to such invasion if there exists some way known to them of avoiding or softening its impact on either of the two aspects of property rights mentioned earlier.

Now despite its forthrightness and simplicity, the view of property cited above has been both challenged and obfuscated by much of the writing on the subject. Most interesting from our present point of view is the potent tradition initiated by some historians in the nineteenth century[2] which advanced the view that primitive society was characterized by communal ownership.[3] This view, understandably, was eagerly adopted and re-emphasized by the socialists.[4] It hardly needs to be pointed out here that the question of the ultimate situs of property rights is basic to much if not most economic discussion and controversy. What is relevant here is that it is of very special significance to the topic of our inquiry. Since a considerable part of the invasions of property originate not in the actions of other individuals but in some action by the community or state, it becomes imperative to pause to consider the validity of the "Maurer-Maine" thesis. For once it is accepted, what have been characterized as invasions of property evaporate altogether. The centrality of this issue calls for far more intensive and systematic inquiry than is possible here; we shall have to be content with merely touching on some of the more obvious flaws in the thesis above.

1. First of all, there is reason to doubt whether, *in fact,* the historical evidence supports the allegation made by Maurer, Maine, et al. Investigations by other, no less com-

petent, historians have led these to cast very serious doubt on the accuracy of the interpretation.[5]

2. Quite aside from the above, it is perhaps significant that the studies which purport to discover communal property are uniformly concerned with property in *land* and are therefore exposed to error on at least two counts:

a. It is by no means clear that land, in very primitive society, is sufficiently qualified by relative scarcity to be regarded as an economic good and therefore suitable to exemplify property rights.[6] It is quite probable that societies in, or just emerged from, a nomadic state have other and better embodiments of property than land.

b. It would appear that the historians involved do not go back far enough analytically. More fundamental by far than property in land is property in one's own person and capacities; and there is no indication that these were ever, or even could be, "communal." Indeed, in this case it is difficult to imagine how Marxians could adopt this view and still, consistently, hold a concept of exploitation based on the labor theory of value.

3. Independently of all the foregoing, there is, it seems to me, a vast irrelevance in the historical "evidence." Imbedded in the adducing of pristine appearances of communal property is the gratuitous assumption that there exists a necessary connection between what is primitive and what is natural and right. This can be little more than the carry-over into political and economic thought of the self-deluding romanticism of the century which sought to express its "mal de siècle" by inventing and venerating a "noble savage." It is not absolutely necessary for private property to have existed from the very first for it to be the best and most productive human arrangement. One can, for example, discover that primitives characteristically practiced cannibalism and still be able to deny that that aboriginal diet is either morally right or more nutritious than fare resorted to later.

The other matter which needs some attending to in the light of our problem is the extent to which financial problems are or are not related to property considerations. In the analysis of incursions into property rights originating in, or related to, financial transactions, it is easy, unless we exercise a little care, to fall into error or, more exactly, into misinterpretation. For example, an extremely important part of the present discussion is whether or not changes in monetary value constitute invasions of property. In an excellent treatment of the subject of invasion of property, Murray Rothbard says:

> The foregoing observations should firmly remind us that what the enforcing agency combats in a free society is invasion of the *physical* person and property, *not* injury to the *values* of property. For physical property is what the person owns; he does not have any ownership in monetary values, which are a function of what *others* will pay for his property.[7]

Now since, in the pursuance of my subject, I am going to insist that, under certain conditions changes in the money values of property are very definitely invasions of property, while Rothbard appears to be saying the opposite, it is once again important to clarify meanings. The fact is that there is no real contradiction between us, a fact which becomes clear once the full import of the term "free society" in the above quotation is appreciated. Elsewhere in this same section, Rothbard says: "*Invasive action* may be defined as any action—violence, theft, or fraud—taking away another's personal freedom or property without his consent." Since he postulates, in the analysis, ". . .a market society unhampered by the use of violence or theft against any man's person or property," his "enforcing agency"—as I am certain he would agree—is something categorically different from any actual agency in existence around us. If the enforcing agency is part of a state which administers a managed money system and engages in fiscal policy—as our government actually does—it not only does not protect *against* invasions of the property rights of individuals, but itself generates massive invasions of this sort, which it then is in a position to enforce.

It is important for our purposes to realize that in any economic system in which money other than full-bodied money is used and in which the acceptability of such money is forced upon the public—by the exercise of legal-tender laws or in some other way—the free market in the sense Rothbard means is to that extent compromised. If one is not free to refuse to accept fiduciary money or to insist on, say, payment in gold, one is not entirely a free agent in determining the conditions of the transactions he takes part in. At best, transactions carried on under such conditions can be said to be under a "constraint"; and it is one of the ironies of our economics that the very pervasiveness of this instance of "taking away another's personal freedom or property without his consent" seems to make most people unwilling to see it as "invasive action."

Given the assumption of a free-market society as postulated by Rothbard, it is, of course, perfectly correct to say that the only enforcement needed is that against injury to physical persons and property, and that the attempt to protect against injury to *values* is, under such conditions, unnecessary and even harmful. But it is also true that under such conditions, financial crises of the sort we are attempting to discuss would not occur, or would at least take an entirely different form. In order to discuss actual financial crises, we must abandon the assumption of free-market conditions; and as soon as this is done, it seems to me, to be no longer true that protection against impairment of *physical* property alone is sufficient. For under these more realistic conditions the same quantity of physical property not only represents a wide variety of different values (as indeed it also would in the Rothbard model), but these variations in value are not fully "negotiable" in the sense of being fully determined as part of the bargaining process among freely exchanging units.

Under actual conditions, therefore, quantities of physical property may not be free to find their own level of relative valuation as they might be expected to do, say, under a barter economy. Actions originating outside the bargaining process itself can and do exert considerable force on the ratios of exchange among commodities—and without appearing to do any violence to the physical commodities themselves. This is a danger inevitably incurred in one way or another in the very process of progressing from less to more efficient systems of exchange; that is, in the emergence, in the first place, of indirect exchanges involving money and, beyond that, in the adoption and extension of the use of fiduciary money. This development makes it possible for the *value* of physical property to undergo changes which are not assignable, in any proximate way, to changes in the physical property itself. Even in the simplest monetary society the surreptitious activities of a counterfeiter do not visit any visible violence on my physical property or person, yet its power to command other goods is impaired in some sense. In the terms so dear to much contemporary economic discourse, an "exogenous" variable (counterfeiting) is added to the interrelations internal to the system itself ("endogenous variables").

It is true, of course, that in the case of a counterfeiter fraud has been perpetrated and that the enforcing agency would, even in a monetary economy, act to prevent his activities. But is it absolutely clear that it would do this precisely and explicitly on the grounds relevant to our discussion, namely, that counterfeiting is an invasion of the property of *everyone* in the community? Is the fraudulence of the case entirely covered by conceiving of it as the attempt on the part of the counterfeiter to misrepresent his product in exchanging it for another particular person's goods or services, to the exclusion of the continuing series of value (price) distortions suffered differentially by all sorts of people up to the point where all prices have adjusted to the change? It seems to me that the latter effect is at least theoretically separable and deserves some attention of itself. Let us now imagine that our counterfeiter, instead of spending his notes, decides to wage a private war on poverty and, with laudable self-effacement, leaves the notes where they are likely to be found by needy and deserving people. The interesting point for us in the present context is not that such acts are outlawed, but the precise reason why they are outlawed. What exactly is the crime committed here, "fraud" or some sort of *lèse-majesté?*

The examples considered above are not intended to be entirely frivolous. History bears witness to the existence of a deepening series of nice escalations involving this more general question of invasion of the property of the community—a line which only begins with examples of crude fraud. Just take the first case we discussed and make the counterfeiter also double as enforcing agent and you have the essential ingredients for the long and unedifying story of coinage debasement. If we then add to the agent's judicial powers those of legal-tender laws, even a metallic money system contains a considerable constraint on the freedom of the market to determine precisely the terms of its own exchanges.

If, in the second illustration, we again include the enforcing agency, add fractional reserve powers, central banking, and liberal amounts of the best intentions of humanitarianism, the whole panoply of the modern state is designed, complete with fiscal and monetary powers and policies. Nor is it wise to assume that we have reached the end of this road. It is therefore imperative that we inquire insistently whether there persists in fact, beneath all the complexities and the blandishments of modern arrangements, the sort of invasion of property referred to earlier.

The fact is, then, that it appears correct to say that individuals living in society clearly have property rights in the money of that society at least to the extent that they hold assets in that form. Moreover, their property rights in money may be more extensive than their rights in the ordinary goods in economic life. If the money concerned is such that its quantity and value are freely established in the marketplace, then property in money is indistinguishable from property in other things; and it is true to say that all they require to be protected from is invasion of their physical property and not from changes in the value of that property. But if, as is the case in the actual order of things, the determination of the quantity and value of the money is not made entirely within the range of activity of those who use it, then it would appear to follow that, unlike property in its more ordinary forms, money *does* imply property rights in *value.* This does not mean, of course, that the value of money can, or even should, be entirely guaranteed. For the variations in the value of money are of two entirely different kinds: the kind of variation which money shares with other goods in the higgling and fortunes of the market, and which does not require any enforcement against invasion; and superimposed on that, additional variation originating in arbitrary or unilateral action outside the market and not subject to the corrective action of the market. It is this latter type of change in value with which we are concerned here.

While, for the purpose of analytical discussion, we have been implying that this special type of variation in value would theoretically justify action by the enforcing agent to prevent incursions against the special property rights which correspond to it, we must now immediately proceed to recognize that, in any practical sense, this is not even remotely likely. To attempt to do this—or even to recognize the right we are referring to—would involve the enforcing agency in a set of nearly intolerable self-denials and contradictions. For one thing, by enforcing such property rights as this, the government would be in the position of offsetting entirely the very actions and intentions which gave rise to this special property right in money; this means nothing less than the complete disestablishment of all monetary and fiscal "policy." And for another, it would be forced to resort entirely to taxation to finance its other activities.

And this brings us full turn into the central issue of this paper. If this special type of property infringement is present and if the usual channels of recourse against property invasions are not available for it, individuals and groups will, to the extent they can, act to protect themselves as best they can against it. And in the process of attempting to do so they cannot fail to create conditions leading to financial crisis. As a group, they cannot conceivably succeed to any substantial extent, for this too would defeat the external forces which occasioned the invasion of property in the first place. But some will succeed much more than others—due to superior knowledge, skill, position, or luck. And it is these differentials which aggravate the injustices involved, though it is no part of our inquiry here to go into this interesting aspect of the matter. All that remains for us to do is to reflect on some of the ways in which this defensive reaction by the holders of money taken as a group makes itself felt in the market and its relation to several types of financial crises.

1. Gresham's Law. The often observed operation of this principle attests to the generality and the potency of the drive to protect the value of one's property in money in the face of suspicion or uncertainty. The usual phrasing of the principle: "Bad money drives good money out of circulation," is misleading and apparently paradoxical and has therefore been deservingly criticized and corrected elsewhere.[8] It is more correct to say, as Rothbard suggests, that "Money overvalued by the state will drive money undervalued by the state out of circulation." But what interests us in the context of the present discussion is *why* this happens. When an individual holds, say, money of two distinct forms, kinds, conditions, etc., and is observed to spend first the sort in which he has less confidence, he is engaging in nothing more mysterious or less understandable than trying to protect his property—in this case, the exchange value of his money assets taken as a whole—by holding on longest to that form of money which, in his view, is likely to prove more permanently valid, acceptable, etc. So strong is this tendency that it applies more widely than even Rothbard's improved formulation would indicate. For the same principle is operating when a person chooses to spend first those notes and coins which are marred, or torn, or dented, even when he has no serious doubt about the official soundness of the money as such. While the latter example of the operation of the law is relatively trivial, it does indicate the power of the motive toward preservation of property. In the more substantial case where exchangers have (or think they have) reason to prefer one sort of currency over another, the preferred sort will either disappear from circulation or at least will circulate much more slowly than the other. In either case, there will be produced to some degree or other a stringency of circulating medium which, if it is carried far enough, will exhibit the characteristics of a financial "crisis."

2. *Debasement of coins.* Countless times in history issuing authorities have resorted to the practice of surreptitiously reducing the amount of monetary metal in the coin of the realm. In whatever interval it took for people to find out about the manipulation, the issuer (not unlike the counterfeiter we mentioned earlier) increased his power to command goods and services relative to that of the community in general—and, indeed, this was the reason for resorting to the practice. Here there was a clear loss of property visited upon the community; but, inasmuch as it was not known or suspected, no defensive action was undertaken. But as soon as some discovered, or even came to suspect, the invasion of property, it inevitably followed that these immediately raised the price of the goods and services they had to sell in order to offset the original invasion. The rapid rise of some prices relative to other prices (those quoted by people who did not yet know and therefore discount) led to many forms of financial stringency.

If under these circumstances there was also available some form of currency which had not been tinkered with, Gresham's law would operate, and some of the pressure which would otherwise have gone into price rises would now be taken up by the hoarding of the preferred currency. However, the mixing of different defensive acts, in this latter case, does not in any way affect the fact that members of the community are attempting, in whatever way seems possible to them, to protect themselves against this sort of loss in the value of their money property. But it goes without saying that some of them will succeed in doing so less than others—and this is especially so in the more complex case—with the result that there will be a redistribution of effective purchasing power, and this in turn sets the stage for a different set of financial difficulties in the market.

3. Bank failures. The applicability of the analysis to the case of paper money is easiest to follow by recalling an era in which the issuers of banknotes were not protected from the defensive reaction of the market to invasions of money property. This was the situation in this country until about a hundred years ago. Private banks were then permitted to issue their own banknotes, subject, however, to having to redeem these notes into specie at any time at the demand of holders of the notes. In this case, a bank might issue more paper money than it was ordinarily called upon to redeem and the practice of fractional reserves was operative. So long as it was able to meet immediately all requests for redemption, the bank was in a position exactly analogous to that of the previously cited debasing agency in the period between the actual debasement and any public awareness of it. In both cases there is a clear invasion of money property and, moreover, one which can persist so long as the victims are not aware of the invasion and therefore do not act to protect themselves.

It frequently happened, however, that banks would overestimate their ability to meet calls for redemption of their notes (more precisely, would underestimate the expected probability that they would be called upon to redeem more than a certain amount). Their inability to meet specific demands for redemption would then cause almost all holders of notes to attempt to protect themselves by presenting notes for redemption, and the resulting "run" on the bank would cause it to fail. This type of financial "crisis" is probably the best known to the man in the street because of its comparative clarity and frequency in our history. What is of particular significance to our analysis, however, is the fact that the immediate cause of the crisis is the "run" on the bank and that this, in turn, is not just an arbitrary or fortuitous act on the part of the public, but the attempt to preserve their property by rescuing it from its present embodiment in the form of banknotes.

Moreover, it should be noted that these attempts to preserve property rights in money can be frustrated—and repeatedly have been—by the action of the state in protecting banks from the consequences of actions which affect their ability to redeem their own currency. This has most frequently taken the form of suspending the right of the holder of paper money to seek redemption. The consequences of such protection need no elaboration here; they were clearly and unequivocally demonstrated by David Ricardo early in the last century in connection with precisely this sort of protection thrown over the note issue of the Bank of England during the Napoleonic War. What does need to be pointed out, perhaps, is that the suspension of specie payments (or other convertibility) shields the banks not only from the consequences of invasions of property already in effect, but also from having to face the results of future similar invasions. Because of this, need for defensive action by the public is all the greater. As people then seek to protect themselves against further erosion of the value of their money property, something they will attempt to do in a number of different ways, the scene is set for the occurrence of all sorts of financial rigidities and imbalance.

4. Crises in Payments Balances. Sharp increases in the outflow of gold, which is still the balancing item in the international balance of payments, are the subject of much current attention. For the purpose of our analysis it is useful to distinguish two forms of this problem: (a) the continuous, more-or-less regular outflow of gold due to the lack of equality of payments to and from foreign countries; and (b) sudden and very sharp increases in demands by foreign holders of money assets of a country for payment—in gold or in the exchange of their own country. The first type does not directly concern us here, though its presence and continuance evidences some serious economic imbalances, often the result of arbitrary interferences with the free play of the market. The second is more directly pertinent to the subject under discussion here.

A person (or organization) holding assets in the form of deposits in a foreign country, if he sees or thinks he sees some imminent danger of loss in the value of those assets, will attempt to protect against this loss. For example, if he fears there will be a serious depreciation in the value of that currency relative to other currencies, or that the country is likely to devalue its currency (i.e., diminish the amount of gold in its monetary unit), he will naturally seek to convert his holdings into gold in advance of such an event. Only by holding his assets in the form of gold or some other stable form can he avoid the loss he would undergo by leaving these assets payable in a depreciating monetary unit.

Now if substantial withdrawals of this sort are made by foreigners who hold deposits in a given country and if there are no other changes tending to offset the drain, there will be a precipitous incremental loss of gold for that country and thus a "crisis" in its international payments position. A recent British experience is an instructive case in point. There was just such a sharp increase in demands by foreigners for payment. Most of the accounts appearing in the press, moreover, made arcane references to supposedly sinister machinations on the part of foreign holders of British deposits. In two instances that I read there was specific reference to an alleged "attack" by Swiss bankers on the British pound sterling.

It is, to say the least, difficult to imagine why these people would want to mount such an *offensive.* Even assuming they could hope to succeed, there would appear little logical reason for them to do so. If, on the other hand, instead of invoking some sort of demonology to explain the phenomenon, one were to imagine that those people were attempting to *preserve their property* against some sort of loss which they saw in the offing (whether correctly or not is beside the point), the whole thing would appear quite ordinary and relatively undramatic. It is, of course, impossible to read the minds of those who "precipitated the crisis," but it is not altogether unreasonable to assume that they may have expected a further devaluation of the pound and were taking measures to protect themselves against loss of property; and, if so, there is nothing nefarious about such action. Indeed, it is another illustration of the point made earlier in this paper: that it may be just such defensive actions which help to explain the occurrence of many types of financial crises rather than the other way around.

5. *Inflation.* A final word may be in order about what is probably the most potentially explosive problem of our day—the possibility of runaway inflation. It is one of the commonplaces of contemporary economic theory and policy to point to—and to attempt to employ—the fact that inflation has, as one of its more immediate and superficial impacts, an "exhilarating" effect on the economy. And there can be little doubt that in the short run this is so; but *why* and under what conditions it is so is, I believe, far more significant and instructive.

A moment's reflection about the nature of inflation will reveal that it essentially consists in the cheapening of money relative to other things. That this should lead to an increase in expenditures—the exchange of money for commodities, equipment and services—is basically tantamount to the operation of Gresham's law on a scale that is grandiose. There is nothing very surprising that, under such circumstances, people should increase their preference for goods over money. And if this were all there was to the problem, it would indeed be true—as some have never tired of assuring us—that a little inflation is a good thing.

But there is, alas, much more. In the first place, since it affects different people and groups neither simultaneously nor to the same degree, inflation has rather marked redistributive effects—and these, as we have seen in another connection above, can have serious disequilibrating results for financial as well as other economic arrangements.

In the second place—and very apposite to our discussion—the differential and other aspects of inflation necessarily involve an incursion into the property rights of members of the exchanging community. To the extent that people so affected realize this, they will act in the way we have been describing—they will attempt to protect themselves against the loss. And one of the main ways in which they can be expected to do this is for them to "discount" the inflation in their economic calculations. The prices for their goods, their services, and their loans will be made to reflect the fall in the relative value of money; and this will be seen to be analogous to the price changes which used to occur in less complex days in response to debasement of currency.

The fact which seems to lull the advocates of "mild" inflation into a false sense of security is that, under ordinary circumstances, the public either does not know the extent of inflation or does not expect it to continue. But there is no reason to assume that this lethargy is unshakable; one has merely to look at the numberless examples of inflation which has gotten out of hand. At some point, the public is likely to become convinced that inflation is going to continue for an indefinite time to come; at this point attempts to "hedge" against it will become general enough to create an immense problem. For the "therapeutic" value of inflation depends on the assumption that people will not attempt to take it systematically into account. As soon as they do, the "exhilaration" is gone and is succeeded by the unedifying rat race to keep ahead of the game—and this is runaway inflation. An examination of the famous German experience of the early twenties or that of the Hungarians in the forties will supply rich detail.

For our purpose it is perhaps sufficient to point out that, here again, what is significant—and in our present circumstances dangerously so—is the inexorable way in which people try to arrange to avoid erosion in the value of their money. And in the unfortunate event that some critical portion of an ever more economically literate public should systematically protect itself against the property invasion which is imbedded in inflation, we shall come face to face with the greatest and most unmanageable of all financial crises—an inflation which feeds itself and against which any ordinary moves only have the effect of increasing its momentum. It is precisely this consideration which made it seem worthwhile to suggest the inverted treatment of the topic we are discussing.

NOTES

1. I. M. Kirzner, *Market Theory and the Price System* (Princeton, 1963) p. 13 (emphasis added).

2. Cf. e.g., G. L. von Maurer, *Geschichte der Markenverfassung in Deutschland* (Erlangen, 1856); Sir Henry Maine, *Ancient Law* (London, 1861) and *Lectures on the Early History of Institutions* (London, 1875); and E. L. V. de Laveleye, *De La Propriété et de ses formes primitives* (Paris, 1874).

3. Cf. for example, Maine (*Ancient Law,* p.279): "We have the strongest reason for thinking that property once belonged not to individuals nor even to isolated families, but to larger societies composed on the patriarchal model. . . ."

4. Notably by F. Engels in *The Origin of the Family, Private Property and the State,* cf. L. von Mises, *Socialism* (New Haven, 1951) p.84; references to primitive communism were also incorporated in the later editions of the *Communist Manifesto.*

5. Cf., e.g., N. D. Fustel de Coulanges, *Histoire des institutions politiques de l'ancienne France,* 6 vols. (Paris, 1875-82); B. H. Baden-Powell, *The Indian Village Community* (London, 1896).

6. Cf., e.g., M. Rothbard, *Man, Economy, and State,* 2 vols. (Princeton, 1962), I, p.78.

7. Rothbard, *op. cit.,* I, pp.152-59; the quotation is from p.157 (emphasis in the original).

8. Cf. L. von Mises, *The Theory of Money and Credit* (New Haven, 1953) pp.75-77; and his *Human Action* (New Haven, 1949) p.432n. Also, especially, M. Rothbard, *op. cit.,* pp. 783-785.

9

Sylvester Petro

FEUDALISM, PROPERTY, AND PRAXEOLOGY

> It is not the business of the scientific historical enquirer to assert good or evil of any particular institution. He deals with its existence and development, not with its expediency. But one conclusion he may properly draw from the facts bearing on the subject before us. Nobody is at liberty to attack several [i.e., private] property and to say at the same time that he values civilization. The history of the two cannot be disentangled. Civilization is nothing more than a name for the old order of the Aryan world, dissolved but perpetually reconstituting itself under a vast variety of solvent influences, of which infinitely the most powerful have been those which have, slowly, and in some parts of the world much less perfectly than others, substituted several property for collective ownership.
>
> —Sir Henry Sumner Maine, *Village Communities* 230 (3d ed., 1890)

Introduction

I PROPOSE to recount here certain features of the land law which prevailed in England from roughly the time of the Norman Conquest to the seventeenth century. My reasons for doing so are several, and each is complicated enough to call for some elaboration.

Ours is a time of extensive and pervasive qualification of the right of private property. It is a time, moreover, in which a current of thought is moving powerfully and swiftly toward ever more extensive and more pervasive qualifications of that right. Almost 150 years ago, Justice Story said for the United States Supreme Court: "We know of no case in which a legislative act to transfer the property of A. to B. without his consent has been held a constitutional exercise of legislative power in any state of the

Union."[1] Today, particularly under the federal urban renewal program and similar state and municipal programs, the kind of transfer to which Justice Story referred is a daily occurrence. Those who object to such manhandling of the right of private property are frequently accused of wishing to "turn back the clock." One of my reasons for examining the land law of England between the eleventh and the sixteenth centuries is to determine whether it is in fact the proponent of broad property rights who wishes to "turn back the clock."

The seventeenth century, the century of the "Glorious Revolution," of the triumph of Parliament and representative government, and of John Locke, was a century in which the Western world's rationales of both personal freedom and the right of private property were conceived, integrated, and set into motion on a theretofore unprecedented scale. A persecuted and misjudged "leveller" of that time, Richard Overton, wrote during one of his terms in Newgate Prison that:

> To every individual in nature is given an individual property by nature, not to be invaded or usurped by any: for every one as he is himselfe, so he hath a selfe propriety, else he could not be himselfe. . . .Mine and thine cannot be, except this be: No man hath power over my rights and liberties and I over no man's; I may be but an individual, enjoy myselfe and my selfe propriety.[2]

It is impossible for a man of the twentieth century to appreciate the immediacy and the force with which such men as Overton conceived the unity of personal integrity, justice, and private property; impossible, that is, without the direct experience of feudal and neofeudal or mercantilist institutions which such men had in the seventeenth century. My second reason for reviewing the feudal property institutions is to remedy this deficiency as best I can in the circumstances. When we have seen how difficult it was to consider men free with the right of private property imperfectly conceived and still less perfectly realized, we shall be in a fair position to judge the probable effects upon freedom of the present trends against private property.

Among the many remarkable achievements of Ludwig von Mises,[3] one of the most enduring must be his demonstration of socialism's incapacity to calculate.[4] Before an economy can operate with any kind of efficiency, Mises demonstrates, it must have some means of evaluating—that is, calculating—production costs; otherwise, production becomes a blind, arbitrary process, in which the resources of the community are certain to be wasted and irrationally developed. But economic calculation is possible only within a society of cooperative exchange—only, that is, within the institutional framework which we refer to as the *market.* The relevance of this contribution of Mises to our subject lies in the fact that private property is the indispensable feature of the market.[5] In purporting to abolish private property in the means of production, socialism would thus deny itself the possibility of operating an economy rationally, that is, efficiently. It should perhaps be emphasized that socialism's abolition of private property would, if consistently pursued, involve the abolition of personal freedom. The fundamental means of production is the human person; the fundamental private-property right, therefore, is the right of control of one's own person. It is no more possible to have a market without personal freedom than it is to have a market without private property in the nonhuman factors of production.

The Western world has never really known what it is to live under socialism, or under any other system not characterized by the right of private property—at least not on any scale larger, say, than the abortive Pilgrim settlements of the seventeenth century in New England. Maine was correct in observing that Western civilization and what he called "several" property are inextricably intermingled in our history. If there is any deficiency in his statement, it lies in the suggestion that the two are merely "entangled." For in truth private property and Western civilization are but two names for the same thing. Voluntary cooperation, specialization, exchange—in short, consensual division of labor—all presuppose private property rights; and those concepts add up to what we traditionally designate the social order of Western civilization. The more comprehensively and coherently property rights have been conceived and practiced, the more fully and productively has this social order been realized: the advances made by Western man since the seventeenth century, when property rights began to enjoy a comprehensive conception, are quite demonstrably a product of the exercise of those rights. While it is true, as I have just remarked, that Western man does not know what it is to live in any but a private-property social order, it is also true that medieval England was characterized by a fragmentary, if not anomalous and indeed contradictory concept of property rights. One would expect, in consequence, that personal freedom, free markets, the division of labor, and other hallmarks of Western civilization would be correspondingly imperfectly realized. My third reason for investigating and recounting the property institutions of feudal England arises from a desire to explore this hypothesis and its implications.

Pre-Norman Land Law

The busy bureaucracy of the Norman kings compiled surprisingly good records of conditions in England after the Conquest. Perhaps even more surprising, enough is known about pre-Norman conditions to establish with a high degree of probability the conclusion that landholding under the Saxons—and, what is more important, the ranking or status of persons—substantially influenced the system which the Normans developed. Holdsworth, together with all other investigators, has concluded that from Saxon times throughout the whole medieval period the fee-simple absolute, the full right of private property in real estate, was not only unknown, but would have been an anomaly.[6] Esmein, the great French legal historian, reached the same conclusion in respect to the *franc alleu,* the French term for the fee simple. The *franc alleu*, he described as "une véritable anomalie dans la société féodale."[7]

It is true, Holdsworth says, that certain forms of landholding under the Saxons (e.g., "bookland" and "laenland") contained the "germs" which were to be developed much later into genuinely free landholding, but on the whole "in the Anglo-Saxon land law we hear little or nothing of any doctrines as to ownership or possession."[8] As a matter of fact the earliest known use of the word "owner" occurs in 1340; significantly, the still more abstract concept "ownership" is not found in use till 1583.[9]

Thus, under the Saxons, the personal relationship to land seems one "not so much [of] ownership as [of] tenure."[10] And, still in Holdsworth's words, "the land is for the most part owned and cultivated according to a customary routine which prevented many of those disputes between individual owners, the existence of which is a condition precedent to [the growth of the more individualistic forms of landholding]."[11]

To adapt Maine's classic formulation, status rather than contract determined the human condition under the Saxons, as well as later. Moreover, this status was largely based on relationship to land.[12] That curious institution, the *wergild*—the price or fine which one had to pay to the kindred of a person he had slain—illustrates this point in an odd way. There are *wergild* records which show, for example, that "a helm and a coat of mail, and a sword ornamented with gold" amounted to "five hides of land."[13] As to contracts and contract law under the Saxons, Holdsworth points out that the existing legal authority was physically incapable of enforcing more than property and criminal law. "The task of enforcing promises involves problems beyond its capacity, and coercive authority beyond its strength."[14]

The relative stasis which sometimes seems to have been a kind of medieval ideal had an odd, perhaps even perverted, egalitarian foundation. An illustration is provided by the fragmented common-field system. A tract of land of several hundred acres, extending over ground ranging widely in terms of contour, fertility, and ease of cultivation, would be divided among various tenants in what can only be described as an extremely awkward way—from the point of view of efficient agricultural techniques. A single tenant would characteristically have his holding of, say, twenty acres distributed among a number of small, disconnected patches—some on the flat, some on the hillside, some rich and loamy, some rocky. Students have generally agreed with Holdsworth that the design of the common-field system, in "giving to each a little bit of the good, a little bit of the indifferent, a little bit of the bad," was egalitarian.[15] It should be emphasized, I believe, that the system, together with the numerous restraints upon alienation which prevailed throughout feudalism, seemed designed also to do that which is, in the long run, impossible: namely, preserve the status quo. Land distribution schemes of the kind associated with our so-called Alliance for Progress have an ancient, if not very promising, lineage.

The Norman Tenures and Their Incidents

William, Duke of Normandy, took England in 1066, and he took it, as the conveyancers say, to "have and to hold." One may infer from his actions that he considered the tight little island largely a personal holding. Before too long, like any good landlord, he had England comprehensively and scrupulously surveyed and each tract carefully recorded in what has come to be known as Domesday Book. He of course did not intend to work the land himself. But as England's principal if not exclusive source of wealth, the land was all nevertheless to serve him. The Domesday survey was based on the assumption that all land had an overlord—"*nulle terre sans seigneur*"—and one qualified as an overlord, or tenant in capite, at least originally, only if he contributed substantially to either William's might or his coffers.[16] Within a century of the conquest, William and his successors had surrounded themselves with a number of bureaucrats, largely imported from Europe, whose job it was mainly to keep track of land holdings. In 1166, for example, the Exchequer made extensive inquiry throughout England as to (1) how many knights had been enfeoffed before and after the death of

Henry I; (2) how many knights, if any, a given fief was deficient in supplying; (3) the names of new knights. "The king intended that he, and not his tenants, should profit by any increase in the capacity of the land to support knights."[17]

The celebrated Norman tenures, when fully developed were: knight-service, frank almoin, serjeanty, socage, and burgage.[18] There were variations and complications; there were even special instances of what amounted virtually to full freeholds. But as a general rule only the king could fully own his land. All other land, according to the formula quoted by Pollock and Maitland, is held of the king: "Z *tenet terram illam de. . .domino Rege*."[19] Thus, to illustrate, A holding directly of the crown, say by knight-service, might enfeoff B to hold by a money rent (socage); B in turn might enfeoff C, an abbey, to hold on terms of praying for the souls of B's ancestors (frank almoin). Knight-service involved the tenant in an obligation to supply a certain number of knights. Tenure by serjeanty was usually held by a (free) servant of the king or a magnate—a cook, banner-carrier, groom, letter-carrier. Burgage tenure was from the earliest times the freest and most unencumbered of all the feudal tenures. It applied exclusively to town lands and came close to involving what we call a marketable title.

A single person might, and sometimes did, hold land in several forms of tenure. Thus Sir Robert de Aguilon, d. 1286, held different tracts of land (a) of the king at a money rent, (b) by knight's fee, and (c) by serjeanty. He also held several tracts in London of the king in chief by socage. The most remarkable feature of the latter holdings is that Sir Robert was explicitly authorized to bequeath them as chattels, a rare privilege at the time.[20]

The person who actually worked the land was called the tenant in demesne. He stood at the bottom of the scale, "the person who seems most like an owner of the land, and who has a general right of doing what he pleases with it."[21] However, it was technically correct as a matter of law under feudalism to conceive of several different persons, naturally in several different senses, as having and holding the same piece of land.[22] Consider, for example, the case of Roger of St. German. Pollock and Maitland, citing an ancient document, tell us that "...in Edward I's day Roger of St. German holds lands at Paxton in Huntingdon Shire of Robert of Bedford, who holds of Richard of Ilchester, who holds of Alan of Chartres, who holds of William le Boteler, who holds of Gilbert Neville, who holds of Devorguil Balliol, who holds of the king of Scotland, who holds of the king of England."[23]

The difference between the feudal tenures and a modern fee-simple-absolute resides mainly, though not exclusively, in how easy it is for land to change hands—in alienability and heritability. Almost all the feudal tenures were markedly deficient in these respects. "Wardship and marriage" were typical restrictions. Politicking went on in the old days, too. Thus the Coronation Charter of Henry I, like a good political platform, made promises. It unctuously declared:

> If any of my barons or other men wishes to give his daughter, or sister, or niece, or cousin in marriage, let him speak with me; but I will neither take anything of his for the licence, nor will I forbid him to give her away, unless it be to an enemy of mine. And if on the death of one of my barons or other men he leaves a daughter as heir, I will give her with her land by the counsel of my barons. If he leaves a widow, who is without children, she shall have her dower and marriage portion and I will not give her in marriage against her will. If she has children, she shall have her dower and marriage portion while she remains chaste, and I will not give her unless with her consent. And the wife or some other relative who has the best claim shall be guardian of the land and of the children. And I bid my barons keep within the same bounds as regards the sons, daughters and wives of their men.[24]

Pollock and Maitland remark of these generous commitments: "That Henry made these promises is certain, that he broke them is equally certain."[25] The important point, however, is that the charter demonstrates the condition of qualified bondage which the imperfect realization of property rights brought about. Land was the principal subject of property rights. With the lord immediately and the king ultimately rested the control. With that control as predicate, even the choice of one's mate could be dictated—and of course was, when vital political interests might be threatened by a marriage contrary to the interests of "the state," *i.e.*, of the king.

Perhaps a word more needs to be said about "wardship" and "marriage." Wardship was the condition which arose when a holder of land died leaving an heir of less than twenty-one years. In such circumstances the lord grantor held the land, taking its rents, if any; he could not commit "waste"; the royal courts were available to prevent that; and he was under obligation to support the ward during his, or her, minority.[26] The "marriage" power, when devolving upon a mere mesne lord, apparently did not mean too much; but the authorities suggest, contrary to Henry I's promises, that where the power resided in the king, it meant a great deal. A widow or heiress-daughter of one holding from the king was likely to encounter real trouble if she married or remarried without the king's consent. Even a male ward was regarded as under a duty to get his lord's consent to his marriage, although a then current maxim held that "marriage should be free."[27]

Two other features of wardship and marriage seem significant. First, the power was a far more marketable asset than the ordinary right in land. According to Pollock and Maitland, "large sums are paid for the wardships and marriages of wealthy heirs; indeed so thoroughly proprietary and pecuniary are these rights that they can be disposed of by will; they pass like chattels to the guardian's executors."[28] Second, not all feudal tenures were subject to wardship and marriage. Socage, burgage, fee farm and nonmilitary tenures in serjeanty were free of those burdens.[29]

Throughout the early feudal centuries, the free tenures were heritable, as we shall see presently in more detail; but they could not be devised at will, except where special grants from the king so provided. Upon the death of the tenant, the "seisin" (the primitive concept of titular right) reverted to the lord-grantor, or to the king if the land was held of him, for the lord-grantor was regarded as having "primer seisin." The heir could perfect his seisin only by paying what was known as "relief" (really a species of death-duty) to the grantor.[30]

The burden of knight's service attaching to the military tenures had an interesting history. The magnates, the great tenants in capite, were given no option, for obvious reasons. If they refused to provide actual military service themselves, and the requisite number of knights, the king could and would distrain (dispossess) or at least impose a heavy "fine."[31] Increasingly from the twelfth century on, however, minor grantees subject to knight's service were allowed to "buy off" from their military obligation. The payment was called "scutage." As the king came to rely upon a more or less professional army, as those holding by knight's service came to be better farmers than men-at-arms, the primitive form of war-tax called "scutage" became a thriving institution.[32]

It would be erroneous to view the feudal situation as one of absolute stasis and simplicity in respect to land-building.[33] Pollock and Maitland found that "the extraordinary license which men enjoyed of creating new tenures gave birth to some wonderful complications," and they offer this illustration:

> If B holds a knight's fee of A, then A can put X between himself and B, so that B will hold of X and X of A; but further, the service by which X will hold of A, need not be the service by which B has hitherto been holding of A and will now hold of X. In Richard's reign Henry de la Pomerai places William Briwere between himself and a number of tenants of his who altogether owe the service of 5 5/24 knights or thereabouts; but William is to hold of Henry by the service of one knight. To "work out the equities" arising between these various persons would be for us a very difficult task: still no good would come of our representing our subject-matter as simpler than it really was.[34]

Yet the restrictions upon transfers were both real and rigorous. Local customs had to be obeyed.[35] The tenant could never free the land of its superior obligation to the lord, or the king,[36] and therefore every conveyance required his concurrence.[37] Moreover, for a long time, subject to a narrowly practiced exception, land could not be devised by will, even though it was heritable by primogeniture; for, as Glanvill said, "Only God can make an heir, not man."[38] The Great Charter of 1215-1216 explains much, in this connection, when it says that "No free man shall henceforth give or sell so much of his land as that out of the residue he may not sufficiently do to the lord of the fee the service due to him which pertains to that fee."[39]

Special grants, usually from the king in chief, might release these restrictions. For example, in 1241 Henry III gave the honor of Richmond to Peter of Savoy "to hold to him and his heirs or to whomsoever among his brothers or cousins he should give, assign, or bequeath it." Twenty years later the king declared formally that Peter of Savoy might bequeath the honor at will. Peter devised the estate to Queen Eleanor, and it did pass to her. The case seemed to have frightened those who saw it as a threat to the income and the power they were deriving from wardship and marriage rights, and a trend toward creating the power of testamentary disposition, which was to be achieved later, was thus aborted in the middle of the thirteenth century.[40]

The omnipresence of Roman law,[41] even well back into the Saxon period, persistently kept in view the concept of a full-fledged property right in land. Those learned in the law have reminded us for centuries that the property right in land conceived by Roman law has never been surpassed in terms of its comprehensiveness and coherence. From Saxon times this concept has been reflected more or less imperfectly in English law. Most forms of landholding in Saxon law were limited broadly in the manner of the Norman feudal tenures; for example numerous instances have survived of petitions to the Saxon kings for the privilege of devising land by will.[42] Yet, as already noted above, "bookland" was a familiar, though not widespread, form of landholding among the Saxons. Holdsworth has cited these as the most significant features of bookland: (1) it was a clean-cut formal mode of conveyancing; (2) it conveyed an absolute property title; (3) important men held land "by the book"; therefore (4) procedure in court cases was more definite and certain where bookland was involved; and (5) thus, the cases involving bookland, being of substantial interest to the crown, a body of well-defined law was developed, creating a learning susceptible of more general application at a later, more propitious time.[43]

The general opinion is, however, that modern conceptions in English law trace more directly to burgage and socage tenure.[44] Burgage, it will be recalled, was the tenure of the burghers, and applied to town lands only. Adam Smith's famous chapter "Of the Rise and Progress of Cities and Towns . . ."[45] tells us that the burghers, "servile soever" they may have been, "arrived at liberty and independency much earlier than the occupiers of land in the country."[46] The burghers wished mainly to be left alone, to trade. They found the landed gentry, the lords, a greater threat to their freedom than the king; and the king found the towns a good source of revenue. Thus an alliance was formed. "The burghers naturally hated and feared the lords. The king hated and feared them, too; but though perhaps he might despise, he had no reason either to hate or fear the burghers. Mutual interest, therefore, disposed them to support the king, and the king to support them against the lords."[47] The towns, and hence the town courts, were administered by the burghers. This fact had much to do with the way in which burgage tenure was developed. The borough courts had a tendency to treat the burgage tenement as an article of commerce; "it is likened to a chattel; not only can it like a chattel be disposed of by will, but it can be sold like a chattel."[48]

Socage, which most scholars think of as the main source, quantitatively speaking, of the ultimate fee-simple-absolute, was the least feudal of the *country*-land tenures. Unlike the copyhold (which somewhat resembled a share-cropper arrangement between dictatorially empowered lord and villein), socage was a "freehold." It was a pure money-rent tenancy—nonspiritual, nonmilitary, and nonserviential;

hence no scutage, no wardship, and no marriage.[49] When, for obvious economic reasons late in the fourteenth century, the incidents of scutage, wardship, and marriage become less attractive to the lords than solid numbers of pure money-rent tenants,[50] "socage begins to swallow up the other tenures and preparation is already made for the day when all, or practically all, tenants will hold by the once humble tenure of the *sokemanni*."[51]

What was happening seems fairly clear. The complex and in some ways contradictory feudal incidents were being sloughed off because they frustrated rather than promoted human action; they got in the way of men's dominant interests. Freedom and full property rights, it was found, served men better than the queer mixture of moralistic and customary restraints which made up the body of feudalism.

Villenage

Villenage shared a good many of the conceptual characteristics of the other feudal institutions: it was vague, complex, and in many ways contradictory and therefore nonviable. The specific origins of villenage in England are unknown, although doubtless associated with the incessant warfare which was a prevailing feature of life in ancient times. We do know, however, that during great disturbances or famines men sold themselves and their children into the limited type of slavery which prevailed under the Anglo-Saxons.[52] Holdsworth makes a number of interesting observations concerning Anglo-Saxon serfdom. He says: "It is probable that at the end of this [Anglo-Saxon] period the class of praedial serfs comprised most of the humble cultivators of the soil. The gebur, the ploughman, the cottar, and their progeny were often serfs attached to the soil, and sold with the soil. They were the most valuable part of the stock of a farm, and their pedigrees were carefully preserved."[53]

According to Holdsworth, conditions at the time were such as to make the difference between a serf and a small farmer inconsequential: "Whether [the serfs] were personally free or not would probably make little material difference in an age in which there was no free market either in labour or land."[54] Again: "The laws of Cnut seem to show that it was easy to confuse the slave and the small free man."[55] He cautions against confusing the sharp Roman conceptions with the vagaries of the medieval theories (although the Roman ideas were later to influence the more learned English commentators): "...the clear conceptions of the Roman law could not be applied to an agricultural community organized on a feudal basis. Still less could they be applied to a community in which the royal power will for many purposes regard the serf as its subject, under the same laws, and liable to perform duties similar to those of free men."[56]

Definitely influenced by the Roman learning which first came to England via Bologna in the eleventh century, Bracton insisted in the middle of the thirteenth century on a sharp difference between free and unfree men: *"Omnes homines aut liberi sunt aut servi."*[57] But the facts went increasingly against him.

Paul Vinogradoff's fine work, *Villainage in England,*[58] demonstrates the shortcomings of Bracton's dictum in a series of pointed statements: (1) "The villain, however near being a chattel, cannot be devised by will because he is considered as an annex to the free tenement of the lord. The connexion with a manor becomes the chief means of establishing and providing seisin of the villain."[59] (2) "I would here recall to attention the main fact, that the opposition between 'free' and 'unfree' rested chiefly on the point of being protected or not being protected by the jurisdiction of the King's Court."[60] (3) "A villain is to a great extent in the power of his lord, not because he is his chattel, but because the courts refuse him an action against the lord. He may have rights recognized by morality and by custom, but he has no means to enforce them; and he has no means to enforce them because feudalism disables the state and prevents it from interfering."[61] (4) "...the wave begins to rise high in favour of liberty even in the thirteenth century. It does not need great perspicuity to notice that, apart from any progress in morals or ideas, apart from any growth of humanitarian notions, the law was carried in this direction by that development of the state which lays a claim to and upon its citizens, and by that development of social intercourse which substitutes agreement for bondage."[62]

Vinogradoff is saying that whether from the point of view of the interests of the state or from the point of view of practical social intercourse, villenage simply did not work very well. Since it had never been a sharply distinct and coherent status, anyway, its breakdown required no sharply revolutionary action.

Let us observe the development more closely. As Vinogradoff pointed out, one of the villein's most significant disabilities lay in the fact that he had to seek his justice in the manorial courts, since the royal courts for centuries had no jurisdiction over him. On the other hand, as against everyone but his own lord, the villein had a rather full complement of rights.[63] It is true that the lord had a technical right, which seems to have been exercised at times, to every chattel which the villein might acquire.[64] But the point is that villeins could own chattels and make transactions involving them. Furthermore, it was not difficult apparently, for villeins to get permission to bequeath their chattels.[65]

These conditions, profoundly contradictory as they were in certain respects, were bound to cause trouble, and they did. "Anyone who claims to hold in villeinage is likely to get good enough justice in the lord's court," Pollock and Maitland point out, and then realistically add—"provided that his opponent be not his lord."[66] Again, the lord's technical right to all of his villein's holdings frequently created an impossible situation for third parties who dealt with villeins. In effect, a serf could sue a third party and get substantial justice in the manorial courts, but the case was frequently different when a third party sued the villein in his lord's court. For the lord could and would upon occasion assert his prior right to all of the villein's worldly goods, thus leaving him judgment-proof—and the third party without recourse.[67]

Pollock and Maitland sum up the situation jocularly, but with a heavy undertone. They say:

> So the law in trying to work out its curious principle of "relative servitude" is driven to treat the serf as a highly privileged person, as one who can sue but cannot be sued upon a contract; and even when it allows that he can be sued, it can give the creditor but a poor chance of getting paid and will hardly prevent collusion between villeins and friendly lords. Again we see the ecclesiastical courts condemning the villein to pay money for his sins, fornication and the like, and then we see the villein getting into trouble with his lord for having thus expended money which in some sort was his lord's. The law with its idea of relative servitude seems to be fighting against the very nature of things and the very nature of persons.[68]

Substantially the same kind of unresolvable contradiction exists in our own contemporary villenage, known as the progressive income tax. Here too the lord, with his deep (and legal) interest in our incomes, becomes greatly disturbed about our expenditures if we register them as expenses offsetting the income to which he lays claim. Our army of bureaucrats, against which the minions of the British lords and kings would cut scarcely any figure at all, are fighting as much against "the nature of things and the very nature of persons" as was the curious villenage principle of "relative servitude." Let us hope that it will not take centuries to remove this contradictory principle.

For it did take Englishmen centuries to slough off villenage. The evolution was much delayed by greedy lords. As markets and therefore wealth increased in England from the thirteenth century onwards, men in villein status tended more and more to steal away from the manors, to make their fortunes as free farmers or tradesmen elsewhere.[69] Wherever they went, however, they carried their villein status with them, a status which accorded to their lord's proprietary rights over whatever they might amass. Some tragic cases are recorded in which lords destroyed men who, though villeins, had built honorable lives and substantial fortunes.[70] In one way or another, however, as time passed, more and more such cases found their way into the royal courts. And those courts, as noted by Bracton in the thirteenth century always ruled in favor of liberty, when in any way they could.[71] Holdsworth opines that by the fifteenth century, villenage was significant mainly because the lord could make money by manumitting the villein (the going rate being about one-third of the villein's holdings), and traces the rest of the development as follows:

> Villein status, then, had become merely a survival of an older social and economic order by the middle of the fifteenth century. Its life had been prolonged to the end of the sixteenth century because it served the purposes of the lawless, and because it sometimes gave to lords valuable rights over persons who prospered either on the land or in some of the other pursuits which afforded careers to the ambitious. When the Tudor dynasty had fulfilled its mission by restoring peace and good government to the country, when lords had made what they could out of their prosperous villeins by selling charters of manumission, this status, always frowned upon by the law, after a long and dishonourable old age, at length died a natural death. The law of villein status was never repealed. It simply fell into disuse because the persons to whom it applied had ceased to exist.[72]

The last case of villein status was decided in 1618. In 1707, a great English judge, Sir John Holt held that "by the common law no man can have a property in another."[74] It was to be many years before the implications of this principle were worked out. The mercantilist system dominated most of the seventeenth and eighteenth centuries, and the brief approximation of laissez faire as a ruling social principle in the nineteenth century was soon to give way to the neomercantilism which now prevails throughout the world. But the realization of the meaning of the right of private property which brought about Sir John Holt's statement has nevertheless had a profoundly significant result. By way of John Locke, David Hume, and the classical and neoclassical economists, it has led for the first time in history to a thoroughly consistent theory of human action; and that theory, again for the first time in history, supplies the framework of a system of political economy oriented with perfect coherence around the first principle of the right of private property: personal freedom.

Conclusion

My last reference is, of course, to the work of Ludwig von Mises, *Human Action.* The general science of human action, praxeology, which Mises has developed in that work, both explains and is itself illuminated by the history we have just surveyed.

Men act. Action means deliberate movement from a less satisfactory to a more satisfactory state of affairs. Satisfaction is subjective. If it is to be striven for effectively and broadly, universal personal freedom is the necessary condition. But freedom without broad, coherent property rights is a contradictory concept; the two are not separate and integrating concepts; they are the same idea analyzed with different ratiocinative techniques. I am not a free man unless I am in broad control of my person, unless I have a full property right in myself and, of course, in that which I acquire without infringing upon the equal right of others. When action is hampered by arbitrary controls, when acquisitions are subjected nonconsensually to fragmented proprietary dominions, freedom is diminished and society characterized by conflict and contradiction.

This was the trouble with feudalism and fully explains its failure to survive. It is the trouble, too, with our own uneasy, unstable neofeudalism or, if you prefer, neomercantilism, and explains why, with its terrible tensions and increasingly bitter conflicts, our present bundle of absurdities—this nonsystem—also will not survive much longer.

NOTES

1. Wilkinson v. Leland, 2 Pet. 657, 658 (1829), cited in Dietze, *In Defense of Property* 85 (1963).

2. From "An Arrow Against All Tyrants and Tyranny Shot from the Prison of Newgate," (1646), quoted in Czajkowski, *The Theory of Private Property in John Locke's Political Philosophy* 20 (Dissertation, Notre Dame University, 1941).

3. Cf. Kirzner, *The Economic Point of View* 146 et seq. (1960) for a valuable critical analysis of the development of economic theory. According to Kirzner, whose point of view I share, we owe to Mises alone among the great economists a thoroughly satisfying explication of the nature of economic science.

4. Mises, *Socialism; Human Action* 201 et seq. (1st ed. 1949). Cf. Hoff, *Economic Calculation in the Socialist Society (passim),* esp. at pp. 129-44 (trans. M. A. Michael, 1949).

5. As Mises himself has pointed out in *The Free and Prosperous Commonwealth* 68 (1962).

6. 2 Holdsworth, *History of English Law* 75—hereinafter cited "H".

7. *Histoire du droit Francais* 249-253, cited 2 H 75.

8. 2 H 76.

9. 2 H 78.

10. 2 H 71.

11. 2 H 76.

12. 2 H 40.

13. 2 H 37, n. 7.

14. 2 H 82. With his unrivalled insights into the conditions of primitive society with respect to consensual arrangements, Henry Maine concluded: "Anciently, the power of contracting is limited on all sides. It is limited by the rights of your family, by the rights of your distant kinsmen, by the rights of your covillagers, by the rights of your tribe, by the rights of your chief, and, if you contract adversely to the Church, by the rights of the Church." *Early History of Institutions* 57-8 (1875).

15. 2 H 61, 75. The probable kinship origin of early communities may have strengthened the egalitarian impulse. Cf. Maine, *Early Hist. Inst.* 72 (1875).

16. 2 H 182-84.

17. Ibid. at 184.

18. These were Glanvill's classifications, ix, c. 4; cf. 2 H 199-201, 379-381 and 3 H 29-30, 206-207, 491-500.

19. 1 Pollock & Maitland, *History of English Law* 210-11, hereinafter cited "P&M."

20. 1 P&M 276-77, citing *Liber de Antiquis Legibus* pp. lxxi-lxxvi.

21. 1 P&M 211.

22. 1 P&M 215.

23. 1 P&M 211, citing *Rot. Hund.*, ii, 673.

24. Coronation Charter of Henry I, c. 3, 4; quoted 1 P&M 306.

25. Ibid.

26. 1 P&M 299 et seq.

27. Ibid.

28. 1 P&M 303.

29. 1 P&M 299 et seq.

30. 1 P&M 288 et seq.

31. 1 P&M 250.

32. 1 P&M 246.
33. 2 H 76-8.
34. 1 P&M 245.
35. 2 H 63.
36. 1 P&M 310-30.
37. Ibid., and see 7 H 43.
38. *Commentaries,* ii, 63; quoted 1 P&M 288.
39. Cf. 1 P&M 313.
40. 2 P&M 27.
41. Cf. 2 H 116-17, 133-49.
42. Incidents from the reigns of Ethelred and Edward the Confessor are cited in 2 H 94.
43. 2 H 116-7.
44. Cf. 1 P&M 275-77, 337.
45. *Wealth of Nations* 373-96 (Mod. Lib.).
46. Ibid., 374.
47. Ibid., 377.
48. 1 P&M 276.
49. 1 P&M 271, 275.
50. "...if the tenant held at a full or even substantial rent, wardship and marriage would be unprofitable rights; the lord wanted rent-paying tenants; he did not want land thrown on his hands together with a troop of girls and boys with claims for food and clothing." 1 P&M 337.
51. Ibid.
52. 2 H 40.
53. 2 H 42.
54. Ibid.
55. Ibid.
56. 2 H 43.
57. Bracton, f. 4b, quoted in 1 P&M 395.
58. (Oxford, 1892).
59. Vinogradoff, 132.
60. Ibid., 131.
61. Ibid., 134.
62. Ibid., 131.
63. 1 P&M 397-98.
64. 1 P&M 399-400.
65. Ibid.
66. 1 P&M 369.
67. 1 P&M 403-4.
68. 1 P&M 404.
69. 3 H 491-509.
70. 3 H 502-4.
71. 1 P&M 400, citing Bracton f. 191 b.
72. 3 H 508.
73. Pigg v. Caley (1618) Noy 27.
74. Smith v. Gould (1707) 2 Ld. Raym. 1274.

10

George I. Mavrodes

PROPERTY

I WANT TO DISCUSS some aspects of the correlative notions of property and ownership, not in the metaphysical sense in which a substance may be said to have a property, but in the social, political, economic, or moral sense in which a person may be said to own an automobile. In this discussion I will make special reference to the socio-political philosophy which is sometimes called Objectivism, and which is particularly associated with the work of Ayn Rand.[1] The notion of private ownership is one of the fundamental concepts of this philosophical system. But it is not merely used in an unexamined way. Rand and her followers have provided a serious and sustained attempt to develop the moral aspects of the notion of ownership, to defend morally a very extensive right of ownership, and to ground this right upon a metaphysical relationship. Consequently, an examination of the relevant Objectivist principles and arguments promises to provide a fruitful approach to the topic at hand.

I will discuss three principal questions:

1. What is the meaning of "property," "ownership," etc? I.e., what philosophical analysis can we give of these terms?

2. How, morally, does one come to own a piece of property (if at all)? Or, to put perhaps the same problem in a different way, what moral justification can be given for ascribing the ownership of a particular thing, say an automobile, to one particular person rather than to another?

3. Is there a way in which the notion of property can be amended (or perhaps replaced) so as to provide us with one or more concepts which are more satisfactory for expressing our moral concerns and judgments?

The first two of these questions are discussed more or less together in the first major section of this chapter. The discussion there is carried forward largely by reference to a fictional, but by no means unrealistic, situation which is developed in various ways to illustrate various hypotheses. In the course of this discussion I argue that Objectivists appear to have overlooked one basic aspect of the institution of property and ownership, an aspect which gives rise to peculiarly difficult problems. I shall also argue that, apparently because of this oversight, Objectivists are mistaken about many of the practical political and social implications of their fundamental principles and lines of reasoning. Taken as they stand, for example, these principles imply that the present legal system of the United States extends the right of private ownership far too widely, providing for the private ownership of many things which, morally, ought never to be subject to such ownership. But this is, of course, just the opposite of the usual complaint of Objectivists about that legal system. I will also suggest that the principles which yield this conclusion are highly plausible and that perhaps they ought to be taken as they stand, with the consequence that our legal system ought to be altered, in at least some of its aspects, in a way just opposite to that commonly suggested by Objectivists.

The third question is explored very briefly in the second major section of this chapter, and there I propose a way in which the notion of property might be replaced in such a way as to provide more flexibility and precision in moral reasoning about the topics to which it has generally been applied.

I

Ownership: Production vs. Seizure

Who owns the chair? Let us turn now to consider a rather simple case, but one which leads rather directly, I think, to crucial questions. A man goes into the forest, selects a tree, and fells it. Then by himself, and by dint of considerable labor, skill, and inventiveness, he converts the wood into furniture—into chairs, tables, and beds. The first question

I want to pose is this: Who owns this furniture?

To Objectivists this must be a question of some importance, for they relate property quite closely to human freedom and to the values of a peculiarly human life. Rand writes, for example,

> The right to life is the source of all rights—and the right to property is their only implementation. Without property rights, no other rights are possible. Since man has to sustain his life by his own effort, the man who has no right to the product of his effort has no means to sustain his life. The man who produces while others dispose of his product is a slave.[2]

In another place she says, "It is the institution of private property that protects and implements the right to disagree—and thus keeps the road open to man's most valuable attribute (valuable personally, socially, and *objectively*): the creative mind."[3]

This line of thought strikes me as rather persuasive in its general thrust, if not in every application to which Objectivists might put it. Human life in the world is concerned, to a substantial degree, with the use and manipulation of physical objects. It is there that, in large part, we develop and exercise our creativity and our freedom of choice. And if we do not have a moral freedom here, if it is not morally open to us to decide effectively what use shall be made of many things, then it must also not be morally open to us to decide upon the preservation and development of our lives. For that preservation and development depends, in part, upon the use of things. I am inclined to agree with Objectivists, therefore, that the question of who owns the chair is representative of a very important class of questions.

What is ownership? The line of thought which I have been sketching assumes at least the rough outline of the answer to another question, that of what ownership consists in. Surely ownership must consist of some moral and/or legal *right* relative to the property which is owned. Here again Objectivists seem to me to be on the right track. Writing of "The New Fascism: Rule by Consensus" Rand says:

> Observe that both "socialism" and "fascism" involve the issue of property rights. The right to property is the right of use and disposal. Observe the difference in those two theories: socialism negates private property rights altogether, and advocates "the vesting of *ownership* and *control*" in the community as a whole, i.e., in the state; fascism leaves *ownership* in the hands of private individuals, but transfers *control* of the property to the government.
>
> Ownership without control is a contradiction in terms: it means "property," without the right to use it or to dispose of it. It means that the citizens retain the responsibility of holding property, without any of its advantages while the government acquires all the advantages without any of the responsibility.[4]

Is there a fairly rigorous way of formulating this point? For the present I propose to say that a certain agent owns a certain object if and only if he has the right to decide upon the disposition to be made of that object. And I will say that the owner's having such a right entails at least two things: (1) the fact that the owner has disposed of the object in a way contrary to some other human agent's preference is not, *per se,* evidence that the owner has done something which he ought not, and (2) the fact that some other human agent has disposed of the object in a way contrary to the owner's preference is, *per se,* evidence that this other agent has done what he ought not.[5] These definitions are not entirely satisfactory as they stand, in that the concept which they define is not as useful as might be desired. But I think they point in the right direction. What defects they have and how they may be amended are subjects for further discussion in this paper.

Production and ownership. Let us turn to our fictional case, then, and ask again, Who owns the chair? Objectivists will, I think, be quick to reply that the craftsman is, or at any rate should be, the true owner of the furniture. Having made it, he properly has the right to dispose of it—perhaps to use it himself or to trade it to one of his fellows. This may in fact be the correct answer to my question, but it will bear some examination. In the first place, it is worth noting that whoever owns this furniture, whether the craftsman or anyone else, did not acquire that ownership by the operation of the market, free or otherwise. No doubt we do come to own many things by acquiring them in the market, by trading for them. But this furniture is one of those pieces of newly created wealth of which the Objectivists properly remind us. If it is ever to have an owner it must have a first owner. But an item can enter the market only if it is already owned. Consequently, no matter how much we may admire the free market or how important it may in fact be, it logically cannot provide the fundamental mechanism of ownership. Unless there is some other way of acquiring property the market will never have a field for operation.

Some people may be tempted to overlook this fact because of the notion that my craftsman, in working to produce a chair, has exchanged his labor, skill, ingenuity, etc., for a chair. If we wish to speak in this way, however, we should be quite clear that the sense of "exchange" here is quite different from that which refers to the market. Of course, it makes perfectly good sense to speak of exchanging one's labor for a chair. One may work and take his pay in chairs, or, much more conveniently, he may take his pay in money and then exchange the money for a chair. One may even labor making chairs, say in a chair factory, and then exchange his pay for a chair. But this is fundamentally different from what a craftsman does. In the first place, what my craftsman does can be done by a single person. Robinson Crusoe can work and make a chair. But in the market sense of "exchange" he cannot exchange his labor, or anything else, for a chair. For there is no one else with whom to trade, and a market exchange logically requires two agents. Furthermore, in a free market the number of chairs which one can obtain for, say, a month's work will be a function of the supply and demand for chairs, of the supply and demand for labor of the sort which one can do, and, perhaps to a lesser degree, of one's skill in bargaining. But the number of chairs which one can *produce* in a month of work is not at all a function of those things. It is rather a function of one's skill in carpentry, of the availability of wood, of the sophistication of one's tools, etc. The market involves a fundamentally different sort of operation from that of the workshop. The Objectivist does well to remind us of the importance of the workshop, of the creation of new wealth. But the workshop also guarantees that the market cannot say the fundamental word on the matter of ownership. Something else must come first.[6]

With this observation in mind let us come back to the suggestion that the craftsman is the first owner of the chair. After all, he is the one who has brought the chair into existence. It is the product of his initiative, his foresight, his inventiveness, his skill, his labor. If it were not for him this chair would not exist at all. Since this is a new piece of wealth, and he is the one who has produced it, why should he not be the owner of it? And anyway, there is no one who appears to have a better claim upon the chair; in fact, it is hard to think of anyone else who has as strong a claim.

This last line of argument, that no one appears to have a better claim than the craftsman, strikes me as unsatisfactory. But it will come up again, and I propose to defer a discussion of it until later. The first line of argument, that one who brings new wealth into existence rightfully has the first claim upon it, I find very powerful and persuasive. I count it as one of the good services which Objectivists are doing for us that they remind us of this sometimes overlooked consideration.

Nevertheless, this consideration cannot be conclusive for the present case. For, alas, the chair is not *solely* the product of the craftsman's labor, etc. That labor, while necessary for the existence of the chair, is by no means sufficient for it. For he made it, we remember, out of a tree. And so this case leads us to a second, and more fundamental, question about ownership—*Who owns the tree?*

Owning what is not produced. At this point some reader may feel that he has been somewhat misled. Of course, he will say, if someone owns the tree and this craftsman has simply seized it without his consent and has converted it to his own use then naturally his title to the resulting product is clouded. The owner of the tree has a rightful claim upon that chair which was made from his tree. Perhaps we should say that he owns a part interest in it, or maybe we should even acknowledge his full ownership of it. The craftsman should first have bought the tree. Then his ownership of the chair would have been unclouded. But the way in which I told the story led the reader to suppose that nothing of the sort was necessary. He envisioned a primitive situation, a few people living on the edge of a vast forest, no one claiming the tree, and so on.

Well, to an extent, I sympathize with such a reader. That is, in fact, the situation which I, too, was imagining. But even so, who owns the tree? If the tree is ever to enter the market then it, too, must sometime have had a first owner who could not have acquired it in the market. Who is that owner and how did he come to own the tree?

One's first reaction, no doubt, is to reply that, in the situation envisaged, the tree had no owner at all, at least prior to its being cut down. This is presumably the answer which Rand herself would give. In discussing homesteading in the United States she says explicitly that the government was not the owner of the vacant western lands but was rather (and properly) the custodian of lands which were unowned until they were claimed by individual homesteaders.[7] In another connection she says, "All wealth is produced by somebody and belongs to somebody."[8] Taken seriously, this entails that the tree as it stands in the forest is not wealth (a peculiar claim to which I will return), and it suggests that perhaps it has no owner because it has not been produced by anyone. This suggestion is made perfectly explicit in one of Rand's novels. There we find the hero making a long speech which Rand later reprinted under the subtitle, "This is the Philosophy of Objectivism." And in that speech the hero, John Galt, says, "The source of property rights is the law of causality. All property and all forms of wealth are produced by man's mind and labor."[9] Now, the law of causality links the chair with the craftsman; he is the cause of the chair and perhaps this may give him a property right in it. But he is not linked in this way with the tree as it stands in the forest. He is not the cause of the tree. It is not, in Rand's words, "produced by man's mind and labor." So if the fictional John Galt is correct about the source of property rights then the tree is not, *and cannot be,* a piece of property. It cannot be owned by the craftsman or by anyone else.

This line of argument, furthermore, is not plausibly to be attributed to a slip of Rand's pen in writing a novel. For she repeats it in another version in a very thoughtful article on copyrights and patents. She explains there that a law of nature cannot be patented by its discoverer though an invention can be patented by its inventor (and it is clear that she thinks this is as it should be). Why cannot the law of nature be patented? Rand gives two reasons, one of which is relevant here. It is that the discoverer has not created the law of nature but only discovered it, while the inventor has created the idea involved in his invention.[10] This argument looks like the complement of the one applied to the craftsman earlier. There it was suggested that perhaps one owns a thing if one creates it; here, that if one does not create a thing then one does not acquire original ownership of it. And, of course, if there is no original ownership there is no transferred ownership either. Such a thing cannot enter the market.

Now, this argument, like its complement, strikes me as rather plausible. It has, however, at least two peculiar consequences. One of them directly concerns the characteristic political, social, and economic proposals of Objectivists. Those familiar with the writings of Rand and others of this school will know that they often complain that our present systems do not give enough scope for private ownership, that many items which should rightly be private property have been seized by governments for "public" ownership. So we hear proposals that the highway system should be sold, the municipal water system should be sold, the fire department should be sold, etc. These writers are, however, not known for insisting that our present legal systems allow for the private ownership of far too much. Yet if Rand's argument is correct then that is clearly the case. For the legal system of the United States and of most modern nations (perhaps the Communist nations are exceptions) clearly vests the ownership of certain trees in certain individuals. And in many of those cases it is perfectly clear that the trees in question have *not* been produced by man's mind and labor. And this is plainly opposed to the principle and the arguments which Rand puts forward. But of course it is not just a matter of trees. The more or less capitalist nations generally recognize and allow the private ownership of land, of mineral deposits, of water rights, and so on. And things of this sort—things whose existence is not the result of human action—commonly bulk very large in the total roster of private property. And therefore, of course, trade involving such items forms a substantial part of the market activities in such nations. Objectivists, however, are not noted for their condemnation of this feature of our legal systems.

This consequence of Rand's principle I take to be of the greatest importance and I shall return to a further discussion of it. I turn here, however, to a consideration of the second peculiar consequence of supposing that the tree, as it stands in the forest, has no owner.

If no one owns the tree then the craftsman does not own the tree. Ownership, however, was defined as the right to decide upon the disposition to be made of the property. Perhaps, then, if the craftsman did not own the tree he did not have the right to decide upon its disposition. But he surely did undertake to make and to implement such a decision. He decided that the tree would be disposed of by being cut down and converted into furniture. And he translated this decision into action—he in fact cut down the tree and constructed the furniture. And in doing so he apparently did what he had no right to do. Now, if one comes into possession of an object by doing what one has no right to do, and if, to make the case stronger, one *could not* have possessed the object without doing what one had no right to do, then surely a doubt is cast over one's claim to be the proper owner of that object. But that seems to be the case here. If no one is the owner of the tree as it stands in the forest then the craftsman's claim to own the chair is seriously clouded.

This result perhaps strikes us as paradoxical. I suspect that part of the reason may be something like this. There is a strong temptation to think of ownership, especially for practical purposes, in terms of legal technicalities and formalities. When someone refers to owning a house, for example, we may think of the carefully executed deed, registered in the county courthouse, etc. And then there is no particular difficulty in thinking that there is some object—a tree, a tract of land, etc.—for which the specified formality has not been performed. But in this discussion we are construing the notion of ownership not in terms of formalities but rather in terms of rights. To claim, then, that no one owns a certain object is to claim that no one has the specified rights relative to that object. And that is a powerful, and troublesome, claim.

It may be possible to avoid this second consequence of the claim that no one owns the tree by examining the notion of ownership more closely. Before trying that, however, let us examine another proposal, that is, that everyone owns the tree as it stands.

In the claim that everyone owns the tree the word "everyone" may be understood either collectively or distributively. The collective sense is not of much use to us here and may be disposed quickly. If the tree was owned by a collective which includes everyone then it was not owned by the craftsman as an individual. But he seized it for his own use. Consequently his claim to the resulting chair is clouded. He should no doubt first have purchased the tree from the collective—say from the tribal department of forests—and then he should have had a clear right to use it.

In the distributive sense there may still be a couple of interpretations possible. It might be held that each individual owns a part interest in the tree. But even if this is construed in such a way as to make it differ from the collective sense (perhaps by referring to a *separable* part interest) it will be of no use to us. For if this were the case then the craftsman, in converting the entire tree to his own use, would have infringed upon those part interests which were not his. Apparently nothing but the full ownership of the entire tree by each individual (distributively) will do.

Now, if each individual owns the tree then the craftsman owns the tree. If the craftsman owns the tree, then he has a right. . ., etc. That seems to be clear sailing. But of course the ownership of the tree by everyone, distributively, is theoretically absurd. For there might be conflicting decisions as to the disposition of the tree. One person might decide that the tree should be felled and made into furniture while another decides that it should stand in the forest as the sacred tree beneath which he shall worship his gods. But it cannot be the case that both of these persons have the right to make the corresponding dispositions of the tree. Consequently, it cannot be true, in any sense which is useful to us here, that everyone owns the tree.

This should not, however, blind us to the fact that, under some circumstances, this absurdity generates very few practical difficulties, and consequently people can proceed as if everyone owned the tree. If the demand for trees is small compared to the number of trees then it will only rarely happen that two people will select the same tree for conflicting uses. And even when they do it will usually be easy for one of them to shift to another tree. Since that solution is cheap, while conflict is expensive, there will usually be a peaceful solution.

It may also be worth noting that the situations we are here exploring are by no means purely hypothetical or limited to primitive situations. Right down to the present time we have proceeded, by and large, as though everyone owned the atmosphere and consequently had a right to do to it whatever he wanted. As long as the practical ways of acting on the atmosphere were small in scope compared to the capacity of the atmosphere the resulting problems were few and small. Occasionally, of course, there might be a conflict. If a heavy smoker settled himself next to a fastidious lady in the railway coach she might slap his face or demand that the conductor eject him. But usually (acting, perhaps, on the principle that he who smokes is more privileged than he who merely breathes) she would simply move away. Now, however, effects upon the atmosphere are no longer small in scope. A single industrial plant may dump enormous volumes of sulphur dioxide and other noxious gases into the air each day. Avoiding these fumes is no longer a matter of moving across town but rather of moving to the southern hemisphere—if, indeed, they can be avoided even there. Those who want to breathe clean air can no longer cheaply avoid conflicts with those who have other uses in mind for the atmosphere. Consequently, such people are now preparing to fight.

One might try to refer the conflict to the market for adjudication. Clean air is a consumer good, it may be said, a commodity just as much as good food and fine wine. If I want it let me trade for it in the free market, and there its value will be determined. Let me buy an air purifying machine, or let me pay the industrialist for his contractual (and enforceable) promise not to pollute.

It would, I think, be a mistake at this juncture to reject this line of argument on the grounds that air is not a commodity, that one ought not to have to pay in order to breathe, etc. It should be countered, rather, by an argument of the same form and appealing to the same principles but whose force lies in just the opposite direction. A dumping ground for industrial wastes is a producer good, just as much as is a drill press or an architectural drawing. The industrialist does not expect someone to give him these latter goods free of charge. Why should he expect to seize the atmosphere for nothing? Let him rather pay me for the privilege of using it as a dump. And if I do not care to sell then let him raise his bid, just as he would on the floor of the New York Stock Exchange. Or, if in the end he thinks my price too high, let him take the alternative which the free market always provides. Let him do without the atmospheric dumping ground—let him keep his sulphur dioxide to himself.

Now, we cannot consistently act upon both of these lines of reasoning, for they lead to quite different results. But we cannot choose between them without deciding the sort of question with which we have been engaged—Who is the first owner of the air and how does he come by that right?

Let us return to the tree as perhaps a more manageable case. The suggestions we have considered so far alike in that they assume that initially everyone has the same relevant relationships with the tree and the same rights (if any) with respect to it. But so far we seem not to have succeeded in generating anyone's special ownership of the chair upon this basis. It is possible that we should begin by assuming that *initially* someone has a special relationship to the tree, perhaps, that of ownership. If such an assumption is true then perhaps everything from then on can be handled well enough by the market and the causality theory of property. The craftsman can buy the tree (unless he happens to be its original owner), he can then make the chair which he will then clearly own, etc. But it is not at all clear how the notion of initially different rights relative to the tree can be worked out. If one believes in God (as I do) and if he believes that God created the world *ex nihilo* (as I also do) then perhaps he will hold that God is the original owner of the tree. This would, I suppose, be a special case of the causality theory of property. If God gave the tree to the craftsman—a special case of the transfer of property rights—then the craftsman would own it. No doubt. But unless we had some reason to think that God has given the tree to the craftsman rather than to his neighbor we seem to be no better off than before. Of course, if we believed that God was interested in morality (as I do), and if we discovered some morally relevant and unique relation which the craftsman (or someone else) has to the tree, then that might serve as a reason for believing that God had given it to him rather than to someone else. But this is just what we have been looking for and have so far failed to find. In fact, it seems that unless we discover such a relation any assertion that people differ initially in their relationship to the tree will be morally arbitrary. Let us therefore make another attempt on the basis of initial similarity.

Rights without ownership. Our definition of ownership presumably entails that the owner of a tree has, among his other rights, the right to cut down the tree. In discussing the suggestion that no one owns the tree we interpreted this to imply that no one has the right to cut it down. But perhaps this was too hasty. If ownership involves a large set of rights then one may fail to own a tree because he does not have the full set of rights relative to it, but he may nevertheless have some right, e.g., the right to cut it down. So while it may be true that initially no one owns the tree it may also be true that initially everyone has some right relative to it. Furthermore, though there is an absurdity in supposing that everyone (distributively) owns the tree there may be some right such that it is not absurd to suppose that everyone has that right relative to the tree. Let me list a few alternative possibilities of rights that apply equally to all, and which resolve the problem of ownership.

1. Everyone has the right to fell any standing tree, and he who does so thereby becomes the owner of the fallen tree.

2. Everyone has the right to fell any standing tree and to trim off its branches, and he who does so is the owner of the resulting log.

3. Everyone has the right to mark any unmarked tree by painting his initials on it, and he thereby acquires ownership of it.

4. Everyone has the right to claim any unowned tree by marking it and then offering a sacrifice on top of Mt. Cloudpiercer. He who does so owns the tree.

5. Everyone has the right to claim any unowned *set* of trees by posting, in the village square, a notice of his claim which defines the set, e.g., "I claim all of the trees which now stand, and which shall stand in the future, in the valley of the Broad River from its source in the mountains to its mouth at the edge of the sea." Whoever does so thereby comes to own all of the trees so specified.

6. Everyone has the right to claim any unowned tree by marking it and then giving a feast for all of his fellows. He who does so comes to own the tree.

7. Everyone has the right to claim any unowned tree by marking it and then giving each of his fellows a useful

tool, such as an axe or a saw. He who does so comes to own the tree.

This list of alternative possible initial rights leading to ownership could be continued indefinitely. It may be instructive, however, to consider this set briefly. They are alike in asserting that until someone takes a specified action relative to a certain tree everyone has the same right relative to that tree, i.e., the right to take that action. They thus assert an initial parity of rights. And so far as I can see the assertion that everyone (distributively) has any one of these initial rights relative to a given tree does not generate any theoretical absurdity. These proposed rights, then, satisfy my first condition.

They appear also to satisfy my second condition for they all specify that anyone who exercises his right by taking the required action thus acquires a new and special right, i.e., he becomes the first owner of something. And this would solve the problem which has thus far troubled us. There is, however, a very important corollary. It is that whenever a person exercises an initial right of this sort then everyone else suffers a corresponding diminution of his rights. In the present case if one person should seize a tree by the exercise of any of these seven rights then no one else could any longer have any of these rights relative to that tree. It seems to me that this is a consequence of the first magnitude. We must soon deal with it.

These features my seven alternative putative rights have in common. From there on, however, these proposals differ. (1) and (2) differ from the others, for example, in that they do not yield ownership of standing trees. They also differ from the others in that they require work to be done on the tree, work of a sort that may reasonably be thought to move in the direction of making the tree more useful to human beings. (They are thus similar to the U.S. homestead laws.) (2) differs from (1) in requiring *more* such work. The others all require something, but what they require is not of itself a start toward converting the tree into something more useful. They are all variants of claiming as distinguished from working.

(5) differs from the remainder in that it offers the acquisition of enormous ownership with a minimum of effort. (3) is somewhat similar but yields more modest results. (4) differs from the others in that it requires a substantial effort on the part of the claimant, but this involves neither working on the tree nor (apparently) conferring a benefit on his fellows. (6) and (7) require such benefits; (7), unlike (6), requires a benefit which might be thought to contribute directly to the advancement of industry and commerce. And so we have here a variety of possible initial rights. But they are not all compatible with each other. If we are to follow out this line then somehow we must choose between these rights (or, of course, we may choose one of the innumerable others which might be added to the list). How could such a choice be made?

No metaphysical criterion. Perhaps the first thing to notice is that there does not seem to be a ready metaphysical principle which yields a clear answer to this question. Perhaps one is tempted to adapt the causality theory to this sort of situation by proposing that one acquires original ownership of only those things which are at least in part the products of one's labor, initiative, skill, etc. One comes to own, that is, these things in which one has "mixed his labor." Such a view would presumably eliminate suggestions (3) through (7). Unfortunately, however, it does not discriminate between (1) and (2), nor between these and their numerous possible variants. And this is a failing of considerable importance. An ordinary human artifact is the result of doing some work upon some raw material or resource. Both the resource and the work are indispensible to the existence of the artifact, but in different artifacts the proportion of the final value which is attributable to the labor varies a great deal. Even for very similar things it varies with different circumstances. When trees are plentiful and the demand for lumber is small then the market value of a log will not greatly exceed the market value of the labor involved in felling and trimming it. In fact, it may not exceed the labor value at all. In that situation there is a good bit of plausibility in vesting the ownership of the log in the woodsman, for the value in the log seems almost entirely attributable to his work. But when trees become scarce and the demand for lumber rises, then the value of a log may greatly exceed the value of the labor in it. (Another way of putting this, of course, is to say that the value of a standing tree has increased.) In this circumstance it will seem implausible that a man should acquire the ownership of a valuable log merely by felling and trimming a tree, for now it will seem that the artifact contains too small a proportion of his own labor. To develop the notion of ownership along these lines requires that we decide how much work is to be "mixed" in a product in order to confer original ownership. But the principle of causality cannot help us with this. Nor does any similar but more suitable principle come to mind.

Perhaps someone thinks of asking why it is implausible that a person should acquire a very valuable log by doing only a small amount of work. Does this judgment rest upon some view of the transcendental value of work? I think not. It rests rather upon the "important corollary" which I mentioned a few paragraphs earlier. When trees are scarce and the demand for lumber is high then the right to acquire first ownership of a tree (or log) is an important and valuable right. But when one person exercises this right all other persons are deprived of the corresponding right. What is implausible is that they should thus suffer the loss of a valuable right without receiving something of comparable value in return.

Now, there is some plausibility in the suggestion that the woodsman's work confers some benefit on his fellows. He contributes his share toward the rise of industry and commerce, and perhaps this is a boon to all. But it is implausible that his fellows should properly suffer the loss of very valuable rights in return for only a small contribution on his part. That is why, if one is attracted to schemes like (1) and (2) at all, one wants to demand a sufficient amount of work. But no metaphysical principle seems to provide a ready answer to the question of how much is sufficient.

Perhaps, therefore, we may be inclined to take suggestions (3) through (7) more seriously. Compared to (1) and (2) they possess at least one marked advantage. They come to grips with the problem of the human ownership of things which are not themselves the result of human action. These suggestions deal directly with that aspect of ownership which involves Man the Seizer more than Man the Producer.

This aspect of ownership seems to fall into a peculiar Objectivist blind spot. In fact, this blind spot is one of the most striking features of Objectivist treatments of the topic of property. I have already quoted Rand's statements that "All wealth is produced by somebody and belongs to somebody" and "All property and all forms of wealth are produced by man's mind and labor." In a discussion of inheritance Nathaniel Branden assumes the same point. He writes, "In considering the issue of inherited wealth, one must begin by recognizing that the crucial right involved is not that of the heir but of the original *producer* of the wealth. . . . When people denounce inherited wealth it is the *right of the producer* that they, in fact, are attacking,"[11] Taken as they stand (and taken as referring to human beings, rather than to God) these assertions are simply and plainly false. There is plenty of wealth which consists of standing timber, lands, mineral deposits, and so on, which was never produced by any human being at all. And plenty of that wealth is inherited. Given the legal and social system of the United States it is just absurd to suppose that all wealth is "produced by man's mind and labor."

One could, of course, try to salvage these claims by providing an arbitrary special definition of the term "wealth." Under this definition an automobile would constitute wealth but the land on which the Empire State Building is built would not. Such a definition would, of course, break completely with common usage. But it has a more serious defect. It would be, in an important way, vacuous. Within our present system it is a fact that land, minerals, timber, etc.—regardless of whether we call them wealth or something else—will be the functional equivalents of wealth. For in a free market they are readily exchangeable for money, automobiles, and other artifacts. And they are exchangeable in this way, of course, because they are valuable. That is a fact which cannot be altered by a definition.

The statements which I quoted above may be interpreted in yet another way—a way, however, which is probably not intended by their authors. We might read them as claiming that, *properly speaking*, only artifacts can be owned and constitute wealth. This would imply that our present social and legal system distorts the true and proper order of ownership. We *ought not* to allow for the ownership of land, minerals, etc. Consequently, if our legal system was as it should be, such things could not enter the market and they would not be exchangeable for artifacts. They would not be, in that case, the functional equivalents of wealth.

This interpretation, as I say, is probably not that intended by Rand and Branden. But we have already seen earlier that it expresses a position which is consistent with—indeed, apparently demanded by—their fundamental principle and lines of argument. It is, however, a farily radical position. Perhaps we should look at the variants of ownership-by-claiming first.

Of these (5) is the least plausible. One puts it first, perhaps, by saying that (5) yields too much for too little effort. But the real reason, I think, is the one we discussed above. (5) takes away too much without a just return. It allows one person to deprive everyone else of an important asset without recompense. So (5) is unsuitable as a moral principle. (3) is not as bad as (5) because it is more modest, but it seems to share the fundamental defect of (5). It allows for one to be deprived of a right without recompense. If (5) is unsuitable then so also is (3).

(4) is somewhat special. If one believes that God is the original owner of the tree, *and* if one also believes that God is interested in trading the tree for a sacrifice, then perhaps (4) is straightforward enough. Or if one believes that everyone will derive some benefit from the offering of the sacrifice then perhaps (4) will seem to be suitable. But otherwise it seems to share the defect of (3) and (5).

(6) and (7) clearly avoid this defect. They require that one confer a benefit on his fellows when, by exercising one of his rights, he reduces the scope of their rights. This strikes me as an advantage, one which (6) and (7) share with (1) and (2), but not with (3), (4), and (5). But there are some other interesting features of (6) and (7). First, they seem very close to, if not identical with, the earlier suggestion that perhaps the tree is initially owned by everyone collectively. For (6) and (7) can be construed as specifying the way in which an individual can purchase a tree from the collective. Or, at least, they seem to be the functional equivalents of such a stipulation. Thus if in the end we opt for something like (6) or (7) we will be, in effect, opting for the view that an initial collective ownership of natural resources is more fundamental than, and basic to, the individual ownership of artifacts.

A second interesting feature is this. (7) does not seem to be clearly superior to (6). And if, as I think, what is operative in (6) and (7) is the principle of recompense for the loss of a valuable right, then there is no reason why (7) should be superior. For while the growth of industry may be one way in which a person might be repaid there is no reason to suppose it is the only way. A feast is also an item of value, and so are many other things, and one might be repaid for his diminished rights in many different ways. But if this is so it reflects back on (1) and (2). If in the end we opt for something like one of them we should do so on the grounds that it provides the most satisfactory repayment for diminished rights, and not on the grounds the new owner has "mixed his labor" in the artifact.

Some consequences. Within the notion of property with which we have been working I can think of no better solution to our problem than to adopt some variant of (1), (2), (6), or (7). That is, we should ascribe to every person a right to acquire original ownership of either certain natural resources or certain artifacts on the basis of some benefit which he confers on his fellows. But I can think of no clean-cut way of deciding just how much, and of what sort, the benefit should be. This must inevitably be a matter of judgment, taking into account an indefinitely large range of factors, many of which can be quantified only very roughly. And, so far as I can see, it must be a political judgment.[12] That is, it must be a judgment made on behalf of whatever group is involved, and made in whatever way that group provides for such judgments. But we must not be surprised if thoughtful people differ in such judgments, nor can we expect all such differences to be resolved by appeals to "rationality," "the facts," or "principles." This is the first consequence which I see. It is, perhaps, mildly disturbing.

The second is perhaps more disturbing. It is that property rights will apparently be relative, not absolute. I have spoken here repeatedly about "others," "one's fellows," "everyone," etc., but without any further elucidation. But these terms are not without their problems. Just who are one's fellows, after all; and to whom does "everyone" refer? Suppose that the tribe decides on some way in which a person can acquire the ownership of a tree and that my craftsman fulfills these requirements. Then he owns the tree, he owns the furniture, etc. Well and good. But what of the tribe which lives across the mountains? Did they also have an initial right relative to that tree, a right which has now been curtailed without recompense to them? It will be true, of course, that they live further away from the tree than does my craftsman's tribe, but it is not easy to see how this geographical fact bears upon their initial moral rights. The geographical fact does, of course, bear upon their probable interest in the tree. They are likely to be unconcerned with what happens to that tree, so no practical problem may arise. But of course they *may* be concerned. They may cross the mountains and think of seizing the furniture. If it comes just to a fight then presumably the stronger will prevail. But what happens if we try morals? The craftsman claims to own the furniture—that is, he claims a moral right to decide upon its disposition. In support of this he points out that he did just what was required. He mixed his labor with the tree, he gave a feast for the tribe, he executed the specified documents, and so on.

He has his case. But against him the newcomers contend that the requirements which he met were not their requirements. And the benefits which he conferred did not accrue to them but to someone else. But he did appropriate for his own use a natural resource to which he had no better right than they. They seem to have a case also. Perhaps we can say that if the newcomers seize the furniture then they will be appropriating his labor for themselves, and that would presumably be unjust. But the craftsman, too, has appropriated something to which these newcomers have a right, and perhaps he therefore rightfully owes them something. What the proper adjustment would be is, of course, another difficult and disputable matter of judgment.[13]

What this problem involves more generally is the likelihood that ownership and property should be construed as relative to a group rather than as absolute. This is because of the likelihood that the requirements will be set by some group which does not include all those whose initial rights are curtailed, and the likelihood that the benefits exacted will also accrue primarily to that limited group. The craftsman's title to the furniture is good relative to his tribe. If one of his fellows should seize his chair it would be a simple case of theft. But against the newcomers his title is clouded. If one of them were to seize his chair the case would be rather more complex. This seems to me a troublesome consequence, but one which apparently follows nevertheless. Perhaps something like it underlies the rather common conviction that whatever may be the morality of military conquest it is not just the same thing as armed robbery.

Recapitulation. Before going on to the second (and shorter) section of this paper perhaps we can review briefly the steps of the argument which we have just followed.

A. The morally justified assignment of property rights in artifacts seems to require a prior assignment of rights to seize and use natural resources.

B. These latter rights cannot be assigned on the basis of causality, production, etc., and no other metaphysical principle comes to mind for the purpose. In the absence of a morally relevant reason for disparity it seems necessary to assign an initial parity of rights in this regard.

C. Any proposed right which will resolve the problem of ownership will be such that its exercise by one person will reduce its scope for all other persons. Hence it seems only just that its exercise be linked to the conferring of a benefit upon those others.

D. A judgment as to what that benefit should be must be a political judgment made on behalf of, and in accordance with the political mechanisms of, some concerned group.

E. The property rights so generated will be relative to that group.

II

Do We Need "Ownership"?

Limited ownership. I have already mentioned Rand's essay on patents and copyrights. In that essay she makes a further provocative suggestion. She notes that these forms of property have a limited life, and, making it clear that she thinks this is proper, she asks why it should be so. Her reply is that the thing patented or copyrighted—e.g., a novel, or the idea embodied in a new machine—unlike a material object, is not consumed and destroyed as it is used. *Hamlet* is not worn out by many readers (though the printed books are worn out), nor is the idea of the wheel destroyed by being often used (though material wheels are so destroyed). These things have a naturally unlimited life. But, she goes on to say, it would be intolerable for us still to be paying royalties to the heirs of the inventer of the wheel. That would give him and his heirs a lien on the work and progress of unlimitea future generations. Such an arrangement, Rand says, "would lead to the opposite of the very principle on which it is based: it would lead, not to the earned reward of achievement, but to the unearned support of parasitism." And to avoid this the life of the ownership should properly be limited.[14]

If I understand the underlying reasoning here it seems to me rather persuasive. I think it goes something like this. A person who writes a novel or invents a new device may do the rest of us a good service thereby. It is therefore only fair that he should have the opportunity to benefit from his own work and ingenuity. Hence we acknowledge his ownership of that idea and he may charge us for its use. But the service which he does us is not unlimited, after all. (We should remember that had the wheel not been invented when it was someone else would probably have invented it later on; had a certain novel not been written some other would have been published, etc.) Since his service to us is limited it is also proper that the right we confer upon him be limited. Now, for material objects it does not matter if we confer an unlimited ownership. Nature itself will put an end to that ownership soon enough. Regardless of what the certificate of title may say, my automobile will rust in a few years and my ownership of it will perish. But since the life of ideas is unlimited the ownership conferred upon their creators must be limited to a specific term. After that they properly pass into the public domain, to be used freely by anyone.

To me this line of argument is persuasive, and its relation to what was sketched earlier will perhaps be obvious. But there is no reason why it should be limited to "intellectual property" (as Rand calls it). If a copyright should properly expire 50 years after the author's death[15] there seems to be no reason why a homesteader should acquire a title which will pass to his heirs and assigns without end. Land, if not as long-lived as ideas, is yet so nearly so as to make the difference inconsequential. It is intolerable, I suggest, that the accidents attending its seizure long ago should burden it forever. If we have not a moral duty to pay royalties to the heirs of the inventor of the wheel then we likewise have no moral duty to pay rent to the heirs of the homesteaders of the Santa Clara valley.

The general principle involved here is perhaps of most interest to us, but it may be worth saying something more about this illustration. It might be objected that there would be insurmountable practical difficulties in returning land to the public domain. A plot of ground cannot be used by everyone as can an idea, etc. Perhaps so, but this means that we must become more ingenious. Maybe, for example, what is needed is a scheme of land taxation which will provide a proper share of the expenses of government, but which will also, over and above those expenses, recover the total value of the land periodically. This additional money might then be made available to the citizens as "opportunity grants," money which could be claimed and used by fulfilling certain requirements, "homesteaded" as it were. So we might seek to provide for every generation the functional equivalent of the open lands in the west.

Fragmented Ownership. The idea of temporally limited ownership seems to me well worth investigation for application in many areas. But it is only one example of a more general strategy. Think for a moment of owning a house. If I own a house I have, probably, a number of rights with respect to it. A right to paint it green, a right to remodel the bathroom, a right to live in it myself, to rent it to someone else, to sell it, or to bequeath it to my heirs at my death. These rights, along with others, are generally lumped together in the notion of owning a house. But there seems to be no reason in logic or in the essential nature of houses or people for supposing that these rights must always go together. There is nothing inherently absurd in supposing that one has a right to live in a house but not to rent it to someone else, or that he has the right to rent it but not to bequeath it to his son. Would not our thinking, then, on these matters be rendered more flexible and precise if we declined to talk of property rights as a whole and turned instead to talk of these several and distinct rights? I suggest that it would.

If we are faced with the problem of deciding who is the proper owner of a certain object we may find a certain person who seems to have a claim in this regard, and no one who has a better claim. In fact, we may find no one else who has as good a claim. The terms in which we set this problem seem to require an all or nothing decision. Someone has to be the owner of the thing, either this person or someone else. But this person, by hypothesis, has the best claim, so we must acknowledge him as the owner. We will thus, perhaps, be forced to ignore entirely those weaker claims which were in competition with his.

If, on the other hand, we could pose the problem in more flexible terms every claim might more readily be given its due. If our conceptual machinery did not require us to lump all of these rights together we might more easily see that this person is justly entitled to some rights, perhaps to more rights than anyone else, but not to every right pertaining to this object. To the others we could also accord their lesser share. There might be good reason, for example, to accord someone the right to live in a certain house until his death, but to deny him the right to bequeath it to his heirs. In some ways that is like what we now call "owning a house," and in other ways it differs. But it is awkward and imprecise to carry on a discussion of this case in terms of whether this person has been denied the right to own this property. He has been accorded some rights and denied others. The discussion should properly focus upon what can be said for and against each of these rights. But the notion of property, as currently understood, is probably too much of a mixed bag to be useful in such a discussion.

I suggest that if we are to think properly about the moral relations of man to his artifacts and to the natural world—indeed, if we are to apply to these problems some of the fundamental principles and arguments of Objectivists—we must be prepared to separate the conglomeration of rights which goes under the name "property." I therefore propose that this concept be phased out of serious discussions and replaced by those elements of which it is composed.

NOTES

1. Thinkers who are largely in sympathy with these views sometimes refer to themselves as "Libertarians," and, particularly when discussing economics, as defenders of "*laissez faire* capitalism" or the "free market." Rand herself says, "The name I have chosen for my philosophy is *Objectivism.*" Ayn Rand, *For the New Intellectual* (New York: Signet Books, 1961), p. viii. I shall follow her choice here.

2. Ayn Rand, *Capitalism: The Unknown Ideal* (New York: Signet Books, 1967), p. 322. This book consists mostly of previously published articles and excerpts.

3. *Ibid.*, p. 19.

4. *Ibid.*, pp. 202, 203.

5. It may be important to notice that rights are here defined by reference to the possible acts and preferences of other *human* agents. Thus, that a snowstorm prevents an owner from getting to his house or that termites reduce it to dust does not constitute an infringement upon that owner's property rights. Those rights can be infringed only by humans.

6. I am not sure whether Rand ever recognizes this distinction. I can recall no explicit mention of it in her writings. In one place her fictional hero, John Galt, speaks of a man on a desert island learning from reality that "life is a value to be bought and that thinking is the only coin noble enough to buy it." (*For the New Intellectual,* pp. 127, 128.) Taken seriously, this passage exhibits the confusion which the distinction would resolve. But perhaps the talk of "buying" here is merely an incautious metaphor.

7. *Capitalism,* p. 123.

8. *Ibid.*, p. 14.

9. *For the New Intellectual,* p. 183.

10. *Capitalism,* p. 130.

11. Nathaniel Branden, "Common Fallacies about Capitalism," in *Capitalism,* p. 92. (Emphasis in the original.)

12. Rand seems to recognize this in her discussion of homesteading. She says that the government "defines objectively impartial rules by which potential owners may acquire them [i.e., ownerless resources]." But the discussion there is very brief and may not be decisive for Rand's views.

13. Of course, the newcomers have probably been appropriating for themselves the resources in their territory so on these grounds they owe my craftsman something too. Perhaps these accounts come out about

even, and no adjustment is morally necessary. But in some cases the accounts clearly are not even. For example, the population of the U.S. appropriates the world's natural resources at a *per capita* rate which vastly exceeds that of Bolivian Indians. Perhaps, therefore, our title to the resulting artifacts is not entirely unclouded as against their claims.

14. *Capitalism,* pp. 130-132.

15. Rand thinks this arrangement, that of Great Britain, is the best for copyrights. *Ibid.*

11

Edwin G. Dolan

ENVIRONMENTAL POLICY AND PROPERTY RIGHTS

THE ONGOING process of social criticism places property institutions under constant attack and review. In the course of this process, advocates of private property are continually called upon to reply to new challenges and to provide renewed justification for the institutions they defend. At the present time one of the strongest challenges to private property institutions comes in the area of environmental policy. There is a growing consensus among environmental economists that the various aspects of the natural environment should be viewed as multiple-purpose, multiple-user, natural assets, owned in common, which must be managed through some collective choice mechanism if they are to be developed, used, and conserved efficiently.

In terms of practical policy, the specific management mechanism most favored is the imposition of residual charges on pollution sources. Now, I would not want to be accused of failure to recognize that a strong case can be made in favor of such charges. The case is particularly strong when it is confined to comparison with the alternative of piecemeal regulation, with the basic common property management approach accepted as a parameter of the discussion. But there is an ingredient missing from much of the policy discussion. This missing ingredient, upon which the present paper will focus, is the case to be made against the whole concept of managing the environment through public policymaking.

Before proceeding to the main analysis, let us pause to review some basic concepts. At the heart of all discussions of environmental economics is the concept of externalities. In the most general sense, an externality can be said to exist whenever an economic activity carried out by some A has an effect on the welfare of some B who is not voluntarily a party to that activity. For our present purposes, such a general definition is too broad. In what follows, we will find it useful to distinguish between three separate species of the genus externality, namely:

Invasions. An invasion will be said to occur whenever party A steals, destroys, or trespasses upon property nominally belonging to party B.

Price effects. A causes B to suffer an adverse price effect when his economic activities increase the demand or decrease the supply for some commodity of which B is a buyer or potential buyer; or increase the supply or decrease the demand for some commodity of which B is a seller or potential seller.

Crowding effects. A causes B to suffer from an adverse crowding effect when his increased use of property held in common with B reduces B's opportunity to use that same property to his own advantage.

(Note that although each of these effects is defined in terms of harm done to B by A, each has its equivalent in terms of beneficial interaction.)

It is important to recognize that this classification of externalities is dependent upon certain conceptions of property rights. Let us use the term *private property* to refer to any arrangement under which a single party is vested with the right to exclude others from the exercise of a given property right, and *common property* to an arrangement under which, within a certain defined community, no individual member has the right to exclude any other member from the exercise of a certain property right. Common property, in turn, can be subdivided into *regulated* and *unregulated* types, according to whether or not some collective choice and enforcement mechanism is used to regulate and control usage. With these definitions in mind, it can be seen that whether a given physical act is classified as an invasion, price effect, or crowding effect depends on the type of property right involved.

A specific illustration will make this clear. Let us suppose that A's factory is situated in such a way that the smoke from his chimney blows down into the airspace surrounding B's house. Suppose that an increase in the market demand for A's product causes him to step up production and consequently increase his smoke emission. Obviously, B suffers from this, but exactly what type of interaction has occurred? There are three possibilities. 1. If B owns his house and land and retains intact the associated air rights, then an invasion has occurred. 2. If A has previously purchased and now has sole ownership of the air rights at B's location, then a price effect has occurred. This is because B can obtain clean air to breathe only by purchase from A (i.e., by paying him to reduce smoke emissions) and the price which A will demand for any given cleanliness of air has risen as a result of the increase in demand for his product and the attendant increase in the marginal value of the disposal activity. 3. If it is the law of the community that air rights are common property, for any citizen to use for breathing, waste disposal, flying, or whatever on a first-come, first-served basis, then it is a crowding effect which has occurred. B's suffering from the smoke is then legally equivalent to his suffering from, say, added traffic on a common road leading both to his house and A's factory.

Using terminology just introduced, the environmental crisis which we face can be characterized as follows. In the past, many natural resources have been treated as unregulated common property. Some have been so treated *de jure,* for example, use of the high seas. Some which are *de jure* in the regulated common class have been in fact unregulated because regulations have not been enforced—for example, uncontrolled sewage disposal in navigable waterways despite the regulatory provisions of the 1899 rivers and harbors act. Still others have been private in principle but unregulated common in practice because of difficulty in securing protection against certain types of invasions. For example, the right of a property owner to clean air has been recognized at least to some extent in principle, but the use of the air as an unregulated sink for the disposal of industrial waste has been able to proceed because of legal structures making it difficult for owners to enforce their rights in court.

Unregulated common property is a system of ownership which works tolerably well as long as crowding effects are minimal, that is, as long as the resource in question is not scarce relative to the demand for it. But as soon as use approaches capacity, the pinch of scarcity is felt and the inefficiencies and inequities of crowding become a great source of contention among the common owners. It would appear that the environmental crisis has come about because people have begun to realize that the capacity limit has been reached or is fast approaching on virtually every one of the natural resources which have up until now held the unregulated common property status, either *de jure* or *de facto.*

When we look at the environmental crisis in this light, the basic problem of environmental policy becomes one of instituting an optimal structure of property rights. Two basic strategies are possible. One is to impose regulation on all the offending unregulated common property; the other is to convert it into securely protected private property.

Implementation of the private property protection strategy would involve two steps. 1. Convert all common property to private status, and 2. take the steps necessary to secure all private property, existing and newly decommunalized, against invasions in any form. These two steps would render crowding effects nonexistent and invasions subject to punitive action. Price effects would become the only remaining form of externality resulting from waste disposal or resource consumption activities, and price effects are essentially benign, since they are incompatible neither with Pareto optimality nor with commutative justice.

The common property management strategy would work somewhat differently. It would be implemented by (1) communalizing all those features of the environment which act as channels for the transmission of economic interactions; and (2) subjecting all common property to rational regulation. The nominal owners of environmental resources currently subject to invasion would have their property rights terminated but, in return, would be promised regulation of the offending activity via the imposition of a residual charge or by some other mechanism. Crowding effects would be mitigated by some form of direct rationing or converted into price effects by the imposition of charges.

Now we come to the central question of the relative merits of these contrasting strategies for dealing with our environmental difficulties. Let us first consider the question from the point of view of positive economics and examine the relative degree of efficiency of resource allocation which might be hoped for under the two regimes.

It has been well established that in a world of zero transactions costs and zero bargaining costs a pure private property system would result in Pareto-optimal resource allocation. This 100 percent efficient allocation of resources would be brought about by private bargaining among property owners who would strive to exploit the opportunities for mutual gain implied by any departure from optimality.

For that matter, it is equally true that in a system of universal unregulated common property, the same 100 percent efficiency would be attained. Of course, the complexity of the bargaining required would be several orders of magnitude greater, since now every single move in the direction of Pareto optimality would require not just a bilateral agreement among private owners but universal unanimous consent by every last one of the holders of common property rights. But if we are going to assume zero bargaining costs, then zero raised by several orders of magnitude is still zero!

What about a regime of universal regulated common property? What ideal condition, equivalent to the assumption of zero transactions costs, would lead to the attainment of a Pareto optimum? Clearly, since in such a system bargaining is replaced by regulation, the required assumption would be zero regulation costs or, perhaps it might better be said, zero information-processing costs. This would include both an ability on the part of the regulators to acquire with perfect accuracy and zero expense all of the data relevant to their decision making, and also the ability costlessly and without error to carry out the computations necessary to solve the global resource allocation problem. This would be the ultimate dream of the regulator—costless and error-free cost/benefit analysis of every conceivable alternative project for resource use.

Given these ideal assumptions, there would, of course, be nothing to choose at least from the point of view of efficiency among the three types of property systems. The relevant question for inhabitants of the real world is whether the inefficiencies arising from nonzero bargaining and transactions costs in a private property system would be more or less serious than those arising from nonzero information-processing costs in the regulated common property world. (We may take it for granted that the unregulated common property alternative would run a poor third except for those rapidly disappearing cases involving nonscarce resources.) It would be the worst sort of policy analysis, of course, to pit the idealized variant of one system against the imperfect version of the other. It should not, for example, be argued that the mere existence of some inefficiencies in the market system arising from nonzero transactions costs is sufficient justification for public regulation of that aspect of resource allocation, nor should the reverse argument be admitted.

In order to avoid this sort of oversimplification let us discuss the relative efficiencies of the two policy strategies with the aid of a couple of examples where realistic assessment of bargaining and regulation costs prevents the attainment of a Pareto optimum under either alternative to the original unregulated common property situation.

In our first example, consider a commonly owned river available for unregulated use as a waste disposal facility by a single large firm and as a swimming facility for several thousands of people who live near it downstream. Suppose the value as a sewage sink is two million dollars, and as a swimming hole, three million, and that the two uses are mutually exclusive. In the unregulated common property system, the river gets used for sewage. Suppose the river is sold to a private party, who decides to operate it in such a way as to maximize his rental income. The firm bids two million. What about the swimmers? Consider two possibilities: (1) the owner can set up turnstiles at selected points along the bank and charge admission, or (2) the swimmers can band together and form a recreation club, which as an organization will enter a competitive bid. In a zero bargaining and transactions cost world, the rent from use as a swimming hole would come to three million either way, but in the real world, it is likely that the suboptimal use would persist.

The turnstile proposal would fail because of excessive transactions costs. The cost of fencing, printing tickets, ticket-takers salaries, and so forth might well total more than a million dollars even if perfect price discrimination could be practiced to bring total revenue up to the maximum three million. The recreation club idea would fail because of the bargaining costs associated with the free rider problem. Once the river were cleaned up, members and nonmembers alike would be able to swim (unless, of course, the club went to the same expense of setting up turnstiles which we have already assumed to be excessive). Thus in this case, a private property regime would fail to put the river to optimal use, and an uneconomically great amount of pollution would persist.

As a second case, let us imagine a factory surrounded by hundreds of homes in a residential community. Let us suppose that under a regime of unregulated common property in air rights the firm gets $10,000 in benefits from pouring its smoke directly into the air, while the total damage to surrounding property owners comes to $5,000, and further, that the marginal damage is $10 per pollution unit while the marginal abatement cost is $0 per unit. Clearly this is a suboptimal situation. Efficiency would require a partial cutback to the point where marginal costs of abatement equaled marginal damage, at which point the total benefit of polluting would exceed the total damage caused by a maximum amount. Unregulated common property thus gives too much pollution in this case. What about the private property solution?

Suppose homeowners were given exclusive rights to their airspace and a legal mechanism for enforcement of these rights. Then any single property owner out of the thousands would be able to obtain a court injunction barring the factory from further invasion by smoke of this person's (and hence all others) property. In a world of zero bargaining costs the firm could, of course, settle out of court with each owner individually, perhaps by purchase of smoke disposal easements. This would in theory result in an optimal solution. In practice, however, it is likely that no such settlement could be arranged. A single stubborn holdout among the property owners could wreck the whole bargain, and indeed each owner would have an incentive to hold out, since by doing so he might hope to get a bigger share of the gains from trade, while risking at worst a situation where pollution would drop to zero, far from disadvantageous to him. Thus the private property solution in this case would most likely result in an uneconomically small amount of smoke emission. The factory would have to spend $10,000 on abatement devices in order to sum a total of only $5,000 in damages.

Now, in the light of this rather gloomy appraisal of the potentialities of the private property approach in these two examples, let us examine the possibility for dealing with the same problems by means of common property regulation. First, it is clear that in both cases, in the world of zero information-processing costs, the optimal position would be attained. In the case of the river, the regulatory agency would simply carry out a cost/benefit analysis of the two alternative uses and decide against issuing a pollution license to the firm in question. In the smoke emission example, the necessary information on the relevant abatement cost and smoke damage functions would be assembled, and pollution would then be reduced to the optimal level, either via a direct order to abate by X percent or by imposition of a residual charge set at just the right level to accomplish the same thing.

Unfortunately, we do not live in a world of zero information-processing costs. We must consider the difficulties which our hypothetical regulator might face in the cases under consideration.

We may begin by looking at the problems which the regulator might encounter in assembling the data necessary for him to carry out his cost/benefit calculations. In principle, he would have at least four alternative sources from which to attempt to draw information on the parameters of the cost and benefit functions under consideration: the private market; survey research techniques; some procedure of democratic voting; and his own seat-of-the-pants intuitive judgments. Let us look at each of these in turn.

1. The possibility of gathering the information needed from the market is eliminated *ex hypothesi* in our examples. If the market could have worked in these cases, there would be no need for regulation in the first place.

2. An attempt by the regulator to obtain the data needed by survey research techniques must also be expected to fail, for the reason that it would encounter in a slightly altered form certain of the bargaining costs which prevented the smooth operation of the private property system. Consider our water pollution example. One alternative considered was formation of a recreation club which would solicit contributions from potential bathers. The main reason such a club would encounter financial difficulties is that strategic considerations would lead each individual potential bather to feign disinterest in the sport when approached for contributions. After all, if he puts nothing in the hat while others do, he will have his cake and eat it too by becoming a free rider. For analogous strategic reasons, this potential bather, when approached by the regulatory poll-taker would attempt to exaggerate as much as possible the benefit which he would gain from clean water. After all, he cannot be sure that his and others' true aggregate

benefits are sufficient to induce withholding of the pollution license, so why not cheat a little and make sure? In short, both the private and regulated property approaches stumble on the fact that when it comes to empirical measurement of subjective utilities and intangible benefits, the only reliable approach is the registration of revealed preference in the market. If the proper market is too costly to set up, then the magnitudes of the utilities and benefits involved just cannot be observed.

3. In principle, democratic voting offers an alternative to markets and surveys as a mechanism for collecting data on preferences. Rather than gathering data on the relevant functions and making an explicit cost/benefit test of a given proposal, our regulator might decide to make an implicit test by submitting the proposal to a referendum or as a bill in the legislature. How well could we expect this approach to work? Here we once more encounter the same sort of result which we have seen before, namely, that in a world of zero bargaining costs, democratic voting would guarantee precise 100 percent efficient resource allocation. The usual explanation runs something like this: Imagine that a vote were about to be taken to approve a project the total costs of which, spread among the majority of beneficiaries and the minority of nonbeneficiaries alike, were greater than the total benefits conferred. Before this issue could come to a vote, those whose share of the costs outweighed their share of the benefit would offer side payments to some members of the majority coalition, who would then switch their vote to one of opposition. By definition, if the losers could raise a sufficiently large bribe to swing the vote, then to undertake the project would not be efficient, and vice versa. In fact, we know that with zero bargaining costs, the outcome of the vote would be optimal regardless of the voting rule in force, whether it be majority rule, the rule of unanimity, the rule of vote, or anything else.

Needless to say, the theorem on the optimality of democratic voting is irrelevant to our case since it is based on the hypothesis of zero bargaining costs in side payments (or logrolling) an obvious departure from reality. Once this assumption is abandoned, there is no reason whatsoever to believe that the outcome of the voting will be efficient. In our water pollution example, a pro-swimming coalition would be formed among all the swimmers, while a pro-pollution coalition would be formed among the owners, workers, and customers of the factory. Whichever side happened by chance to be the more numerous would win. Exactly the same thing would happen in our air pollution example, where the outcome of majority voting would most likely be one or the other extreme solution, rather than the intermediate efficient point of X percent abatement.

4. Finally, we come to the possibility that the regulator might base his cost/benefit calculations on parameters which he simply pulls out of the air. This is quite common practice. For example, a recent Sierra Club publication reports an instance of cost/benefit calculation for construction of a highway, in which the engineer in charge used the figures of 0.5¢ per vehicle mile for increased comfort and convenience to motorists, $1.50 per hour for the value of time saved in travel, and zero for the aesthetic effects of the project. He explicitly admitted that the numbers chosen were completely arbitrary—well, no, not quite arbitrary. He admitted to having raised the figure for time saved from $1.00 to $1.50, since the lower figure had proved insufficient to push the benefit/cost ratio up to the cutoff point mandated for the department where he was employed.

It is necessary to dwell on the evils of regulation on the basis of fabricated data, since no pretense for defending the efficiency of the procedure can be found. Such regulation is pure paternalism, projecting the regulator's own preferences upon those regulated. Perhaps this explains why the practice is so widespread—it is the one procedure guaranteed to maximize the regulator's own welfare.

The preceding analysis appears to lead us to the conclusion that although in certain circumstances nonzero bargaining and transactions costs might prevent the attainment of efficient resources allocation in a private property system, *these very same circumstances,* when present, would prevent the would-be regulator from gathering the data needed to carry out his function efficiently.

So far, in considering the effects of nonzero information-processing costs on the efficiency of regulation, we have looked only at the problem of data gathering and omitted the problem of computation. Here we enter upon the ground of the famous "socialist controversy"—how is the regulatory agency going to solve all those "millions of simultaneous equations"? It is important to recognize that the simultaneity problem is a real one for environmental regulation. Remember the law of the second best—Thou Shalt Not Optimize Piecemeal. The environmental regulation problem is an inextricable part of the general equilibrium problem for the economy as a whole.

Now, the outcome of the socialist controversy was to establish that the polycentric decision-making of the market did indeed do a better job of computing solutions to those equations than any central planner could. For our analysis, this leads to an interesting possibility. Suppose, for a moment, that contrary to what we have just argued, an environmental regulator were able to obtain the necessary data on the parameters of these equations. Then we would be faced with the comparison between a regulator who could compute only imperfect solutions on the basis of perfect data on the one hand and, on the other, a market which, although working with prices which imperfectly reflected underlying preference functions, could much more accurately compute solutions given this limitation. Thus even by giving the regulator a patently absurd concession with regard to the validity of his data, we still could not be sure that his performance would be superior to that of a private property system.

Finally, we come to one last difficulty with the regulated common property solution to the environmental problem. Remember that the scheme, as originally outlined, involved the communalization of all environmental resources involved in the transmission of interactive effects sufficient to cause significant inefficiencies and inequities. We have not yet discussed the problem of how to decide exactly which property to communalize and which to leave in private hands. Unless, as some would have it, we communalize and regulate all property of every type, the decisions have to be made on a case by case basis. Given the type of political institutions which we are familiar with, it is difficult to imagine this critical decision—the decision on which activities to shift to the public sector—being made on any other than a democratic basis. But there is no reason to place any great faith in the ability of the democratic process to decide issues of this type in an efficient manner. The best we could hope for would be that the impact of voting behavior on collectivization programs would be completely random, that is, that on the average about as many activities would be communalized which should not be as those which would not be communalized and should be. However, the situation is probably even less satisfactory than this. There are reasons to believe that the democratic process works with a bias toward excessive communalization in cases of this type. Thus it might well be true that even if it were desirable to switch some property to the regulated common status, to introduce such a possibility as a constitutionally permissible alternative in a democratic regime might mean simply exchanging an excessively small regulated sector for an excessively large one.

Up to this point, we have examined the relative advantages and disadvantages of alternative environmental strategies solely in terms of the criterion of economic efficiency. This is far from the whole story, however, and in closing I would like to examine briefly some of the normative implications of the two alternatives. To put the matter simply, it is my contention that aside from all considerations of efficiency, the regulatory solution is incompatible with the maintenance of a free society. In this connection, two points should be made.

First, the increase in the proportion of total property belonging to the regulated common category would imply an extension of the principle of authority and reduce the scope of the principle of autonomy. An autonomous man adjusts his behavior according to a pattern of his own creation, skillfully or poorly designed to serve his own ends as he sees them. A person subject to authority, on the other hand, adjusts his behavior in accordance with the design of another, and his welfare becomes dependent upon the degree of obedience to the other's directives. Autonomy is, of course, not quite the same thing as freedom; the free man's right to submit voluntarily to authority must be recognized. The two are incompatible in an absolute sense only when the authority is imposed by force. Yet it would be unwise to think that the proponent of individual liberty can be indifferent to the extension of authority even when it is of the voluntary or constitutional variety. Institutions for the exercise of authority, even when voluntarily created for the most benign of purposes, have an unfortunate and often observed tendency to get out of hand.

The second normative objection to the regulatory approach is that its original introduction would involve a great many invasions and confiscations of property. Let us take a simple example, that of automobile exhaust pollution. We have noted the reason we have a problem with this in the first place is that the right to dispose of gaseous wastes in the air has been treated *de facto* as an unregulated common property right. But just because motorists have acted as if they owned the air and had a right to dispose of their exhaust wherever they pleased, this does not mean that property holders have recognized and acquiesced to that right. Far from it! Individuals stubbornly insist on believing that they have a right to clean air to breathe, certainly at least when they are sitting in the confines of their own homes. It is difficult to convince these people that a motorist who pumps noxious gases into their living rooms is not committing an invasion, and that it is anything but a defect in the legal system that the motorist cannot be made to cease and desist or at least to pay damages.

This stubborn private property mentality is illustrated well by an objection often raised by environmentalists against the idea of residual charges as a means of pollution control. It is protested that such charges constitute a "license to pollute." Eminent economists are prone to ridicule this charge and ascribe it to the ignorance and lack of sophistication of the man on the street, yet I think that the license-to-pollute charge stands up to scrutiny and is a telling objection to residual charges.

First of all, it is ridiculous to deny that residual charges are in fact a form of license to pollute. A policy implementing such charges is one which allows certain economic activities to be carried out by those who pay an appropriate fee to some governmental authority, and by no one else. Wherein lies any legal or analytical difference distinguishing this policy from the granting of licenses to operate liquor stores or drive taxicabs?

Rather than engaging in a battle of semantics, it would make more sense for the advocates of residual charges to admit that a license is a license, but that, in this case, the license is a good and beneficial one. This would clear the way to examine the real thrust of the license-to-pollute charge and bring clearly into focus the fundamentally different ethical bases upon which the private property protection and common property management strategies rest. The private property system is based on the conception that an individual has an absolute right to the exclusive employment of his own property to advance his own ends as he sees fit. The regulatory approach, in contrast, is built on the idea that property belongs to whoever can make best use of it, regardless of whether his right to use it has or has not been previously established by production or contract or exchange or any form of voluntary process.

Consider the position of an individual who is left choking on the fumes of a factory which finds it more profitable to pay and pollute than to abate. What consolation is it to him to know that the charge paid is equal to the marginal disutility of choking, as determined by some remote government functionary? What consolation is it to him to know that a certain percentage of distant factories, facing somewhat different technical conditions, have been in-duced to abate rather than to pay and pollute? The victim knows only that he continues to choke and that he is powerless to seek redress because his claim to ownership of the air he breathes has been denied.

As a *reductio ad absurdum,* consider the following point: If it is good to sell licenses to pollute, why not licenses to rape? Suppose it could be determined, accurately, that the mean marginal value of suffering to a rape victim were, say, $518. If the license fee were set at exactly $518, would not the resulting pattern of behavior be Pareto optimal? Could one not argue that all sorts of bargaining and transactions and litigation costs would be economized upon by treating the resource in question as regulated common property rather than as private property?

The ethical basis for the common property management strategy of environmental regulation is an example of what I call Raskolnikovism. Just as Raskolnikov murdered and robbed the old lady on the grounds that his life and purposes were more important than her life and purposes, the regulator who issues you a license to pollute my airspace or my drinking water is making the arbitrary decision that my property can better be used to serve your ends than it can to serve my own. It is this idea lying at the basis of so many current recommendations in the field of environmental policy which I find more than any other to be fundamentally subversive.

12

James M. Smith

THE SCOPE OF PROPERTY RIGHTS

> Though the earth and all inferior creatures be common to all men, yet every man has a property in his own person; this nobody has any right to but himself. The labour of his body and the work of his hands we may say are properly his. Whatsoever, then, he removes out of the state that nature hath provided and left it in, he hath mixed his labour with, and joined to it something that is his own, and thereby makes it his property. It being by him removed from the common state nature placed it in, it hath by this labour something annexed to it that excludes the common right of other men. For this labour being the questionable property of the labourer, no man but he can have a right to what that is once joined to, at least where there is enough and as good left in common for others.[1]

THIS VERY familiar and very influential passage from Locke has been commented on, discussed, interpreted and criticized as much as any passage in modern political philosophy. In what follows, I do not propose to add to the extensive literature devoted to these tasks. Instead, I shall focus entirely on one concept introduced by Locke, namely, self-ownership. Beginning with some rather speculative suggestions about Locke's reasons for using this problematic notion and some general remarks about the right to property conceived as a natural right, I shall move with as much dispatch as possible to the development of my main theses: 1. That the concept of self-ownership is incoherent. 2. That the adoption of the view that a person is property, even self-owned, leads to morally unacceptable consequences. And 3. that an understanding of why the first two theses are true helps us to understand the special immorality of slavery and raises some important questions about the role of labor in a market system. I am not concerned to interpret, defend or criticize Locke, so the peculiar merits or defects of his view will not be germane to the discussion.

The right of individuals to own and dispose of property (what I shall call for short, property rights) was clearly a cornerstone of political philosophers in the seventeenth and eighteenth centuries. The right to property was claimed as a natural right in the seventeenth century, which is to say almost from the beginning of modern natural right theories. Its status as a natural right was vigorously defended throughout the seventeenth and eighteenth centuries and this status declined only as natural right theory itself declined under attack from English philosophers and continental politicians.

First, the necessity of protecting property rights and fairly adjudicating disputes about them justified the very existence of government. Without that necessity, Locke suggests that the state of nature was a very tolerable mode of existence for men. Second, the fact (if it was a fact) that the state did protect property rights established an obligation on the part of the citizen (at least *qua* property owner) to obey the laws established by the state. Having accepted this benefit, Locke argued, one had tacitly consented to the rules established by the state. Finally, though ambiguously, the existence of private property provided a basis for limiting the power of the state. If the *raison d'être* of the state was the protection of private property and if the obligation of the citizen also derived from this service, surely an invasion by the state itself of those rights would justify opposition and perhaps even revolution.

Why would Locke or anyone rest such a crucial right on self-ownership? I suggest the following considerations which make such a foundation for a natural right to property seem promising or even necessary.

If one wishes to claim that property rights do not depend on the willingness of particular states to grant them, if, indeed, a state which does not grant them is to be judged illegitimate, then the basis for such rights must be independent of the legal systems of particular states. The fundamental case of ownership must be a "natural" not an "artificial" relation. But what can such a relation be? Even the principle that I own what I produce or work on seems to depend on a system of property or contracts. But what of the relation between myself and my labor? That I have produced or worked on something, say picking apples or sawing wood, is surely a natural fact, untainted by legal conventions. And it is equally certain that my labor is *mine,* that is, that I own it. And, as Locke argues, to the extent that my labor is necessary to what I have produced (a bushel of picked apples, a cut log) I own it as well. But why distinguish between my labor and any other aspect of myself—my character, my abilities, my attitudes, my beliefs, and so forth? They are mine whatever any state says, and hence I own them "naturally." Thus I have a basis in nature for asserting a property right and, by extension, for judging the political and legal systems of states which interfere with or refuse to protect that right.

Of course, one of the reasons for asserting a natural right is to claim a basis for making such judgments. In that respect, asserting a natural right is like describing an ideal state to which actual states can be compared, inevitably to their disadvantage. The description of an ideal does not, by itself, constitute a demand or a limit on the action of others. But the assertion of a right is precisely these things: a demand that others act or refrain from acting and, hence, a limit on their action. A natural right is a limit not contingent on the particular circumstances of a given state or social status or individual merits or defects, but deriving solely from one's status as a person. If a right, such as the right to property, is regarded as central or fundamental among natural rights, it is because it serves to limit the action of others in ways crucial to the interests of the possessor of the rights. Certainly property rights were so regarded by Locke and those he influenced in the seventeenth and eighteenth centuries. This attitude, however, was not itself fundamental. Rather, it arose out of a view of human nature and an estimation of the political and social arrangements possible at the time. For a rational, self-interested and independent person, motivated by pleasure and pain, the possession of property was both necessary and sufficient protection in the political and social circumstances of the eighteenth century.

Very few indeed would now give property such a central position. If the question of justifying the existence of government is raised at all, it is much more likely to be settled in terms of the protection of individual interests or even in terms of individual fulfillment than in terms of the protection of property. It is the Marxist who most frequently accepts Locke's view that the state exists to protect property and then only in order to stand Locke's argument on its head. Although consent and the provision of individual benefits still play a substantial role in establishing political obligation, neither of these is taken to be tied to the protection of property in any intimate way. Finally, property rights are so far from being regarded as an absolute limit on state action that many theorists—non-Marxists as well as Marxists—seem to regard the ability of the state to limit and direct the use of property as a test of its ability to serve the general interest or the common good.

Thus, from being regarded as a fundamental—perhaps the most fundamental—natural right, property rights have declined in importance to the point that a wide range of writers regard them as marginal in importance and some even regard them as inimical to basic human interests. At the same time, the concept of natural rights has once again assumed a central position in political theory. A number of recent articles,[2] while disagreeing in detail, agree persuasively on a number of contentions. First, the concept of a right beyond those guaranteed by a particular legal system is coherent and morally defensible (perhaps even essential). Second, while the common theological and metaphysical bases for natural rights are not adequate, there is a basis in human nature for rights which apply to all human beings regardless of their membership or status in a particular legal system. Thus, these rights can be regarded as human rights not just in the sense that all rights are human, but in the stronger sense that every human being has them. Third, these rights, like their "natural" ancestors, can be asserted "against the world," that is, they constitute valid demands even though they are not actually met at a given time or place, and if they are not met within a particular legal order that fact constitutes a criticism of that legal order.

Finally, although the basis in human nature for these rights is described differently by different writers, and these differences are not trivial, there is an impressive overlap in those human characteristics which the various authors cite. Needs are perhaps the most frequently cited bases and some include certain fundamental human relations, such as parent-child, or sibling-sibling. The equality of human worth and (less importantly) the inequality of human merit also are regarded as potential bases for these fundamental human rights. But the absence of property rights as human rights is striking. There is discussion of the use of property and of its distribution. But neither the right to own nor the right to acquire property as such is regarded as sufficiently central to human needs to deserve inclusion.

In both the eighteenth and the twentieth centuries, then, natural or human rights are claimed both to call attention to interests of persons independent of their citizenship in a particular state or membership in a particular society and to provide a basis for criticizing a state or society which refuses to protect these interests. What has changed is the eighteenth-century belief that property rights served to protect central human interests. This change is the result not only of different political and economic circumstances, but different conceptions of human nature. That our conception is central to our position on the whole range of social or economic issues can be seen by examining certain features of arguments between proponents of different social or economic systems. When the individualist (if I may use this term undefined) asserts the necessity of initiative, nonconformity, and freedom from social constraints, for example, the collectivist (similarly undefined) may respond by asserting the necessity of social concern, social cohesion and cooperation. If we ask "Necessary for what?," we may very well receive the "same" answer from both sides, namely, for the interest or benefit of the persons involved.

My suggestion is not that this indicates a fundamental agreement between the individualist and the collectivist. Far from it. Rather, it shows that the argument as so far conducted has not even penetrated to the level where the crucial divergence in views occurs, namely, in the concept of the person for whose good both the individualist and the collectivist argue. A similar situation is found, I think, in the more specific argument concerning the role of property. Individualism, in one of its more important historical varieties, regards private property as an essential element in a good society. Collectivism, in one of its more important varieties, regards the right to private property as inimical to a good society. Good for whom? For the persons who compose the society. Once again, the giving of the "same" answer suggests not a basic agreement but rather a disagreement at a level more fundamental than the argument reaches.

My premise is that some aspects of this more fundamental disagreement can be revealed by considering the logical and moral difficulty involved in self-ownership. I want first to consider the question of whether one can own himself in the full sense of "own." Professor A. M. Honore[3] notes eleven incidents of the "liberal concept of ownership" whose "basic" model is "...a single human being owning...a single material thing. Ownership [he writes] comprises the right to possess, the right to use, the right to manage, the right to the income of the thing, the right to the capital, the right to security, the rights or incidence of transmissibility and absence of term, the prohibition of harmful use, liability to execution, and the incident of residuarity. No doubt [he continues] the concentration in the same person of the right (liberty) of using as one wishes, the right to exclude others, the power of alienating and an immunity to expropriation is a cardinal feature of the institution."[4] How is the claim that an individual has property in his own person to be judged against this concept of property?

Nothing is to be gained at this point by concentrating uncritically on the use of the various parts of the English verb "to have," reflexive or possessive pronouns like "myself" and "himself," "my" and "his," and the preposition "of." As reflection will show, and as P. J. Day[5] has argued, we *have* many things we do not *own* (colds, ancestors, toothaches), and the king of the Hellenes, the travels of Marco Polo, and the patience of Job were not owned by anyone, including the Hellenes, Marco Polo, and Job. It has been notorious since Aristotle that the verb "to be" has many uses besides asserting identity, and it should be apparent by now that the verb "to have" has many uses besides asserting ownership. It would thus be question-begging to assert that Jones owned his personality because we truly say "Jones has a pleasing personality." The question is whether the "has" here expresses (or can express) ownership or some other relation. Similar points could be made about "of" and the reflexive and possessive pronouns.

The semantic or logical point about "to have" in its relation to ownership is similar to the one about "to be" in its relation to identity. But there is a further point to be made about the concept of ownership. It is akin to the point that Hume makes when he calls justice an artificial virtue. Ownership is an artificial concept, not just in the sense that it is technical as, for example, "square root" is technical, but in the further sense that it is embedded in what Rawls calls a practice: "a[ny] form of activity specified by a system of rules which defines offices, roles, moves, penalties, defenses, and so on, and which gives the activity its structure. As examples one may think of games and rituals, trials and parliaments." "Jones owns the book" may thus be compared with "Jones has Smith in check." Although the combinations of shapes and sounds (what we sometimes call the words) "owns" and "check" may occur independent of their respective practices ("Check my addition." "I've come into my own.") they cannot be understood in the same way without either taking the practice (chess or property law) for granted or surreptitiously relying on their rules to provide the proper sense. Of course, this doesn't show that "John owns himself" *doesn't* make sense. But it does show that any attempt to construct a system of property rights on that claim is doomed to circularity. For, if it does make sense, it can only do so within a system of property rights.

On the other hand, there is an important distinction to be made between the institution of private property and the game of chess. Although they are both defined and governed by rules and (explicit or implicit) authorities, the rules of property have an external reference lacked by those of chess. That is, they, along with the broader legal system of which they are a part, are intended to have a bearing on human interests, desires, conflicts, and so on, which exist independently of the institution, though the institution may play a role in giving them the form they have. Thus, the relative scarcity of resources, the various desires and attitudes people have, the fact that we suffer pain, and so forth, all play a role in the development of the law of property and, of course, the law of property produces and directs attitudes and desires and our conception of conflict at the same time. Although we can give chess (or any game) such "external" connections, they don't normally have them.

One consequence of this is a difference in attitude toward critics or reformers. If someone insists he is not in check, though the rules indicate that he is, we either regard him as lacking in understanding of the rules or as simply silly and infantile. If he proposes a radical change in the game, for example, that pawns should be allowed to move like rooks, we can either regard him as proposing a new game (either more or less interesting) or, again, as not understanding the game of chess.

But in a practice with external connections, proposals for change are not only more important but more ambiguous in their import. When Proudhon says "Property is theft" the paradox seems as much moral as logical or legal, and the response has an appropriate ambiguity: is it nonsense or immorality? Well, both and neither. He clearly intends a moral reevaluation of the practice. But since the practice itself provides the only available terms for criticism, he resorts to paradox, that is, literal nonsense, to make the point.

Another example of radical criticism of an institution is provided by Butler in his novel *Erewhon.* Perhaps we could say, for Butler, "Punishment is assault."[7] Just as there are connections between the institution of property and noninstitutional goals and conflicts, so there are various noninstitutional concepts which serve as "natural" bases for the application of institutional concepts. So the fact that I have the book serves as a basis for a claim to possess which serves as a basis for a claim to own. (Compare also "Jones attacked Brown" and "Jones assaulted Brown," "Jones killed Brown" and "Jones murdered Brown.")

J. P. Day, in the article already referred to, argues that "Jones owns himself" is absurd because "Jones has exclusive use of himself" is absurd and having exclusive use is an essential element in ownership. The reason for regarding it absurd to say that Jones has exclusive use of himself is, according to Day, that using is an irreflexive relation, that is, no individual can have the relation to himself. Thus, any sentence of the form "X uses X" must be false.

Although I am sympathetic with Day's ultimate conclusion, namely, that one cannot own oneself, I am not wholly convinced by his line of argument. For one thing, he depends on the claim that "[exclusive] use is the most important part of the meaning of property." He grants, rather too easily as I shall argue, that alienation and destruction are not irreflexive since one can commit suicide or sell himself into slavery. Thus, the alleged absurdity of my using myself and its centrality to ownership is crucial to his case. I am inclined to agree with Honore that no single incident of the eleven he cites is necessary to a property claim, though the eleven together are certainly sufficient. If we grant, as Day does, that alienation of oneself is possible, even what Honore calls the cardinal features of property would not be totally lacking in the putative case of self-ownership. Indeed, how could we sell (into slavery) what we never owned?

It appears that Day assumes that "uses" is a univocal

term so that, for example, if I cannot use myself in the same way I use a tool or a plot of land, then I cannot use myself at all. But no one denies that I can own a picture or a copyright or a government bond, though none of these is used as land or tools are used. Given the wide range of meanings that the notion of use has in uncontroversial cases of ownership, it seems unwarranted to conclude that "I use myself" is absurd in any logically important way merely because the expression seems bizarre in ordinary usage—as I think it does. To reach such a conclusion we must first consider a wider range of the incidents of property. The logical barrier to self-ownership is the contingent relation which holds between property and its owner. That relationship can be made clearer by a consideration of a second possible reflexive property relation, namely, self-alienation.

To understand self-alienation in a full sense, I think we must understand selling oneself into slavery, for it is in that case that I am treating myself as a piece of property in the full "liberal" sense, subject to all the standard incidents listed by Honore. There is more than one kind of slavery, of course. But it is chattel slavery that is most clearly associated with a system of private property rights, and so it is chattel slavery on which I shall focus.

The legal system in which one could be said to sell himself into slavery would have to be an extended system, at least in recognizing the double classification inherent in slavery: some creatures are both pieces of property and persons. If slaves were not persons at all, the institution would not be peculiar or present any logical or moral problems. It would merely be the extension of rules of property to new and unique objects. On the other hand, there is also a difficulty in regarding slaves as persons in the full sense. Consider the distinction between being a slave and having a lifetime contract to perform some range of services. On what could we rest the distinction? Historically, the majority of slaves have been treated harshly and cruelly and the benefits they have derived have been meager indeed. But this does not seem to be a conceptual requirement of a system of slavery. Individual slave owners allegedly were kind and generous, and there seems to be no logical barrier to generalizing their behavior rather than the behavior of their fellow slave owners. On the other hand, there are well-known examples of low wages, wretched working conditions and the like outside the system of slavery. The crucial difference seems to be between an agreement in which the pursuit of self-interest by both parties is limited, however formally or inadequately, by the interests of the other, and a situation in which one party's interests are given full consideration while those of the other party are disregarded completely, and his rational powers, capacities and talents are completely at the service of the other. This difference would not be affected by the fact (if it were a fact) that most or even all slave owners refrained from "taking advantage of their situation," that is, were solicitous for the welfare of their slaves, and consulted their wishes whenever possible. For any conduct of that kind would be completely at the discretion of the slave owner. Should he lapse into historically more common behavior, the slave would have no right violated. Indeed, he is not the sort of being who could have a right to violate. This point should not be blunted by the fact that the slave owner might have duties with respect to the slave, for example, to refrain from certain acts of cruelty or offensive public displays. Such duties are just the sort we have toward animals. Their existence confers rights, not on the animals (or the slave), but on other (official) nonslaves to restrain or censure the slave owner's conduct. It is the offense to the nonslave which determines the slave owner's duties, not the invasion of the interests of the slave. Thus slave owning, even benevolent slave owning, should not be confused with a paternalistic arrangement in which one person is charged with protecting the interest of another even if the interests are threatened by the person himself. In that case, one party is conceded to have rights and interests but is regarded as incapable of appreciating or protecting them. It is this incapacity which leads to the imposition of paternalistic duty on others. But any consultation of the slaves' interests is supererogatory on the part of the slave owner. Indeed, an even stronger claim is justified: the recognition that the slave has interests (as opposed to feelings, wishes, cares, etc.) is incompatible with regarding him as property.[8]

It is now clear why, and in what sense, the double classification necessary to a system of slavery is problematic. For it is a central aspect of our concept of a person that he has interests distinct from those of other persons, the capacity to understand those interests, and the ability to direct his conduct to protect and serve those interests. To the extent that a creature falls short of these standards, he is regarded as defective as a person or, as in the case of children, not yet (fully) a person. One person's interests may coincide with the interests of others as well as conflict, of course. He may even renounce his interests in some cause he regards as worthy. But even renunciation of interest requires that one's interest be weighed. To be a slave is to have no interest to put in the scale.

From this account also emerges a clearer reason for regarding selling oneself into slavery as a fundamentally incoherent notion. Selling, at least as it is envisaged in the liberal sense of ownership, is a voluntary action of a person. Moreover, it is a crucial feature of selling that there be consideration—some benefit to the seller. How then are we to conceive the act of someone selling himself into slavery? It must be performed by one with distinct interests, capable of appreciating and protecting them. The act itself must be one in which the agent is aware of his interests and which requires a consideration in exchange for whatever interests he surrenders. And yet the result of the sale requires the seller to be a being with no distinct interests. Indeed, even that does not quite capture the situation. For becoming a slave requires not only that one surrender his interests, but that he place the capacities and abilities which were formerly employed in their pursuit unconditionally in the hands of another. Nor can this be regarded as simply extinguishing one's interests as mystics are said to do. One might extinguish one's interests by committing suicide or by engaging in some extraordinary religious discipline in which he would come to wholly identify his interests with some (as we might say) impersonal force or entity. (It is interesting to note here that those religions in which such an identification is sought regard the individual self, identified by distinct interests, as unreal, that is, both insubstantial and unworthy.) One might come to identify his interests utterly with those of his buyer-master. But given our criteria for personal identity and for voluntary action, we would be likely to regard such an identification as pathological rather than voluntary.

The institution of chattel slavery, then, is conceptually unstable since it requires us to classify slaves in two incompatible ways: as persons, with interests and the capacity for pursuing those interests, and as pieces of property, wholly lacking in interests and valued only for their utility in furthering the interests of others. This conceptual problem is mirrored both in moral and practical terms. The moral restraints which slaves as persons impose on their masters constantly conflict with the attempt to maximize the benefits allegedly to be derived from the most efficient use of their capacities. Yet, those features of slaves which make them most valuable as property, for example, the power of self-direction, the ability to follow orders, to respond critically, also constantly remind us of the fact that they are not property at all, but persons.

The concept of property in a person is thus inherently unstable in application. The objects to which it is applied are always liable to be regarded as persons only—producing moral outrage at the institution—or as property only—producing moral outrages in the institution. To regard myself as property, I must thus have two conflicting conceptions of myself. Though this may not yield a contradiction, I think the act of selling myself is akin to the issuing of utterances like "It is raining, but I don't believe it" or "I am not as smart as I think I am." For the presuppositions under which one can give my action (the offer of sale) its normal sense, are also those which make the total situation incoherent.

These conclusions also serve as an improved basis for the claim that slavery is unjust. The claim that slavery treated men as means instead of ends has always seemed to me more suggestive than informative, at least until some interpretation is given. On the other hand, while the suffering of the slaves and the corruption of their masters certainly justifies the condemnation of slavery, they do not establish the claim that it is unjust. Nor does the charge that the slave was given too small a share in the fruits of his labor seem to me satisfactory as it stands. First of all, by resting the claim of injustice on the unfairness of distribution, it assimilates slavery to a host of other social arrangements which are also unfair in their distribution of benefits, thereby minimizing the injustice of slavery. But more importantly it misses the point. For no conceivable distribution of benefits within the institution of slavery could change the nature of the institution itself, and the central injustice stems from that nature. It is in fact an injustice compounded. For it is unjust to treat beings who have interests which they recognize as though they had none, and it compounds that injustice to derive benefits from the very capacities one denies: the capacity for self-direction and understanding and adjustment to human needs in others. Since chattel slavery rests on this very combination it is necessarily unjust regardless of the attitudes or actions of those within the system.

To what extent do these arguments apply to ownership of aspects or parts of persons? We do not normally speak of a person owning his body or even parts of his body. On the other hand, there is clearly a market for human hair, blood and probably detachable or replaceable organs, such as kidneys and perhaps ovaries. No doubt sperm and ova will soon be added to the list. As the art of transplants is further developed, we can expect eyes, hearts and other nondetachable or replaceable organs also to be purchased for delivery after death. In general, however, I think that conceptual and moral difficulties attend any attempt to conceive of ownership applying to central aspects of a person. The body can be bequeathed, of course, but not sold or otherwise transferred. It may be destroyed, as in suicide, but I suggest that we do not conceive of the suicide as destroying his property, but himself. Again, aspects of myself, such as my reputation and good will, can be sold, used, bequeathed, but only insofar as they become attached in the minds of others, to objects external to me, such as my business or a product.

There is however, one aspect of myself which has special interest as property, if only because the best known enemy of private property has considered it so thoroughly. Marx rests a large part of his attack on capitalism on the fact that the wage-laborer must sell his labor-power in order to live. Now, I am no more interested here in interpreting Marx than in interpreting Locke (and I am no more qualified to do so). What I shall do is propose an argument (which I think is Marxist in its basic thrust) without claiming that it is what Marx really said. The argument, however, has an intrinsic interest for us, and if it can be made stronger or criticized more cogently by reference to Marx, that will provide a basis for further discussion.

However equal the distribution of property was to begin with (the argument begins), it is now developed in advanced industrial capitalism in such a way that some own property apart from and detachable from themselves which can be used (sold or invested or rented) to advance and protect their interests. Others, however, have little or no property of that sort and, therefore, can only survive (or, at any rate, pursue their interests) by selling a part or aspect of themselves, namely, their labor-power. This is not to be understood as the product of their labor (which would be the case where a potter sells his pots or a shoemaker his shoes) nor as their laboring on a particular occasion or occasions (which would be the case where someone was interested either in a particular product or in a performance of some sort, say singing or dancing). Rather, to sell one's labor-power is to sell the right to direct, control and profit from one's power to produce valuable products. To put it another way, it is to give up to the discretion of another the use of the talents, abilities and capacities which would normally be used to protect and further one's own interests. Hence, it is to sacrifice (to that extent) one's ability to pursue one's interests and to provide the buyer with the power to use that capacity (by directing it in any direction he chooses) for his own interests. Now this sale of labor-power has the following characteristics:

1. It is a sale of a central, perhaps the central, element of the seller's person, that is, direction over his creative power.

2. It is a forced sale, that is, although no particular person can demand this control, the laborer must sell to some buyer in order to survive.

3. Moreover, whatever buyer gets it, the use of that power will be hostile to the interests of the laborer, for it will be used, directly or indirectly, to maintain the laborer in a position in which he must sell his labor-power.

Now, some may quarrel with the distribution of the benefits of this system, but this is not the crucial wrong. For, however well the laborer was paid for his sale and however favorable his conditions were within the system, its essential character and, hence, essential evil would remain: the laborer (and the buyers of his labor) would be in the position of regarding himself as a commodity, a piece of property. And, at the same time, it is the capacity he has as a person to create valuable products that makes him a useful piece of property, and it is precisely that capacity from which others benefit and which is used in opposition to his own fundamental interests as a human being, namely, to control and direct his creative capacities as he sees fit. And is this not almost exactly the evil that was pointed out in the system of chattel slavery?

Three questions are appropriate here: 1. In what sense is the laborer forced to regard himself as property in order to sell his labor-power? 2. To what extent is the sale involuntary? 3. To what extent does the sale of labor result in its use in ways hostile to the laborer's interests? A full answer to these three questions would go beyond the scope of this paper. What I shall try to do briefly is indicate the issues which a response must face.

The crucial issue raised by the first question is the extent to which the direction of one's labor is central to one's character as a human being. On the one hand, one might hold that it was so central that no matter how much its use as directed by another benefited you in other ways, the very fact of its being under the control of another would be dehumanizing. Curiously, this is not only the position I see in Marx, but it is suggested by a very individualistic thinker such as Mill, though not in any direct way.

On the other hand, it is possible though difficult to hold that control over one's labor is so marginally an aspect of oneself that it does not matter who controls it, so long as the consequences are beneficial in other ways. One who held that men were essentially consumers might take such a position, or perhaps one who held that concern for one's earthly welfare was inappropriate. A third alternative, which seems to me to have promise, is to agree that control of one's labor is essential, but that this can be provided *via* the extension of political power to the worker and control by the political process of the process of production. The extent to which this response is compatible with a recognizable system of private property or capitalism is another matter.

Finally, a number of contemporary sociologists and psychologists suggest that men are so utterly plastic and so amenable to various social influences, that the question, as I have formulated it, is inappropriate. What a person *is* is totally dependent on the social arrangements in force at a given time. Thus, *Walden Two* or *Brave New World* are equally compatible with happy men if the men are trained properly. I must confess that I am repelled by this response without knowing how to answer it to my satisfaction.

The answer to question two is intimately tied to the answer to question one. If control of my labor is regarded as central to myself, then any conditions which could induce me to alienate it will be regarded as *prima facie* making the alienation involuntary. (Compare the discussion above with that of voluntarily selling oneself into slavery.) If control of one's labor is marginal, any reasonable benefit could be regarded as sufficient to establish the *prima facie* voluntariness of the sale. The question is made more complex by the fact that the market system itself can be differently related to the voluntary acts of the participants. If we regard it as substantially the product of the voluntary action of the participants, then our view of particular hard decisions within it will be very different from what it would be if we regard the desires and interests of the participants themselves as products of the system.

Finally, whether the use of alienated labor-power is necessarily hostile to the laborer will depend on the theory of classes one adopts. For Marx, of course, that it is necessarily hostile follows from the definition of classes together with the proposition that an individual's interest is essentially determined by his class membership. If it could be maintained that one's interest were determined by other factors, or by the individual alone, then, although a particular use might be hostile, it could not be regarded as a necessary consequence of the market system itself. And any political arrangement which gives the laborer control over the market system would not only provide him with control over his labor, but could also guarantee that its use would not be hostile to his interests.

NOTES

1. J. Locke, *Second Treatise of Government,* 1690, ch. 5, sec. 27: J. S. Mill, *Principles of Political Economy,* 7th ed., 1871, bk. 2, ch. 1, sec. 1; ch. 2, sec. 6.

2. See Melden, A. I. (ed.), *Human Rights* (Belmont: Wadsworth, 1970).

3. Honore, A. M., "Ownership" in Guest, A. G. (ed.), *Oxford Essays in Jurisprudence,* Oxford University Press, Oxford, 1961, pp. 107-147.

4. Ibid., p. 113.

5. Day, J.P., "Locke on Property," *Philosophical Quarterly,* Vol. 16, 1966, pp. 207-221.

6. Rawls, John. "Two Concepts of Rules," *Philosophical Review,* Vol. LXIV, No. 1, p. 3.

7. On this point, see also Searle, "How to Derive 'Ought' From 'Is'," *Philosophical Review,* LXXIII, No. 1, pp. 43-58. Searle compares Proudhon's "Property is theft" with "Law is a crime," "Marriage is adultery," etc.

8. The distinction between having interests and feeling pain, being frustrated and the like is easiest to make in the case of animals. Out of consideration for the public interest not being offended, I am forbidden to inflict needless pain on my horse. But only consideration of my own interest requires me to include the welfare of the horse in my deliberations. The horse has no right to such consideration and, hence, no interest to protect.

13

Israel M. Kirzner

PRODUCER, ENTREPRENEUR, AND THE RIGHT TO PROPERTY

"THE INSTITUTION of property," John Stuart Mill remarked, "when limited to its essential elements, consists in the recognition, in each person, of a right to the exclusive disposal of what he or she have produced by their own exertions, or received either by gift or by fair agreement, without force or fraud, from those who produced it. The foundation of the whole is the right of my producers to what they themselves have produced."[1] My purpose is to point out the ambiguity of the phrase "what a man has produced," and to draw attention, in particular, to one significant, economically valid, meaning of the term, a meaning involving the concept of entrepreneurship, which seems to have been overlooked almost entirely.

Precision in applying the term "what a man has produced" seems to be of considerable importance. The ethical views associated with widely disparate ideologies, relating both to the justifiability of private rights to property, and to the problem of justice in the distribution of incomes, appear to involve in some form the notion of "what a man has produced." Thus the Lockean theory of private property, which came to serve as the source of the moral case for capitalism,[2] has been understood as depending on the view that man has the right to the "fruits of his work."[3] As Milton Friedman has pointed out, the capitalist ethic (which he identifies as holding that "a man deserves what he produces"[4]) is shared by Marx, since Marx's view on the exploitation of labor, resting on the premise that labor produces the whole product, is valid "only if labor is entitled to what it produces."[5]

Without necessarily accepting, therefore, any one of these ethical positions, it seems worthwhile to achieve clarity by seeking to understand what exactly the notion "what a man has produced" is to mean. The literature seems to have perceived production *insofar as it flows from factors of production,* so that by the statement "what a man has produced" has been intended "what has been produced by those factors of production identified with the man with whom we are concerned." Briefly, a man is a producer insofar as he is himself considered a factor of production, or as he is the owner of factors viewed as responsible for output. Thus Friedman seems to further identify the capitalist ethic with the view that "an individual deserves what is produced by the resources he owns."[6] J. B. Clark rested "the right of society to exist in its present form" on his marginal productivity theory of distribution, seeing it as satisfying the requirement that each man gets what he produces.[7] Locke's labor theory of property begins from the premise that "every man has a property in his own person.... The labor of his body and the work of his hands we may say are properly his."[8] Production is made possible only by the ownership of agents of production.

It follows that if we perceive production as flowing from factors of production, and if we correspondingly relate the ethical implication of "what a man has produced" strictly to that which derives from the factors of production which that man owns (including, of course, his own labor capacity), then the exercise of pure entrepreneurship in production (i.e., seen as involving no element of factor ownership) carries with it none of the favorable ethical connotations attached to "that which a man has produced." This conclusion, the questioning of which is the purpose of this paper, requires some elaboration.

Factor-Ownership and Entrepreneurship

It is well known that economic literature suffers from insufficient attention paid to the entrepreneurial role, so that we find few careful attempts to define precisely what this role consists of. In the more sophisticated discussions of entrepreneurship, a fairly sharp distinction has emerged between the factors of production on the one hand and entrepreneurship on the other. In Schumpeter's classic discussion, for example, the means of production include *all* agents required to produce the product in the state of circular flow (equilibrium). In equilibrium there is the tendency "for the entrepreneur to make neither profit nor loss. . .he has no function of a special kind there, he simply does not exist."[9] In disequilibrium, on the other hand, innovations in product quality and in methods of production are attributable to the initiative of pioneering Schumpeterian entrepreneurs. Although, that is to say, the new products or the new productive techniques require *no* resources beyond those consistent with the state of equilibrium, these new products and techniques would not have appeared at all in the first place, had it not been for entrepreneurial daring and drive.

It follows that there is a built-in ambiguity, therefore, concerning the sense in which pure entrepreneurship can be considered a resource necessary for the emergence of the product. And it is this ambiguity which is no doubt partly responsible for the disagreement among economists as to whether to treat entrepreneurship as a factor of production.[10]

On the other hand, as we have seen, until a product or technique has in fact been introduced, possession of all necessary means of production (including relevant knowledge) guarantees nothing without the presence of entrepreneurial initiative. So that even Schumpeter recognizes that entrepreneurship "may be conceived as a means of production."[11] On the other hand, if a would-be producer asks the question: "Supposing I decide to produce product X (or to utilize production technique Y), what means of production will it be necessary for me to obtain?", then it is clear that the answer will not include "the decision to produce product X (or to use technique Y)." And this is undoubtedly why Schumpeter stated that "ordinarily" he did *not* conceive of entrepreneurship as a factor of production.[12]

Clearly a sharp distinction must be drawn between means of production ordinarily conceived and entrepreneurship. The latter is *not* similar to factors of production insofar as concerns the theory of marginal productivity.[13] More fundamentally, entrepreneurship, even if considered a means of production, *cannot be purchased or hired by the entrepreneur,* that is, it is never perceived by the potential entrepreneur as either an available productive factor or as a necessary productive factor. Either the entrepreneur is prepared to take the initiative or he is not.[14] If he is not prepared to take the initiative, the would-be entrepreneur simply sees the project as, on balance, one not worth undertaking. He does not see it as a project for which a needed resource is unavailable. If he is determined to take the initiative again, then all he needs to obtain are the factors that would be required in the entrepreneurless state of equilibrium. Or, to put the matter in a slightly different form, the engineer asked to identify the productive agents to which a product is to be attributed, may indeed include intangibles such as "knowledge," but will *not* list "initiative" (since the very notion of attribution presupposes the decision to produce). Accordingly, since the entire product can be attributed to the "other" means of production, it follows that entrepreneurship is in fact not a means of production at all and cannot be credited with having contributed anything to the product.

To sum up, the literature revolving around the ethical implications of "what a man has produced," is concerned with what has been produced by the factors of production which a man owns (or even more narrowly, by the man himself seen as a factor of production). If one perceives pure entrepreneurship as not being a productive factor, it follows that it cannot share in the favorable ethical implications of being responsible for the product. On the other hand, if one views entrepreneurship as a productive factor, attributing some portion of the product's value to the initiative of the entrepreneur, parallel with the contributions made by the other factors, then that portion (however calculated or evaluated)—*but no more than that portion*—may be considered as having been produced by the entrepreneur and relevant, therefore, to the corresponding ethical implications.

We will, in the following pages, draw attention to the possibility for a position almost precisely opposite in all respects to that just presented. In the position to be offered for consideration, the favorable implications of the phrase "what a man has produced" *do not apply at all to factors of production.* Rather, on this position, pure entrepreneurship is responsible—in the sense relevant to the ethical connotations of "what a man has produced"—to the *entire* product. (Moreover, this way of seeing matters is only helped by insight into the sense in which entrepreneurship is *not* to be considered a factor of production. In other words, paradoxically enough, the entrepreneur is to be considered the sole "producer" of the entire product—in the ethically relevant sense—precisely because he makes *no* contribution to production in the sense relevant to the theory of marginal productivity.) A sentence from Knight presents, I believe, the essence of what this argument is all about. Much of it can be viewed as a commentary on the following: "Under the enterprise system, a special social class, the businessmen, direct economic activity; *they are in the strict sense the producers, while the great mass of the population merely furnish them with productive services, placing their persons and their property at the disposal of this class;* the entrepreneurs *also* guarantee to those who furnish productive services a fixed remuneration."[15]

Some Observations on the Lockean Theory of Property

A philosopher-critic of Locke's theory of property has summed up the theory as follows: (1) Every man has a (moral) right to own his person; therefore (2) every man has a (moral) right to own the labor of his person; therefore (3) every man has a (moral) right to own that which he has mixed the labor of his person with.[16] This summary will serve us conveniently in our discussion.

Apparently Locke took it for granted that, since a man has a moral right to his own labor (in the sense of "working"), he has also a moral right to that which his labor produces. This view, which we call proposition (3a), (and which we have cited above as an example of the ethical values attached to the notion of "what a man has produced"), seems implicit in proposition (3).[17] However proposition (3) goes beyond the view that what a man has produced is morally his own. Proposition (3) asserts that when a man mixes his labor with unowned natural resources, in the "natural state" in which there is "still enough and as good left,"[18] he is to be considered as the natural private owner of what results from the mixing. Clearly it is the ambitious proposition (3) which is of the greatest importance for Locke's own thesis. It is however with the more modest proposition (3a) that we are ourselves concerned.

That in proposition (3a) Locke has in mind labor-as-factor-of-production seems clear from his often cited extension of his proposition (3) to include hired labor. "Thus. . .the turfs my servant has cut, and the ore I have dug in any place where I have a right to them in common with others, become my property without the assignation or consent of anybody."[19] A man's own labor is his own in a sense no different from that in which the labor of his servant is an employer's. That which has been produced by a man's own labor is his own in the same sense in which that which has been produced by an employee's labor is the employer's.

It is true that Day is sharply critical of Locke, denying that one can talk significantly of owning labor (in the sense of "working"). Laboring, Day contends, is an activity, "and although activities can be engaged in, performed or done, they cannot be owned."[20] However, economists will find Locke's use of terms quite familiar and acceptable. Economists speak of agents of production (in the sense of *stocks*), and of the "services" of agents of production (in the flow sense). A man who "owns" an agent of production is considered by economists to own, by that token, also the services flowing from that agent. Again, by hiring the services of a productive agent, a producer is considered by economists to have acquired ownership of the service flow, by purchase from the previous owner of that flow (that is, the owner of the agent "itself"). In speaking of owning the services of an employee, therefore, the economist does not in fact have in mind the ownership of the *activity* of working, nor the ownership of that which the activity of working produces, nor even the ownership of the *capacity* for working.[21] Rather the economist is perceiving the employee as a stock of human capital, capable of generating a flow of services. So that, to the various different meanings Day discovers to be attached to the word "labor," should be added: "labor" viewed as the flow of abstract productive service generated by a human being.

Viewed in this "economist's" sense, therefore, Locke's theory seems to say, quite understandably: (1′) Every man has a (moral) right to own the human capital represented by his person; therefore (2′) every man has a (moral) right to own the flow of labor services associated with his person; therefore (3a′) every man has a right to the product produced by these labor services—(just as he has the right to the product produced by the labor services he has hired from an employee).

Clearly, therefore, proposition (3a′), with which we are ourselves concerned, relates to labor viewed as a physical factor of production. It appears moreover that even the notion of labor as *sacrifice*—a notion which might permit one to regard the product as being deserved by the laborer in the sense of reward for sacrifice—is foreign to Locke's theory. Thus as Myrdal has pointed out, Locke's view "that labor is the source of property has nothing to do with pain and sacrifice but follows from the idea of labor as a natural property of the worker and as the cause and creator of value."[22] So that Locke, at any rate, is not arguing his proposition (3a′) on the basis of any ethically merited *reward* for the pain or sacrifice of labor. Instead, it appears, Locke's proposition (3a′) rests on the ethical view that the product *physically derived from a man's property* should belong to him in the same sense that the natural growth from a man's property may be deemed to belong to him naturally.[23] This is entirely consistent with the usual interpretation of Locke-type ethical arguments, as presented by modern economists, in terms of the language of the theory of marginal productivity.[24] We shall see below that there are grounds for discovering, however, elements of an alternative perception of the ethical meaningfulness of production in Locke.

Human Will and the Acquisition of Property

Contrasted with the notion of the product as *physically* produced by man (with or without the use of other productive resources), is the perception of the product as resulting from the *human will.* As discussed briefly above, we shall be arguing that for the purposes of ethically justifying property in products, it may be of relevance to draw attention to the sense in which the product finds its source in entrepreneurial decision making rather than to the sense in which it is derived from factor ownership. While explicit recognition of this insight is almost entirely absent from the literature, it is possible to discover a number of remarks and views which suggest an "entrepreneurial" approach to a justification for property.

Thus in Locke's own century Pufendorf emphasized the distinction between an action which is forced and that which is performed freely. Only the latter is properly a *human* action, involving "an element of subjective spontaneity" and a "free project of the self."[25] A century later Kant's theory of the acquisition of property through labor saw the labor itself as almost irrelevant to the act of acquisition. "When it is a question of the first acquisition of a thing, the cultivation or modification of it by labour forms nothing more than an external sign of the fact that it has been taken into possession. . . ."[26] It is not the mixing of labor with an object which makes it one's own, but "the transcendental operation of directing [one's] will upon [it]."[27] Hegel too saw in the human will the true source of property rights and moreover saw it as providing a justification for the acquisition of natural resources which is superior to that depending upon the mixing of labor.[28]

Moreover, it has seemed to some writers that Locke's labor theory of property too (as well as the labor theory of value of the later classical economists)[29] cannot be properly understood unless one recognizes the special character of labor, the *human* factor, as compared with other factors of production. So that if one accepts their view, it turns out to be not quite correct to interpret Locke's theory of property as depending on the view that the product arises physically from an owned factor of production which happens to be labor. Thus Weisskopf, in his psychological analysis of classical economics, viewed as deriving from Locke, emphasizes labor as *an activity of the person.* Following on Myrdal,[30] Weisskopf points out that in the classical view nature is seen as dead, with only human labor seen as the *active* agent. Petty's dictum comparing labor to the father, the active principle of wealth, with land seen as the mother, is used by Weisskopf to explain the Locke-classical treatment of labor as the sole origin of wealth for purposes of justifying property rights and of explaining the determination of value.[31]

If Weisskopf's view of the matter is correct, then Locke's labor theory does not relate to that aspect of labor in which it is seen merely as a physical source of the product, but rather to the aspect of labor in which it is seen as inseparable from the active human will of the laborer. Plausible though Weisskopf's view may be for an understanding of the classical preoccupation with labor, it seems difficult to reconcile it with Locke's treatment of hired labor as being as complete a justification for property rights in the product as one's own labor. If Locke's treatment of hired labor envisages the employer as hiring not only the physical labor services of the employee, but also the active, spontaneous, human elements associated with these services, then, of course, he is not understanding these elements in their purely entrepreneurial sense (in which, by definition, they cannot be hired at all).[32] We shall return to offer further brief remarks on Locke later in this paper.

Finally, we notice that more recently Oliver, in drawing attention to the inadequacy of Marxian labor theory for a doctrine of "earned-income" (in which a man is entitled to what he has produced), argues that Marx leaves no room for the role of the free will exercised by the laborer in his work, when such a role is essential for the very concept of "earning."[33] We have thus an example of the recognition of the role of the human will in ethical evaluation of "what a man has produced."

Production—Automatic Growth or Human Creation?

From the foregoing discussion it will have become apparent that we are confronted with two quite different views on the nature of production. We turn now to spell out explicitly what these two views are and to consider briefly their plausibility to serve as foundations for the ethical view that what a man has produced ought to be his.

1. *Production as Automatic Growth from the Factors of Production:* The one view sees production as it would occur in the state of equilibrium. In such a state each producing firm has already been fully adjusted to the conditions of the market. The services of necessary inputs (including the services of managers) flow smoothly into the firm in synchronized fashion, with the corresponding output flow emerging with equal smoothness. The market value of the input flow corresponds exactly to that of the output flow; alternative uses for input services offer no higher factor prices, alternative sources of input-supply promise no savings. Certainly one can say that the output has been produced by the productive input services. But because there has, in such a state, been no room for entrepreneurship, output must be seen as emerging *automatically,* as it were, from the combined input flow, exactly as fruit might grow from a tree without direction from the owner of the tree. To rest an ethical case for ownership in a product on the circumstance that a man's productive resources have pro-

duced it, in *this* sense, is to claim that the product is his not on the grounds that *he* has permitted his factors to create the product, but on the grounds that the product has grown—as it were automatically—from the factor services he owns.

2. *Production as a Human Creation:* The alternative view refuses to see the product as emerging automatically from a given combination of factor services. In this view the product has come into being only because some human being has *decided* to bring together the necessary productive factors. In deciding to initiate the process of production, this human being has *created* the product. In his creation of the product this entrepreneur-producer has *used* the factors of production which his vision has brought together. He has not cooperated jointly with these factors (so that this view does not see the entrepreneur's contribution as consisting of a portion of the value of the product, with the remaining portion being the contributions of "other" productive agents.) He has produced *the whole product entirely on his own,* being able to do so by his initiative, daring and drive in identifying and taking advantage of the available productive factors. In this view, an ethical case for ownership in a product, based on one's having "created" it, depends strictly on one's *not* having been the owner of one of the cooperating input factors. (To the extent that an entrepreneur was also a factor-owner he is credited with the creation of the product only in the sense that he "purchases" his factor services from himself, so to speak, rather than permitting them to serve alternative purposes.)

If one uses the first of these two views on production as the basis for an ethical case for property in the product, or in the distribution of income, it is entirely relevant to use a Clarkian marginal productivity approach. The contribution of a factor of production must somehow be disentangled from the contributions of other factors, and the theory of marginal productivity may, with greater or lesser success, be called upon for this purpose. But if it is the second ("creation") view which is to be used, then marginal productivity is entirely irrelevant (except in a sense to be discussed below). On this second view the (necessarily indivisible) entrepreneur is responsible for the entire product. The contributions of the factor inputs, being without any entrepreneurial component, are irrelevant for the ethical position being taken.

Of course, it is true that also on this second view, the entrepreneur-producer must, in order to "create" the product, acquire the services of the necessary productive factors. (And in fact competition may force him to compensate them to the full extent of their respective marginal products.) However, it should be plain that this view does not claim rights in the product for the entrepreneur on the grounds that, since he has fairly purchased these factor services, production has now been carried on with *his* factor services. In this view the entrepreneur's rights rest strictly on the vision and initiative with which, at the time when he owned *no* productive resources, he undertook to marshall them for his purposes.

It is not the purpose of this paper to choose between these two interpretations of the ethical implications of "producing." Our purpose has been rather to draw attention to the existence of the second view and to emphasize its diametrically opposed character as compared with that of the first view. In choosing which of these views to endorse (if, indeed, one wishes to endorse either of them at all) or which of them to ascribe to particular writers, it is necessary to consider carefully whether it is the active human *creativity* of the producer which is to be underlined and recognized or rather the ownership of the physical or other *ingredients of production.*

Finders, Keepers, and Speculative Profits

The points made in the preceding section may perhaps throw light on certain matters raised in discussions concerning the ethics of property and income distribution. Oliver[34] has noted that sometimes writers presenting ethical positions based on "what a man has produced," introduce the notion of "finders, keepers." "The man . . . that first discovers and claims title to natural resources thereby gains ownership." Oliver points out that Locke's position bases ownership in natural resources (with which one has mixed one's labor) partly on "discovery." For Oliver "finders, keepers" is a rule which bears no relation at all to the ethical deservingness associated with having produced something. Our insight into the "entrepreneurial" view on production may perhaps be of some help in this respect.

Briefly, it seems that Locke's labor theory of property rights is best understood as involving a combination, possibly a confusion, of *both* the "factorial" and the "entrepreneurial" views on production. We recall our earlier reference to Myrdal's and Weisskopf's understanding of Locke in terms of the contrast between active, live labor and passive, dead nature. This certainly supports the theory that Locke viewed labor as not merely a factor of production, but as also involving the uniquely human element which we have identified with entrepreneurship. Again, the initially puzzling view which Locke presents, in which title to natural resources is acquired by the mixing of labor, becomes understandable when the mixing of labor with the natural resource is perceived as the grasping of the "entrepreneurial" opportunity offered by the available but as yet unappropriated resources. The "finders, keepers," rule which Oliver discovers in Locke thus represents essentially the same ethical view as that underlying the entrepreneurial view on production. In this view a producer is entitled to what he has produced not because he has contributed anything to its physical fabrication, but because *he perceived and grasped the opportunity* for its fabrication (by utilizing the resources available in the market). This is clearly an example of "finding, keeping."

These insights appear relevant to some comments by Samuelson on the normative aspects of speculative profits. Where a crop failure generates speculative profits, Samuelson points out that the successful speculator need only be a trifle quicker than his rivals in order to make his fortune. In his absence, the socially advantageous consequences of his speculation (i.e., the curtailment of relatively less urgently needed consumption at earlier dates, making possible some more urgently needed consumption at later dates) would occur seconds later through the activities of other speculators. Even if one accepts "a Clarkian naive-productivity theory of ethical deservingness," Samuelson remarks, one can hardly justify the capture of all the profits by the successful speculator who saved society from no more than a few seconds of unwise consumption. Without commenting on the substance of Samuelson's normative criticism of speculative profits,[35] it seems useful to remark that, as we have seen, a Clarkian ethical approach is wholly inappropriate anyway in dealing with entrepreneurial profits. What *might* be of greater relevance would be the entrepreneurial view which, as we have seen, consists essentially in precisely a "finders, keepers" ethic. On such an ethic an opportunity perceived and grasped confers ethical deservingness. Necessarily this perceives the gain from grasping the opportunity as having been deserved, despite the possibility or even the likelihood that others might have perceived and grasped the same opportunity seconds later. No one is bound, of course, to subscribe to this entrepreneurial ethic; in fact one may reject it precisely on Samuelson's grounds, if one chooses. But it does seem appropriate to judge the deservingness of one particular example of entrepreneurial profit on the approach relevant to a defense of the deservingness of entrepreneurial profits in general.[36]

The Entrepreneurial Element in Factor-Owners' Decisions

Although we have been at pains to emphasize the distinction between the factor-of-production view on production on the one hand and the "creation" entrepreneurial view on the other, it seems wise to point out a circumstance which operates to blur, to some extent, the sharp line we have drawn between these views. This circumstance is the presence of an entrepreneurial element in *every* human action and decision including, especially for our purposes, the decisions of factor owners.

The isolation of a purely entrepreneurial element in production is, of course, an analytical device. Human action in its totality is made up of an "entrepreneurial" element (to which is attributable the decision maker's awareness of the ends-means framework within which he is free to operate), *and* an "economizing" element (to which we attribute the efficiency, with respect to the perceived ends-means framework, of the decision taken).[37] Analytically we conceive of factor owners as pure "economizers" operating within an already perceived market framework. Entrepreneurs, on the other hand, we perceive as becoming aware (with no resources of their own at all) of changed patterns of resource availability, of technological possibilities, and of possibilities for new products that will be attractive to consumers. But flesh and blood resource owners are, of course, also to *some* extent, their own entrepreneurs, (just as flesh and blood entrepreneurs are likely to be owners of some factor services themselves).

It follows that when a producer hires the services of productive agents, entrepreneurship has in fact been exercised, not only by "the" entrepreneur, but also by the factor owners in deciding to sell. While productive services may be viewed as flowing "passively" from the productive agent, it is the factor owner's decision (from which all elements of entrepreneurship cannot be entirely absent) which permits the flow to proceed in the adopted channel rather than in alternative processes of production. In the case of labor in particular, the factor owner's decision to permit the service flow is required at every minute of his service. So that when we say in an apparently "factor-of-production" view of the matter that a factor has produced a product, we are, *in real-world cases,* referring *both* to the factor as producer and to the factor owner as, at least to some extent, entrepreneur. Now, it seems of great importance to emphasize the two quite different senses of production so involved. It seems, at the same time, helpful to notice how easily the two views on production can become combined and/or confused. This will perhaps account not only for the view which our interpretation has ascribed to

Locke, but also for the circumstance that the literature has failed almost entirely to notice explicitly the possibility of an entrepreneurial, factorless view of the ethical implications of producing. The single but outstanding exception is the sentence in Knight cited earlier, in which it is the entrepreneurs who are seen "in the strict sense" as "the producers," with the factor owners merely furnishing them with productive services.

NOTES

1. J. S. Mill, *Principles of Political Economy*, ed. William J. Ashley, (London, 1923), p. 218.

2. See G. Myrdal, *The Political Element in the Development of Economic Theory* (Harvard, 1954), p. 71f; R. Schlatter, *Private Property, The History of an Idea,* (Rutgers University Press, 1951) Chapter 7; C. B. Macpherson, "The Social Bearing of Locke's Political Theory," *Western Political Quarterly* (1954); A. Ryan, "Locke and the Dictatorship of the Bourgeoisie" *Political Studies* (1965).

3. Myrdal, *Ibid.* Strictly speaking, Locke did not actually assert that, by mixing his labor with a nature-given resource, he has thereby "produced" the result. However, he has certainly been understood as having implied as much. Thus, commenting on the notion "that, if a man 'makes' something, it is his," Oliver cites Locke as having given expression to this idea in his labor theory of property rights. (H. M. Oliver, *A Critique of Socioeconomic Goals,* Indiana University Press, 1954, p. 27). See further later in this paper.

4. M. Friedman, *Price Theory, A Provisional Text* (Aldine, 1962), p. 196.

5. M. Friedman, *Capitalism and Freedom* (University of Chicago Press, 1962), p. 167. On this see also Oliver (*op. cit.,* p.37). In an extensive critique of Oliver's discussion, Rothbard *(Power and Market, Government and the Economy,* Institute for Humane Studies, 1970, p. 183) makes it clear that he supports the same underlying ethic.

6. *Price Theory,* p. 196.

7. J. B. Clark, *The Distribution of Wealth* (Kelley, 1899), p. 3.

8. J. Locke, *An Essay Concerning the True Original, Extent and End of Civil Government,* paragraph 27.

9. J. A. Schumpeter, *The Theory of Economic Development* (Harvard, 1934), p. 76.

10. On this see, for example, the discussion in F. Machlup, *The Economics of Sellers' Competition* (Johns Hopkins Press, 1952), pp. 226-228.

11. Schumpeter, *op. cit.,* p. 143.

12. *Ibid.*

13. See Schumpeter, *op. cit.*, p. 153; Machlup, *op. cit.*, p. 226; F. H. Knight, *Risk, Uncertainty and Profit,* p. 271.

14. On all this see the writer's *Competition and Entrepreneurship* (University of Chicago Press, forthcoming), Chapter 2.

15. F. H. Knight, *Risk, Uncertainty and Profit,* p. 271; emphasis on the central clause supplied. Similar statements are to be found in F. Hawley, *Enterprise and the Productive Process* (New York: Putnam, 1907), pp. 85, 102, 112, 127.

16. J. P. Day, "Locke on Property" (*Philosophical Quarterly,* 1966) reprinted in G. J. Schochet, (Editor) *Life, Liberty, and Property, Essays on Locke's Political Ideas,* (Belmont, California: Wadsworth Publishing Company), p. 109. All page references will be to this reprint.

17. See Day, pp. 109-110; and see above note 3.

18. Locke, *op. cit.,* paragraph 33.

19. Locke, paragraph 28.

20. Day, *op. cit.,* pp. 113f.

21. On all this see Day, *Ibid.*

22. G. Myrdal, *The Political Element in the Development of Economic Theory,* p. 74. It should be noted, however, that just as the later classical economists used expressions like "trouble," "sacrifice," "pain" synonymously with "labor"—and are for this reason described by Myrdal as having viewed labor strictly as the "trouble caused by effort" (Myrdal, *Ibid.*)—so too does Locke occasionally (see paragraphs 30, 34) seem to identify the justification for ownership of the product of one's labor as resting on one's having been he "who takes pains about it."

23. See the reference in E. Halevy, *The Growth of Philosophic Radicalism* (Boston: The Beacon Press), p. 45, to Hume's view that "we are the proprietors of the fruits of our garden, and of the dung of our flock by virtue of the normal operation of the laws of association."

24. See Oliver, A *Critique of Socioeconomic Goals,* (Kraus repr., 1954) p. 33; see also the sources referred to above notes 4, 7.

25. See A. C. Cutler, "Some Concepts of Human Rights and Obligations in Classical Protestantism," in A. L. Harding (Editor) *Natural Law and Natural Rights* (Dallas: Southern Methodist University Press, 1955), p. 16.

26. I. Kant, *Philosophy of Law* (Edited by Hastie, Edinburgh, 1887), p. 92.

27. R. Schlatter, *Private Property,* p. 256.

28. See Schlatter, *Ibid.*

29. On the question of the impact of Locke's labor theory of property on the later classical labor theory of value, there has been controversy. Myrdal (*The Political Element in the Development of Economic Theory,* pp. 71f), Halevy (*The Growth of Philosophic Radicalism,* p. 44), and W. A. Weisskopf (*The Psychology of Economics,* University of Chicago Press, 1955, pp. 22ff, p. 145) all assert a direct influence. See, however, J. A.

Schumpeter, *History of Economic Analysis* (Oxford University Press, 1954), pp. 120, 310-311; see also I. M. Kirzner, *The Economic Point of View,* (Van Nostrand, 1960), pp. 25, 190, notes 8, 9.

30. Myrdal, *The Political Element,* p. 72; see especially Myrdal's reference to Rodbertus.

31. Weisskopf, *The Psychology of Economics,* pp. 25, 145.

32. For further discussion of the entrepreneurial element in the decisions of factor owners, see below pp. 10ff.

33. Oliver, *A Critique of Socioeconomic Goals,* p. 37.

34. *Ibid.,* p. 42.

35. Samuelson's discussion is in his "Intertemporal Price Equilibrium: A Prologue to the Theory of Speculation," *Weltwirtschaftliches Archiv* (December, 1957), p. 209. For further comment see the writer's *Competition and Entrepreneurship* (University of Chicago Press, forthcoming), Chapter 6.

36. See Schlatter, *Private Property,* p. 191, note 2, for references to use made of Locke's labor theory to condemn the ethical status of entrepreneurial profit.

37. See further the writer's *Competition and Entrepreneurship,* Chapter 2.

CONTRIBUTORS

ROBERT L. CUNNINGHAM, Professor of Philosophy, University of San Francisco. He earned his Ph.D. at Laval University, Quebec (1951). He is author of *Situationism and the New Morality* (1970) and a contributor to the *New Catholic Encyclopedia* (1967). His articles have appeared in the *New Individualist Review, The Personalist,* and *Modern Age.* He is a member of the American Catholic Philosophical Association, the Mont Pelerin Society, and the Council of Advisers of the Institute for Humane Studies. He was born in Birmingham, Alabama, in 1926.

EDWIN G. DOLAN, Assistant Professor, Department of Economics, Dartmouth College. His works include *TANSTAAFL: An Economic Strategy for the Environmental Crisis* (1971) and, with co-author David E. Lindsey, *Basic Microeconomics: Principles and Reality* (1974) and *Basic Macroeconomics: Principles and Reality* (1974). He earned his Ph.D. at Yale (1969). He was born in 1943.

F. A. HARPER, President, Institute for Humane Studies, Menlo Park, California (1966–73). He earned his Ph.D. at Cornell University (1932) and spent twelve years (1946–58) as an economist with the Foundation for Economic Education. His works include *Liberty, A Path to Its Recovery* (1949), *Why Wages Rise* (1957), *Morals and Liberty* (1965), and *Defending Private Property: You and Devaluation* (1968). His articles have appeared in *Farm Economics, Vital Speeches, National Review,* and *The Freeman.* He was a fellow of the American Association for the Advancement of Science and a member of the Mont Pelerin Society. He was born in Middleville, Michigan, in 1905 and died in California in 1973.

CARL F. H. HENRY, Editor, *Christianity Today.* Dr. Henry holds a Th.D. from Northern Baptist Theological Seminary and a Ph.D. from Boston University. He has taught at Wheaton College, Gordon College, Northern Baptist Theological Seminary and is president of the Institute for Advanced Christian Studies. He is the author of some twenty books.

ARTHUR KEMP, Charles M. Stone Professor of Money and Credit, Claremont Men's College, Claremont, California. His works include *The Legal Qualities of Money* (1956), and a monograph *The Role of Gold* (1963). He earned his Ph.D. at New York University (1949). He is a member of the American Economic Association and the Mont Pelerin Society. He was born in Buffalo, New York, in 1916.

ISRAEL M. KIRZNER, Professor of Economics, New York University. His works include *The Economic Point of View* (1960), *Market Theory and the Price System* (1963), *Competition and Entrepreneurship* (1973). He earned his Ph.D. at New York University (1957). He is a member of the Mont Pelerin Society, American Economic Association, and Royal Economic Association. He was born in London in 1930.

LEOPOLD KOHR was born in 1909 in Oberndorf-Salzburg, Austria-Hungary. He earned his LL.D. at the University of Innsbruck in 1933. He has been Assistant Professor of Economics at Rutgers University (1946–55) and Associate Professor of Economics at the University of Puerto Rico (1955–57). His works include *The Breakdown of Nations* (1957) and *Customs Union, a Tool for Peace* (1949).

GEORGE I. MAVRODES, Professor, Department of Philosophy, University of Michigan. His works include *Problems and Perspectives in the Philosophy of Religion* (edited with Stuart C. Hackett) (1967), *The Nationality of Belief in God* (editor) (1970), *Belief in God: A Study in the Epistemology of Religion* (1970). He was born in 1926.

A. NEIL MCLEOD has been affiliated with The Institute of Paper Chemistry since 1955. He earned his M.S. at Harvard Business School (1948) and his Ph.D. at Cornell University (1950). He is a member of the Mont Pelerin Society and chairman of the Council of Advisers of the Institute for Humane Studies. He was born in Canada in 1917.

SYLVESTER PETRO, Professor of Law, Wake Forest University, School of Law. His works include *The Labor Policy of the Free Society* (1957), *Power Unlimited: The Corruption of Union Leadership* (1959), *The Kohler Strike* (1961), *The Kingsport Strike* (1967). He was professor of law at New York University (1950–73) and is a member of the Mont Pelerin Society and a trustee of the Foundation for Economic Education. He was born in Chicago in 1917.

MURRAY N. ROTHBARD, Professor of Economics, Polytechnic Institute of New York. His books include *Man, Economy, and State* (1962), *America's Great Depression* (1963), and *For a New Liberty* (1973). He is editor of the *Libertarian Forum* and a member of the Mont Pelerin Society, American Historical Association, and Board of Academic Advisers, Institute for Humane Studies. He was born in New York City in 1926.

JAMES A. SADOWSKY, S. J., Assistant Professor of Theology, Fordham University. He earned both his B. A. and M. A. at Fordham University and his S.T.L. at the Facultés S. Albert, Louvain, Belgium. He is a priest in the Roman Catholic Church and a member of the Society of Jesus.

JAMES M. SMITH, Professor and Chairman, Department of Philosophy, Fresno State College. He earned his Ph.D. at Brown University (1960). Previous to joining Fresno State College, he was Assistant Professor at the University of Washington (1966–69). His papers have been published in *Ethics, Analytical Philosophy, Theology Today,* and *Religious Studies.* He is a member of the American Philosophical Association.

LOUIS M. SPADARO, Professor of Economics and Dean, Martino Graduate School of Business Administration, Fordham University. He is author of *Economics: An Introductory View.* He is a member of the Mont Pelerin Society, the American Economic Association and the American Statistical Association. He was born in New York City.

JAMES W. WIGGINS, Dana Distinguished Professor of Economics and Sociology, Converse College. His works include *The New Argument in Economics, Relativism and the Study of Man,* and *Central Planning and Neomercantilism.* He is a member of the Mont Pelerin Society, the Economic Advisory Committee of the American Medical Association, and the Educational Advisory Council of the National Association of Manufacturers.

INDEX

Note: An italicized number (Arabic or Roman numeral) indicates a page on which a term is defined.